Pink Tanks and
Velvet Hangovers

Pink Tanks and Velvet Hangovers

An American in Prague

Douglas Lytle

Frog, Ltd.
Berkeley, California

Pink Tanks and Velvet Hangovers: An American In Prague

Copyright © 1995 by Douglas Lytle. No portion of this book, except for brief review, may be reproduced in any form without written permission of the publisher. For information contact Frog, Ltd. c/o North Atlantic Books.

Published by Frog, Ltd.

Frog, Ltd. books are distributed by
North Atlantic Books
P.O. Box 12327
Berkeley, California 94712

Cover photo by Jim Galvin
Maps on pages xiv–xvi by Nenad Vitas
Cover and book design by Paula Morrison
Typeset by Catherine Campaigne
Printed in the United States of America by Malloy Lithographing

Library of Congress Cataloging-in-Publication Data

Lytle, Douglas.
    Pink tanks and velvet hangovers : an American in Prague /
    Douglas Lytle
        p.   cm.
    ISBN 1-883319-24-2
        1. Prague—Description and travel.   2. Lytle, Douglas—Homes
    and haunts—Czech Republic—Prague.   3. Prague
    (Czechoslovakia)—Social life and customs.   4. Prague
    (Czechoslovakia)—Intellectual life.   5. Prague (Czechoslovakia)—
    Economic conditions.   6. Prague (Czechoslovakia)—Social
    conditions.   I. Title.
    DB2614.L97   1994
    943.71'2—dc20   94–41644
                                                       CIP

1   2   3   4   5   6   7   8   9 / 99   98   97   96   95

For my Mother
Who would have loved all this
And my Father
Whose support has meant everything to me

Song of the Native Land

Beautiful as on a jug a painted flower
is the land that bore you, gave you life,
beautiful as on a jug a painted flower,
sweeter than a loaf from fresh ground flour
into which you've deeply sunk your knife.

Countless times disheartened, disappointed.
always newly you return to it,
countless times disheartened, disappointed,
to this land so rich and sun-anointed,
poor like springtime in a gravel-pit.

Beautiful as on a jug a painted flower,
heavy as our guilt that will not go away
— never can its memory decay.
At the end, at our final hour
we shall slumber in its bitter clay.

— Jaroslav Seifert

Table of Contents

"The motive of a journey deserves a little attention. It is not the fully conscious mind which chooses West Africa in preference to Switzerland. The psychoanalyst, who takes the images of a dream one by one—'You dreamed you were asleep in a forest. What is your first association to forest?'—finds that some images have immediate associations; to others, the patient can bring out nothing at all; his brain is like a cinema in which the warning 'Fire' has been cried; the exits are jammed with too many people trying to escape, and when I say that to me Africa has always seemed an important image, I suppose that is what I mean, that it represented more than I could say, 'You dreamed you were in Africa. Of what do you think first when I say the word Africa?' and a crowd of words and images, witches and death, unhappiness and the Gare St. Lazare, the huge smoky viaduct over a Paris slum, crowd together and block the way to full consciousness."

—Graham Greene, *Journey Without Maps*

"I am a camera with the shutter open, quite passive, recording, not thinking. Recording the man shaving at the window opposite and the woman in the kimono washing her hair. Some day, all this will have to be developed, carefully printed, fixed."

—Christopher Isherwood, *Goodbye to Berlin*

Acknowledgments

Almost the first thing new acquaintances ask is how I ever got the idea to move to Czechoslovakia. As I have no connection to the region, no relatives to guide me there or prior interest that would make such a move self-evident, their questions are understandable. The plain fact is, one doesn't just plan on moving to Czechoslovakia. I certainly didn't. You see, there was this Czech woman that I met and a faint sense of obsession and I was a little bit bored with my life as a reporter and well … you just don't *plan* on these things.

Not surprisingly, I was at a loss to explain to my friends exactly why I was leaving a decent, if low-paying, reporting position to go off and live in a country that was just beginning to emerge from underneath forty years of totalitarianism.

In reflection, although I was blind and naive about the magnitude of what I was jumping into, coming to Prague has made an immensely positive difference in my life, both professionally and personally. I arrived ostensibly to teach English and write the occasional news article, but have lingered long enough to participate in the launch of *The Prague Post,* a successful weekly, English-language newspaper and also watch Prague turn into something of a haven for American youth seeking a temporary respite from declining job prospects back at home. The exodus to Prague does not appear to be waning, with new arrivals continuing to replace those who return home. In addition, some Americans are settling in for the long haul by forging relationships or starting businesses.

I originally expected that writing a book about Czechoslovakia after communism would be relatively straightforward: a few historical dollops about the past, reminisces about what I saw and descriptions of how people adapt to an open society once again. But the division of Czechoslovakia on January 1, 1993, into the Czech Republic and Slovakia turned my story upside down and helped create a book that is both a reminder of the past and a warning for the future. We should not underestimate the importance of the Czech and Slovak nations, simply because of their diminished size. Most, if not all, of the identifiable fissure points facing the former Soviet satellites have surfaced to varying degrees in both the Czech Republic and Slovakia: nationalism, resurgent anti-Semitism, doubts about economic reform and the *vox populi's* withering faith in the ability of democratic leadership to solve overwhelming problems.

Grammatically, the split of the country presented me with the difficult problem of how to refer to the new countries throughout the text of this book. I am not alone in this regard, as Czechs and foreigners often stumble in conversation when speaking about the Czech Republic and Slovakia. It is also not uncommon to see the name Czechoslovakia still pop up (albeit incorrectly) in foreign news stories and on television. Hence, I often use "Czechoslovakia" as a place and region, especially when discussing events that occurred before the split of the country on January 1, 1993.

I have used traditional English spellings of towns and places (Pilzen vs. the Czech Plzeň, Wenceslas Square vs. the Czech Václavské náměstí., etc.) instead of the Czech spellings as the chances are the casual reader may be more familiar with the former.

With the exception of writing about the political and nationalist tensions between Czechs and Slovaks, I have concentrated primarily on documenting the Czech cultural and social perspective, as I have lived and worked only in Prague. The Slovaks would make fascinating and important subjects on their own and I earnestly hope someone produces an account of their recent history soon.

This book would never have seen the light of day without the generous help of the many good Czech people who have made me feel welcome in their country. They have shared stories of their years under communism, opened their homes to me, given me support and left me with many good memories. As much of what they told me was extraordinarily personal, I have changed some names and places throughout the text to protect their privacy.

I am indebted to the following organizations for help and resources while I was engaged in final research and writing: Lisa A. Frankenberg and the staff and offices of *The Prague Post,* the *American Cultural Center* and the *Center For Independent Journalism* in Prague, the *Czech News Agency* (ČTK), and to various faculties at Charles University in Prague. Concurrently, I would like to thank Daniel DeLuce (for encouraging me to reveal), Linda Keller, Jennifer Rudy, Revan Schendler, Alan Levy, Ross Crockford, M. Thea Selby, Cathy Křižíková, Barbara Freitas, Melissa Morrison, John Allison at *Prognosis,* Jaroslava Severová, Ivan Malý and Kevin Gibbons for their assistance and indefatigable support. In addition, I thank all my friends and relatives who sent me clippings over the last several years as each has proved invaluable.

I am forever grateful to Jiří Pilucha for his especially close reading of the text with regard to the Czech language and various historical events. For his good work, I owe him far more beers than my salary can accommodate. I also thank Lindy Hough and Richard Grossinger at North Atlantic Books for their steadfast belief in this project.

Finally, my appreciation and much love is sent to Renáta Nováková and her family, who have put up with more than three years of whining, whimpering, complaining, questions, grievances, incessant babble and chatter about life—especially the smallest details—in Prague. Renáta helped me tremendously during the final push to finish this book and all of her comments and criticisms have helped make this a much better story.

Douglas Lytle
Prague, The Czech Republic
Fall, 1994

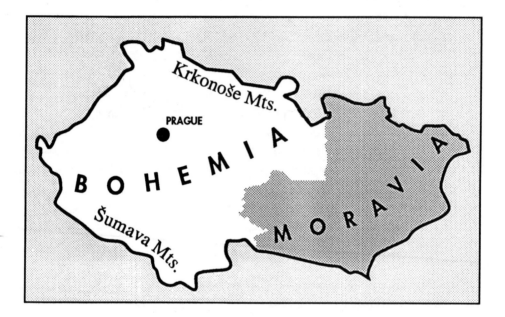

The Czech Republic

Czechoslovakia before 1993

The Czech Republic and Slovakia after 1993

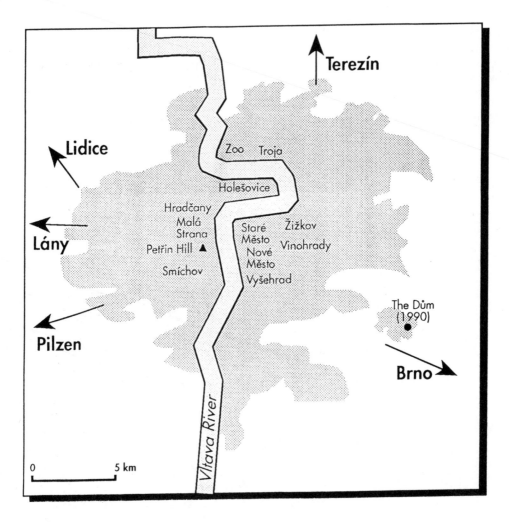

Terezín

Lidice

Lány

Pilzen

Zoo   Troja

Holešovice

Hradčany
Malá
Strana
Petřin Hill ▲

Smíchov

Staré
Město
Nové
Město
Vyšehrad

Žižkov

Vinohrady

The Dům
(1990)

Brno

0   5 km

Vltava River

Prague

1

A Train into Bohemia

Moments after my train crossed into Czechoslovakia from Germany, I felt like I had climbed aboard a roller coaster. I'd been a nervous wreck for weeks, but on this afternoon in late August, 1990, my stomach was shaking as a badly as the train.

It was hot and I was drenched, sweating from pores I didn't even know existed. Despite the boiling humidity, I was convinced my fragile mental condition was more to blame for my ceaseless perspiration.

Woozy and drained after a long plane flight from Los Angeles, I was only vaguely cognizant of the green Bohemian forest that flicked by as we rattled along through the westernmost portion of the country. Instead of concentrating on my new surroundings, I was trying to determine whether or not I was crazy for dumping my job and running away with a woman who I had only known for six months. Or had it been five?

Until I met Nikola, my world had revolved around my job as an entertainment reporter for a daily newspaper in the San Francisco Bay Area. I generally didn't take chances, preferring instead to keeping my head down and doing my work as best I could. My life was reasonably simple, ordered around my friends and good music and books and the respective fates of the San Francisco Giants in the spring and summer and the 49ers in the winter. But every so often, someone comes along who changes your life. Nikola was that person.

A Czech-American who had moved to the United States with her parents following the Soviet invasion of Czechoslovakia in 1968,

1

Nikola was wild, eccentric, lively and entertaining—a somewhat mysterious personality hidden behind a flying mass of blonde hair, high cheekbones and lovely, cream-colored skin and dark clothes. I began by inviting her in the early spring to a Madonna concert that I was dreading attending alone. One evening led to another, and soon she had endured more than a handful of other horrible concerts I was forced to review, including a particularly awful Milli Vanilli show.

Once, when I was at her house, she showed me pictures of Václav Havel, a former playwright and philosopher who had become President of Czechoslovakia in December, 1989. A playwright and dissident who had spent several years in prison, Havel's ascension to the presidency came at the end of the Velvet Revolution, a three-week series of strikes and public actions which brought an end to the forty-year Communist dictatorship.

Nikola read me Czech poems and discussed her recent trip to Prague, where she had visited her relatives. Later, we went and saw a performance of Havel's play, *Audience,* at a theater in San Francisco.

Although her Czechness was an interesting facet to her personality, I didn't give it much thought until she announced in early summer that she was leaving to teach English in Prague with her sister, Dora.

The idea of my accompanying her to Czechoslovakia had begun innocently enough during one of our late-night phone conversations. First, there was some banter about what an interesting trip it would be for her and a discussion of how different our lives would be when we separated. The usual *gee-it'll-be-too-bad* words were exchanged as we both considered the fact we soon would be parting.

Somehow, the talk turned to exploring the possibility of my going along on the trip and then the conversation ended and I went to sleep. The next morning, I awoke and laughed to myself about the stupidity of just picking up and leaving my job. What a joke: go to a country I don't know a thing about. Less than two months later, I found myself riding this dusty train towards Prague.

I looked across the train compartment at Nikola, who was sleep-
~ fetal ball on one of the train's plastic red couches. Here
idn't know until early in the spring and who since
to turn my life upside down. And this *association*

2

between us, this so-called relationship, had become less than stable. Half the time I couldn't stand her, half the time I was obsessed. Though my mind had been firmly camped in the former for several weeks, I had vowed to press on, regardless of my feelings.

Don't go anywhere because of a woman, some of my friends told me before leaving, and their advice was right. But I wasn't following anybody, although this was, of course, partially a lie. As I watched her sleep, I reasoned that there was nothing wrong with either of us that couldn't be solved by going our own separate ways. Sometimes people don't mesh very well, and in this case, our respective personalities and quirky moods and tempers seemed to clash more often than meld.

But I got myself on this voyage, and I was determined to succeed on my own, rather than turn tail and head home. The Berlin Wall had fallen, the Cold War was over and the Soviet Union was pulling out its troops. I was not going to miss this chance at a unique experience.

A few minutes earlier, the Czechoslovak border control had swept through the train, big soldiers in olive-drab uniforms and green caps. There were no delays, no thorough customs check and few questions. A stamp into my blue passport, a thin smile from each soldier, a touch of the green caps with an index finger and then they were gone.

Our train passed through tiny, rural villages and shallow ravines overgrown with rhododendrons and thick vines and ferns. Buildings, some yellowed and blotchy with age, crumbling and cracked from disrepair, moved by, faded laundry hanging from every balcony and window. In wide, rolling fields a single tractor trundled across acres of brown soil, its smokestack belching tiny curls of brown exhaust into a sky streaked with high white clouds. Softened by a hazy light and enveloped in a rich, sticky humidity, everything seemed green beyond recognition, all cast in a unreal, impressionistic glow.

The door to our train compartment opened and Dora, Nikola's sister, entered from outside, where she had been smoking a cigarette. She laughed, after taking in my sorry appearance which was highlighted by my sweat streaked face and drenched shirt.

"You look like you've been swimming with your clothes on!" she giggled and I managed a half smile. I had met Dora for the first time precisely two days before in Los Angeles and still felt unsure of what

3

to say to her. So I looked out the window and thought about the elderly man at Frankfurt airport I had nearly killed earlier in the day. Nikola, Dora and I had been trying to move our piles of luggage down to the train station below the airport when one of my suitcases fell from my grasp and rolled down a long escalator. About twenty feet below, an elderly man with a cane and a woman—presumably his wife—were carefully making their way off the escalator when my heavy, black duffel bag came tumbling along, cutting him down in the back of the knees.

Amazingly, the man was not injured and was also reasonably understanding, given that he had narrowly avoided being crushed by a falling piece of luggage.

"I'm never coming to this fucking airport again!" his wife said, fixing me with an angry stare and giving me a wide berth, even as I blurted out my apologies.

Thinking back about the incident, I laughed suddenly in the quiet of the train compartment at the elderly woman's profanity which had been as unexpected as my flying suitcase. Dora looked at me quizzically and I could see she had probably arrived at the conclusion that her sister had invited a delirious, sweating lunatic to Czechoslovakia.

Gradually, my mind turned to the challenges that lay ahead. Like Nikola and Dora, I would be teaching English in a public school in Prague. I also planned on writing articles about the changes in Central and Eastern Europe. For the first few days or weeks, we would live with Nikola's uncle at his apartment. And beyond those half-baked, less than concrete plans, there was a disturbing, empty void.

To me, the teaching opportunity was still open to question, as I hadn't received confirmation from the school board in Prague. But Nikola had assured me there would be some kind of job waiting for me. Czechoslovakia was less than six months into its first democratic government since 1948 and the need for English teachers was critical. For the last forty years, the main second language in the schools had been Russian.

"There should be plenty of teaching jobs available somewhere even if you can't teach in a proper school," Nikola had said one night over dinner at my house in San Francisco. "Nobody speaks English— well, hardly anyone—and they need all the help they can get." She

4

held up a huge, old-fashioned iron key, the kind used to open dungeons and gates in black and white movies.

"They even still use these kinds of keys in a lot of their homes!" Nikola said, setting it on the table and then pulling out pictures of Prague with the buildings all dotted with golden spires and red tiles and cobblestoned streets. I could see gas lamps and tiny, mysterious alleyways. Over a bottle of good California wine and flickering candlelight, it had sounded so romantic, so foreign, so mystical. I was hooked, seduced by Nikola's personality and good looks and my desire to suddenly do something radically different with my life. Suddenly, my job covering rock and roll, film and larger-than-life celebrities like Roseanne Barr and Madonna seemed so empty, so unnecessary. Bland music, over hyped big-budget films, pre-recorded concerts, banal television—who needed it! And then there was the traffic, telephones, bills and the tedious enjoinments that defined my life from sunrise to sunset.

The fact that I knew next to nothing about Czechoslovakia gradually faded as a concern. I was excited about the possibility of learning an entire language and culture from scratch. I have had a long and abiding interest in Russian literature, politics and the Slavic languages. At the University of Southern California, I spent some time attempting to learn Russian and master its difficult, intricate Cyrillic alphabet. Like earlier, aborted forays into Spanish and French, I eventually abandoned Russian and instead took degrees in journalism and Creative Writing. Despite not being good at learning languages, I never lost my enthusiasm for the Slavic culture. So, when the late 1989 revolutions swept through the Warsaw Pact countries, I watched with more than idle curiosity as first Poland and then East Germany and Hungary slowly opened. What an opportunity for a journalist! To grab a chunk of the Berlin Wall or explore deep into once-forbidden societies!

Still, I heard more than a few, "You're going where?" comments in the month before I left. Some friends enthusiastically endorsed the move, saying that it could do wonders for my career and self-esteem.

"Imagine all the things you'll see," one friend said. "You can eat strange foods you don't know the name of and fall in love with wild, exotic women! You can drink vodka until it runs out of your ears!"

5

A Czech émigré told me: "I envy you, that you will be living in my homeland. There is so much to see. There is such a history. And the wonderful beer! And then there are the dumplings. Terrific! But don't eat too many as they are dripping with cholesterol and other things that are so bad for you."

Others were more cautionary.

"Hmmn. Seems a bit flaky," a fellow reporter told me. "Are you sure you have thought this through?" One cynical fellow (whose wife is Czech) put it in the most earthy terms possible: "Doug, you *fucking* fool. It's a Communist country. Jesus, take a second look at your atlas and find a better country."

Even the police thought I was a bit demented. The night before I left San Francisco, I had a going-away party at my house. Shortly after one in the morning, a police car, called by the loud blasts of rhythm and blues and funk emanating from the house (and no doubt, a few calls from the neighbors), pulled up in front. I was sitting on the porch with some friends. The two officers politely requested that we lower the volume of the music. One of my friends slapped me one the back and told the police about my relocation plans.

"You're going where?" one of the officers asked.

"To Czechoslovakia," I replied, with the slight grin and air of casualness that I had used to answer and deflect all previous questions about my plans. "To teach English."

"Jesus, have a good party. You're going to need it," one officer said, heading back to the patrol car. "Good luck."

Their comments were little more than static in my ears. I left most of my worldly material possessions, including a huge record collection, in the safe keeping of a friend. I stuffed a typewriter, a dictionary, two travel books on Czechoslovakia, a worn Russian-English dictionary (just in case), dozens of cassettes, clothes, an electric shaver and a toothbrush into three bags.

One long plane flight later—wham—here we were on the train. No wonder I was delirious.

Unable to sleep on the train like Nikola, I pulled out some materials I had found about the country and read some statistics about the region. Prague was the largest city with a population of 1,191,000, while the entire country contained 15.6 million people. Life expectancy for males was 68 years, 75 for women. Infant mortality was an astonishing 13.9 deaths out of 1,000. The country was ethnically divided between Czechs (64%), Slovaks (31%), Hungarians (4%) and Germans (1%). Before the Communists took power in 1948, more than 77 percent of the country was Catholic, while 20 percent was Protestant and two percent was Jewish Orthodox. Before World War II, there were hundreds of thousands of Jews living in the country, and Prague had a flourishing Jewish quarter. But, as in Poland and in Hungary, the Nazis destroyed the Jewish population.[1]

Interestingly, after the 1989 revolution, 24.5 percent of the nation said they had no religious affiliation, which 46 percent said they were Catholic and about 17 percent was Lutheran, Protestant or Hussite. It was the first new survey on religious values since the Communists had come to power in 1948.[2]

These facts brought me no closer to an understanding of just who the Czechs and Slovaks were. An extraordinarily old guidebook cheerfully told me, without much elaboration: "The Czechs, in fact, were long ago nicknamed 'the Yankees of Europe.' The sober, diligent rough-hewn Czech feels more at home in a mine, mill or factory. Like a New Englander or Scotsman, he loves to build machinery, and his homeland, Bohemia-Moravia, is one of the world's most highly industrialized areas." Judging by this screed, I would be meeting a lot of happy mechanics who would take me into the basement after dinner to show me their favorite tools and drills. I also wasn't so sure how good I would be at discussing differing theories of irrigation.

As our train rattled on, I was treated to a vast panorama of crumbling buildings, huge factories belching dark smoke into the sky and tall, identical apartment buildings. Dora leaned over and described how these apartment buildings were called *paneláks* because of their unique panel construction.

But then the buildings drifted off into the distance and the scenery reverted back into gentle countryside split in places by primitively paved roads and dirt and gravel roads. In spots, tall, waving poles and

7

lines sagging with hops covered the countryside. Hops, as any beer fanatic will tell you, are the nucleus for good beer. The thought of beer reminded me that I was thirsty beyond belief. I suggested to Dora that we search for some refreshments.

Dora reached into her luggage and dug out a handful of Czechoslovak *koruny*—crowns—left over from their visit earlier in the year. The currency was faded and crumpled, a jumble of blue and dark green notes. Several of them, most notably the 100 crown note, were larger than American money. At the time, one American dollar was worth about 35 crowns.

As we headed to the dining car to buy several bottles of Czech-made lemonade, Dora pointed out the various politicians whose faces were printed on the money, including a serious-looking man named Klement Gottwald, a long-time Communist who had engineered the peaceful overthrow of the democratic government in 1948. In the restaurant car Dora spoke to the steward in Czech. Their incoherent conversation made me realize that the "Teach Yourself Czech" cassette tapes I had been listening to for several weeks probably wouldn't be enough to teach me how to speak properly. The tape had been full of useful phrases like, "Is it a comedy or tragedy?" and "Please tell the manager to prepare my bill."

"I'm going to try and learn one new word a day," I said with confidence several minutes later as we settled back into our seats with the drinks. Dora looked out the window and sipped her drink through a straw.

"Perhaps if you tried to learn two, you might acquire a larger vocabulary in half the time," she said with only a trace of irony. I grasped her point.

Dusk faded into dark. We sat and drank the sodas while Nikola lay zonked out next to us. I thought about a conversation I had had on the plane flight from Los Angeles to Frankfurt with Eddie Ochagavia, a middle-aged man who had emigrated in the 1970s from the Soviet Union to the United Kingdom. Now he worked as an announcer on the *BBC World Service,* broadcasting news to the Soviet Union in

Russian. Eddie was a fierce defender of Thatcher, Tories, the West and Capitalism (perhaps all in that order), and spent some of the trip arguing about England's economic woes with a young pretty Englishwoman who backed Labour.

And, Eddie could drink. After giving me his card and a brochure outlining his work at the BBC, he proceeded to drink his way through a small pile of those tiny bottles of vodka that the airlines give you.

As the inflight movie ended and many of the people around us slumbered, I asked him about Mikhail Gorbachev's plan to reduce alcoholism in the Soviet Union by reducing vodka production.

"It was a complete failure," he said, twisting open a fresh bottle of vodka. "We can never stop drinking. Gorbachev failed to remember a basic Russian proverb: "To drink is to live." With a great flourish, he poured the bottle into his plastic glass and settled into his seat. He was quite interested to hear that I was moving to Prague.

"Go there," he said. "Go there and see what life is like. Then you will understand what happened there, and everywhere. And, you will understand your life in America better." His words were cautionary and continued to haunt me as I looked out the train window into the dark night.

Prague came in a rush. One minute we were passing open fields and grassy embankments with the occasional glow from villages and streetlights, and the next we found ourselves surrounded in acres of these identical apartment buildings, factories—a living, breathing metropolis.

Shortly after 10:30, the train ground to a stop at Prague's railroad station, Hlavní nádraží (Main Station). Exhausted, dirty and bearing what must have been half a ton of luggage, the three of us clambered off the train.

Opened in 1909 when the country was still ruled by the Austro-Hungarian Empire, Hlavní nádraží has held a variety of names, depending on who was ruling the country at that point. It was first known as *Franz Josef Bahnhof* under the Austria-Hungarian Empire. After the end of World War I and the creation of the first Czechoslovak state, the space was renamed *Woodrow Wilson Station,* as President Wilson had had much to do with the creation of the country. Not long after, on November 23, 1923, Wilson wrote to President T. G. Masaryk, the first President of Czechoslovakia:

> "I yesterday received at the hands of the Charge of the Czechoslovak delegation here the really magnificent volumes in which you have so thoughtfully had bound photographs or places and objects which citizens of Czechoslovakia have been so gracious as to name for me. I feel highly honored at such evidences of their confidence and friendship, and shall treasure the albums as among my most valuable possessions. I hope everything goes happily with yourself and the admirable little republic over which you preside. It is a matter of intense pride with me to have had some part in bringing it into the family of nations."[3]

If Wilson had only known what the next 60 years would bring! During World War II, while the Nazis ruled the country, Wilson's name was dumped in favor of *Hauptbahnhof*. The station was again renamed Hlavní nádraží after the war and has remained ever since.[4]

Alighting at Hlavní was jarring. The main hall was apparently the crossroads of Eastern Europe: it seemed every Romanian, Ukrainian, Bulgarian, Turk and Russian in the region had decided to take a holiday with the whole family at the same instant.

Captivated by the station's alternately spooky and mysterious atmosphere, I gazed up at tall arching ceilings carved in an elaborate Art Nouveau style. The station obviously had been sumptuous, with elegant brown marble walls that now echoed with train information being read in Czech.

Floors were covered with an endless sea of baggage, boxes, vinyl bags and rolled up sleeping bags. The air was pungent with cheap cigarettes and liquor and the halls resounded with the sound of children crying, running, yelling and playing, couples arguing, men trading cigarettes or furtively changing money, playing cards and drinking moonshine from tall bottles.

As train stations in former socialist countries go, Hlavní nádraží was, in retrospect, actually fairly benign, compared to the scenes of near panic I have since witnessed in Moscow and Belgrade, where disorderly ticket lines stretch for yards and people literally fight each other for seats by crawling in through train windows.

Sadly, Prague's elaborate station had been supplanted by a post-modern, gray concrete and metal addition that architectural critics like Prince Charles would deplore as a "barnacle." Completed in the early 1980s, the modern addition—like so much socialist architecture I would see later—was aesthetically ugly, unfunctional and already falling to pieces. Birds nested in the brown beams of the new hall's high metal roof, their droppings fouling the floors. Fluorescent lights flickered across cracked stone floors. The atmosphere was cold and threatening.

While I was waiting for Nikola and Dora to telephone their uncle, I made my way upstairs into the older portion of the station and discovered that the construction of the modern addition also ensured that most passengers no longer used this more grand area. Consequently, most of its former glory was gone; the dark art nouveau ceilings had turned gloomy and faded, the marble walls cracked and ruined. With the exception of a few restaurants and *hernas* (gaming halls), the hall was mostly empty. Spooked by the emptiness, and also by a group of Gypsies watching me from the shadows, I beat a hasty exit back down the stairs.

An abortive attempt to use the bathroom ended when I discovered that you needed several *koruny* to use the toilet. Having no Czechoslovak money yet, I decided to "hold" it. I felt even better about my decision when I got downwind of the bathroom and received a whiff. I also discovered that most of the signs in the station were written only in German, Czech and Russian. English speaking people like me were definitely out of luck.

Presently, a porter, sporting a jaunty navy blue cap pushed far back on his head and wearing a powder blue shirt framed with huge sweat rings and dark black polyester pants, came with a small motorized truck to move our things to the curbside. I followed it, soaked with sweat, out past a host of strange looking signs emblazoned in Cyrillic and Czech, to the curbside, where I found Nikola and Dora arguing in Czech with a handful of male taxi drivers.

Since it was late, many taxis had stopped for the night and the few available didn't want to take us and our assortment of luggage across town to where we would be staying until we found permanent accommodation. There were too many people, they said, and far too much luggage.

Nikola and Dora described the cab drivers as being engaged in a socialist game of sorts, the "to není možné" ("It's not possible") game in which each player shrugs his shoulders and repeats "it's not possible" over and over like a kind of mantra. The winner of "It's not possible" game got to go back to watching his black and white television. Losers had to unhappily do whatever one was asking for. That is, unless the taxi driver had now moved on to socialist game #2: "I'm now going to rip you off."

As Nikola and Dora talked to the drivers, another group of drivers sat nearby drinking beer from tall, half-liter unmarked brown bottles. The night was boiling with humidity and the men, clad in sweat-stained undershirts, hair damp and swept back against their foreheads, passed packs of cigarettes around. One of them looked up and smiled broadly when he saw my peaked condition. He offered me a swig of his beer and a cigarette. I politely declined both.

By that point, I didn't care much about anything, except to take a cold shower and change into some clean clothes. As that refreshing prospect was still hours away, I meekly sank down on a huge pile of luggage and try to fathom what the hell I was doing there.

2

Prague: My New Home

Two taxis, one for us and one for our luggage, were finally agreed upon and we left the confines of the main station. The driver chattered away in Czech with Nikola while he drove with one arm like a maniac. The other arm kept a succession of cigarettes going from mouth to ashtray and back again. He looked a little like Lech Walesa with a thick walrus-like mustache that only Slavic men can seem to sprout.

We roared off down towards a bridge across the Vltava, the river that divides Prague and provides a good chunk of its mythic history.

Although guide books about Czechoslovakia go overboard in describing the Vltava as "a source of inspiration to artists, poets and dreamers," it does resonate with a special quality. It is not wide, like the Danube cutting through Vienna or Budapest, but neither is it inconsequential, and provides Prague with a center of reference and an emotional heart.

The beauty of the Vltava is enhanced by the presence of Hradčany Castle that overlooks Prague from high on a hill over the left bank of the Vltava. The Castle is a sprawling mixture of architectural structures from the medieval and Renaissance periods. In the center of the buildings is the massive Gothic St. Vitus Cathedral. Portions of the Castle date back to the ninth century when Prince Bořivoj of the Czech Přemysl dynasty first built a wooden fort on the hill.

During the 18th century, when Bohemia was considered to be the musical capital of Europe, musicians drew inspiration from the Vltava and the Castle. They were educated in Prague's conservatories and at night performed in the theaters. Mozart, it is said, loved Prague more than Vienna or Salzburg and wrote his Symphony no. 38 for the city and the Vltava. Smetana composed the tone poem *Má Vlast* (My Country) and several others for the Czech nation with the Vltava in mind.

The Castle has been home to a whole host of interesting characters, occupying governments, ruthless scoundrels and out-and-out criminals including Bohemian rulers, Hussite kings, Hapsburg elite, the first democratic government of Czechoslovakia in 1918, Nazis, Communists and as of December, 1989, the new democratic government of Czechoslovakia.

The Soviet army marched to the Castle to take control of the country on a warm night in August, 1968. And, when the Communist government fell in December of 1989, thousands of people gathered in the cold night in Prague's squares to gleefully cry, "Havel na Hrad!" ("Havel to the Castle!") The Castle is the singularly most recognizable structure in the city; its brooding presence dominates the skyline and defines the city's architectural traditions.

As our taxi veered off a side street onto a rough, cobblestone riverfront road, I saw Hradčany's silhouette for the first time. Achingly beautiful and massive, it seemed to float above Prague, its lights reflecting gold and silver onto the shimmering Vltava. Streetlights from each side of the river cast off an orange glow. Red and white streetcars rumbled along the edge of the river with their electrical contacts arcing and throwing off a shower of blue sparks at uneven contact points.

From that moment on, regardless of how depressed I ever became, however homesick or how bad a day I might have had, a stroll along the Vltava with its view of the mighty Castle never failed to lift my spirits.

After crossing across the Vltava, we pulled up in front of a long stretch of apartment buildings on the embankment. In the dark, I could only just make out the details of the architecture, but it was plain that the apartments were beautiful, built before the turn of the century, with detailed cutwork all over the facade.

It was a measure of my cultural ignorance that I wasn't able to properly identify the architectural motifs running along the building, or any of the other buildings in the city. I didn't know Baroque from Modernist, Rococo from Italian Renaissance. Before coming to Prague, a building was, well, just a building.

My naiveté about matters architectural pointed up perhaps a still greater problem: I was too much of an Americentrist. While I consider myself an expert on Pop Culture (some of my friends tell me sadly this isn't something to be proud of), when I arrived in Prague I realized so much of the world had passed me by. I had never seen Mozart's *Die Zauberflöte,* never thought about much about the history of Europe before World War I, never wondered why people live or dress the way they do in different cultures and I certainly didn't know much about the current state of Europe and the issue of economic integration.

Presumably, these topics had been presented to me at one time or another; obviously, they had simply gone in one ear and out the other. Well, here it all was at my fingertips and I felt like my education was going to begin again—quickly.

Nikola and Dora's uncle, František Honzák, was waiting for the taxis under a flickering streetlight near his apartment. He ran over to open the door for us and unload our bags. There was a bad moment when he had a slight row with one of the cab drivers for overcharging us. They pointed at the excessive amount of luggage I was helping to remove from the cars and then František seemed to understand.

Lean and gaunt, with shoulder-length long hair that was slightly streaked with grey, František sported the same kind of thick bushy mustache as the cab driver and a pair of the saddest, weariest eyes I had ever seen. His worn face displayed a set of slightly buck teeth, which gave him a goofy expression whenever he smiled. He seemed friendly and generous.

In the heat of the evening, František—whose nickname was Faust—was dressed in ragged, faded jeans and a dark-blue, short-sleeve shirt covered with tropical-looking white swirls. In Hawaii, he might have fit in as the quintessential beachcomber and driftwood artist. He shook my hand warmly and said good evening to me in Czech: "Dobrý večer."

15

We clambered up a tall, dark staircase to the fourth floor where Nikola and Dora's grandmother, Blanka, was waiting in the entryway of their apartment. By the time I got to the top, I was thoroughly winded.

Compared to many Czech apartments I would see later, their apartment was very large, with a kitchen, storeroom, three rather spacious bedrooms and a large, airy center room. However, Faust, his wife, their children and the grandmother all lived here, so the flat seemed pretty small.

Like a cat exploring fresh territory, I took tentative steps through the house, searching out the toilet, which, European style, was located separate from the wash basin in a small space the size of a closet.

Over the years, Faust had collected an impressive array of *splachovadla,* otherwise known as pull chains. There were chains fashioned from wood, from steel, chains with carvings and chains with pictures. Sadly, the real chain for the toilet was only made of heavy plastic.

We would be sleeping in the children's room. Their mother had taken them away to their cottage in the country for the weekend. The space was lined with kids' books, toys and cheerful posters. A pine wood bunk bed ran against one wall. Other rooms were tastefully furnished with older, antique tables and tapestries.

Presently, we all gathered around a small table in the kitchen. Blanka moved about the room, assembling a late snack of bread, ham and cheese. As she set each item on the table she repeated its name to me in Czech: bread was *chleba,* ham, *sunka,* and the white cheese, *syr.* Faust opened some red wine, and the girls asked him at length about his new job with the government.

Before the revolution, Faust had worked at Albatros, the state publishing house for children's books, writing and editing books. But after the fall of the government, he had taken a job helping to sift through the huge mound of secret papers left behind by the government, and especially, the StB (Státní tajná Bezpečnost), which was the Czech equivalent of the KGB.

Faust said that, although it was a long and difficult task trying to figure out who did what and where, they were slowly piecing together

16

the past. Even though StB officials had done a good job trying to shred as many documents as they could, Faust said there had been too many documents to try and destroy.

The small kitchen was dark, with only one old fixture spreading light across the room. The gloomy darkness reminded me of nights I had spent with my grandparents as a child, watching *Lawrence Welk* or Mutual of Omaha's *Wild Kingdom* on a Saturday night.

Noticing my worried expression at the incoherent babble of Czech, Faust smiled and went out of the room, returning a moment later with a slim, red book called "Easy Czech Phrases for the Traveler." He and the others laughed as I stumbled my way through basic sentences like, "Prosím, platím (Please, I'd like to pay)."

"Sorry, I cannot," Faust said, slowly, looking at me, "speak English. You must learn Czech!" I gave Faust an Oakland A's baseball hat which I had brought from the Bay Area, and was disappointed to discover that he wasn't much interested in baseball.

"He doesn't go in for sports much," Nikola said, translating for Faust. He was, however, quite a collector of foreign money, and so I gave him an assortment of American change that I had in my pocket. He rushed to get his collection out and add the pennies, nickels and dimes into his book.

Faust asked about Nikola and Dora's mother, who lived in Los Angeles. As they all discussed recent family events, I thought of her mother, who had seen us off at the airport the day before.

"Remember Douglas, I think you're doing something important and useful for these people," she said in her heavily accented English. "You'll do fine, and you will see that the people will be very grateful." She had promised to come visit Prague on her next holiday.

After about an hour of banter in the dark kitchen, we collapsed into bed. I slept fitfully for several hours, swaddled in the bottom half of the bunk bed. My body's circadian rhythm, still tuned to California time, woke me up shortly after four in the morning.

In the dark, I fumbled for my shortwave radio and headphones. Dialing along the bands, I searched for a program in English, but all I could find was a babble of Slavic languages, including Czech and Slovak. Other languages sounded similar, but I couldn't tell if they

17

were Polish, Bulgarian, Serbo-Croatian or Russian. Occasionally a German voice glided by, but for the most part, the languages were foreign and unfamiliar.

Suddenly, home seemed a long way away. After I began to get that nervous, quaky feeling in my stomach again, I got up and went to the window which faced out towards the river. Across the water, on the other embankment, a tram rumbled by. Beyond, in a small square, a huge digital clock installed on the side of a building flashed the time (4:03) in huge lights that were almost a story tall.

Peering out at the water, which shimmered under the yellow street-lights, I felt far away from everything I had known before. Calculating the time in my head, I imagined the things that were taking place in California. People at my newspaper were taking phone calls, writing stories, traveling around the Bay Area and living a normal life. What was I doing here? I wasn't Czech. I had never planned on being a teacher. What was I saying? I wasn't a teacher.

Rather than allow myself to panic too much, I went back to bed and again tried scanning across the FM band of my radio.

Before I left the United States, a friend had kiddingly said the former Warsaw Pact countries were probably so backward the Czechs and Slovaks were probably still listening to disco music. The first local station I came across that night was playing Van McCoy's "The Hustle" which ushered in the golden age of disco back in 1974. The station followed up that blockbuster with Abba's "Waterloo," another big hit from the early 1970s. I made a mental note to check and see if *Saturday Night Fever* or *Thank God It's Friday* was playing in Prague movie theaters.

Early the next morning, following a light breakfast of processed ham, brown bread and orange drink that tasted like Tang, only better, I had a shower and shaved.

As plumbing in many Prague apartments was installed before World War II, the bathrooms have extremely limited water pressure and hot water. I climbed into the tub carefully and, holding the telephone-like attachment in one hand, I doused myself as carefully as I

18

could because there was no curtain. Eventually it dawned on me that one had to sit down while bathing or else spray water all over the bathroom.

After my shower, Nikola told me to be happy for the shower, as older apartments sometimes didn't have hot water or shower facilities. Some months later, I met a Czech woman whose darling apartment had been constructed before 1820 and fell into this severe category. Every day she showered at friends' homes.

The plan for our first day in Prague was simple: determine whether we really had been assigned teaching jobs. Since I still didn't know whether this included me, I dressed in a suit and tie in hopes of making the best possible impression on my (I hoped) future employers. School would be starting in less than a week, so we had to move quickly if we wanted to get settled in before the first day of classes.

I walked out to the kitchen where the grandmother Blanka was reading a newspaper and listening to the radio. Strong sunlight was streaming in through the window and the kitchen seemed friendlier than the night before. Blanka smiled at me as I entered and I said good morning, "Dobrý den," using up all my Czech. I sat down at the table and pulled out the phrase book again, hoping to find something useful to say. After discarding possibilities like "My car has had a breakdown and I need help" and "Could you please shine these for me?" I came across a great one: "Jsem nervosní." (I'm nervous.) Blanka smiled again and rattled off a 15 second speech in Czech that was probably meant to reassure me. I smiled dumbly and agreed with her.

With Blanka leading the way, Nikola, Dora and I headed off to the main school office that was responsible for organizing the various school assignments for foreigners. Dressed in our Sunday best, we trooped downstairs and out onto the street. The day was clear, with a few heavy, thunderstorm-like clouds dancing far off in the horizon. It appeared it would dreadfully hot again. Blanka went into a *tabák* (tobacco and cigarette store) to buy some tickets for the tram.

Buses, trams and the subway are all on the honor system. To ride, one must have a monthly pass or purchase a "one ride" ticket somewhere. Those caught without either a ticket or expired ride coupon are fined on the spot.

19

I followed along behind Nikola, Dora and the grandmother like some idiot cousin. Details stood out which had I had never seen before—a whole new culture. An old man stood at the corner, a cane balanced between his legs while he plumped his beret before setting it on his head. Wide trucks with dirty canvas tops hurtled ominously through the streets, throwing up a curtain of exhaust and dust. Women with plaid bandannas and floral work coats carried sacks of groceries home in the early morning sunshine. I stood transfixed. I was 12 the last time I had been in Europe and was far too much of an egocentric youngster to appreciate the countries we had visited.

While Blanka consulted tram times, I gaped at the hustle and bustle around me. There were strange smells: diesel and fresh bread, garbage and dust. A woman moved by, leading a dachshund on a leash. It looked like a sausage on wheels. Then a man passed by carrying an armful of fresh bread. I craned my neck to see the character of the buildings with their faded facades and little awnings.

A long red and white tram rumbled to a stop and we clambered aboard. Three large steps get you into the main compartment. It's a bit of a step for younger people; for the elderly and handicapped, it's a humiliating and difficult climb.

Trams don't offer a smooth ride, especially on some of the city's more uneven cobblestone streets. You really have to hold on, if you can't sit down, which is often, as trams always seem to be overcrowded. Despite looking like they were designed and built shortly after the onset of communism in 1948, the trams actually date back to the mid-1970s.

The elderly and handicapped are automatically given seats on the trams. As we rattled along, Nikola said that the trams are easier for the elderly than the underground subway, which has no elevators and more steps. The previous government neglected to do much for the needs of the handicapped.

"They said handicapped people only existed in capitalist countries!" Nikola said.

Depending on the quality of the driver and the tram, it's quite easy to fall down, especially if you aren't paying attention or holding on. The first time I fell down on a tram was while I was gamely trying to punch my "one ride" ticket in one of the little ticket machines mounted in the trams. After the tram took an unusually hard turn, I suddenly found myself sprawled on the floor.

As people and shops whizzed by, Dora pointed out a huge line snaking out of store. A ha! My first socialist line!

At each stop, a loudspeaker in the tram gave an ominous-sounding metallic chime and then a recording announced the name of the stop. People clambered heavily up and down the tram's three large steps, with the elderly surging towards open seats. And then the tram sluggishly started off again.

Dora pointed out other shops, including a *maso* (meat) store that had cords of blood-red sausages and hunks of beef hanging in the window. A shoe store. And a bookstore—*knihkupectví*. Everything was called exactly what it was. Under the rules of the previous government, few businesses were allowed to have unique or individual names, so a meat store was "meat store" and *pánské oděvy* was exactly what it was: men's clothes. When you needed something for the kitchen, you went on over to the "kitchen needs" store and if your children wanted paper for school, you took them to the "school needs" store. And then, for big celebrations, everyone trotted out to the "restaurant." If it was a big affair, you could go to the one and only "Chinese restaurant" in the center of town. It all seemed like the world's largest generic city.

We arrived at the main school office and were greeted with smiles from several staffers working in the office. Yes, they said, there were jobs for Nikola and Dora, and yes, we have a job for the strange American man who decided to quit his job and come to a country where he couldn't speak the language. Actually, they just smiled at me and said, yes, we have a school for you to teach in.

More chatter. Then Nikola turned to me with a big smile. It seemed the government had arranged for us all to live on the outskirts of town in a building that had been designated for the foreign teachers. It all seemed too good to be true.

"For the first time, I think everything is going to work out," Nikola said, sitting down next to me. She patted my hand reassuringly while I felt my stomach ease back into a normal working order. Here I was, nearly alone in a foreign city and in less than 24 hours had a full-time job and a place to live. My parents would be extremely pleased, I thought, as we turned and headed back down the stairs.

Blanka said something to Nikola and Dora. They laughed and looked at me.

"Blanka says now you can see that Czechs *can* provide for Americans!" Dora said.

We went first to Dora's school, which was a large elementary school just out of the center of Prague that specialized in teaching math and science. We stayed about a half an hour while Dora was introduced to an applauding staff as a rarity—a native English speaker who could also speak Czech fluently!

Blanka, satisfied that our jobs had been confirmed, went back to their apartment and the school custodian at Dora's school was given the responsibility of transporting us off to the other schools. We drove us off through more tree-lined, narrow streets and across a boulevard lined with several large ugly apartment complexes and a row of stores. Less than two minutes later, we pulled up in front of a building that was my school—Základní Škola Prokopová (Prokopová Elementary School).

Grey and imposing, the front of Prokopová featured flat, unadorned architecture. Set on the corner of a large boulevard, it looked out over a row of apartments and a construction site. The school had been constructed to be a hospital during World War I and looked like it could take a day's worth of mortar fire and not lose a brick. The custodian left Dora and I off at the school and then drove Nikola off to visit her school, which also was located in the neighborhood.

Once inside, through a huge set of oak doors, we were greeted by the principal, a plump woman with short brown wavy hair. She ushered us up to the second floor where she and another teacher of about forty, were drinking coffee.

"Hello," the teacher said effusively while rising to her feet. "We've been waiting anxiously for you."

Waiting for me? I was more than amazed.

"Yes, the school office called us last week and said there would be an American teaching here. We were most pleased to learn of this, you know."

The teacher, whose name was Dana Vránová, explained that they didn't have many English teachers, even though the school supposedly specialized in teaching languages. She and the other English teachers on the staff were very happy to finally have a native English speaker who could help them rebuild their language department.

"You know, English was sort of forbidden here before. We did teach it, but not many people learned how to speak it very well," Dana said, her words coming quickly in a rush. She had very serious eyes that were hidden behind large glasses. Her face was equally serious, set off by dark, wavy hair.

"Of course, we have plenty of Russian teachers!" she said, giggling and gesturing towards the principal. "Our principal here is just such a teacher!" The principal grinned and said nothing.

"She doesn't speak English," Dana said, inviting me and Dora to sit. Dana produced a sheaf of papers and explained that I would have a full schedule of classes every day.

"Just like a real Czech teacher!" Dana said, touching my leg and giggling again. She had a nice laugh, a cross between a giggle and a full chuckle.

"But, you know," I said, looking worried. "I've never taught before."

"We'll help you," Dana said reassuringly. "We know you'll have a lot to learn. And maybe, we can learn from you, too. There is such a change going on here in our country, you see." Her English was perfectly correct and sounded almost British, except that she had a habit of throwing the words "such" and "you see" into her conversation. The principal continued to say nothing—even in Czech—during this first meeting; she merely sat behind her desk and fiddled with papers or smiled while looking at me.

As the school secretary served us a cups of thick "Turkish" coffee, in which boiling water is poured right over the grounds, Dana asked me questions about where I was from and what I used to do in the United States.

"I have never been to the United States," Dana said. "This, I think you will find, is quite normal, as most of us never were allowed to go there, and even if we could have, you see, we never had the money for such trips. But I have been in London. In fact, I studied English there for several months. It is such a beautiful country."

While she and the principal went over some papers for my work permit, Dora and I waited and drank our coffees. When I reached the bottom of the small cup, I nearly spit on the floor. Dora looked at me sympathetically.

"You don't have to drink the grounds in the bottom of the cup."

Just then, Dana came back with the school papers I would need to take to the authorities.

"What do your parents think of you being in such a strange country like Czechoslovakia?" Dana asked, handing me the documents. I didn't want to say that they probably thought I should be committed, so I merely said they were very interested in my travels.

Dana seemed to be all nervous energy and action. She clapped her hands and nearly clucked at me and Dora, "Well, well, let's have a tour of the school, shall we?"

We walked about the school, looking in classrooms and ascending a wide set of stairs. Teachers were busy preparing their rooms for fall, counting out textbooks, putting up student artwork from the previous year onto yellow-and-white walls and arranging desks and chairs.

With its painted cement floors and school books and student work displayed in cabinets, Prokopová could have passed for any school in the United States. It was old and faded but felt right: chalk smells and pencil shavings, echoing ceilings. The classrooms looked like they had seen generations of children coming in and out every day.

If my old elementary school teachers could have seen me, busily inspecting the classrooms with their green blackboards and sturdy desks, they would have laughed—I am the most unlikely teacher.

Until the eighth grade, I hated school and hated riding the ugly yellow bus. I genuinely fantasized about the school burning down or collapsing during an earthquake—preferably with my teachers in it. I was a bit of a smart aleck who wondered why he hadn't been appointed to do something more useful instead of sit in a classroom all day. My grades didn't reflect my self-image of inner brilliance, and I was forced to constantly prove my case to an ignorant world.

Just then, Nikola arrived back with the school custodian with instructions that we were to go to our housing. As we left, Dana told me not to worry much about school just that day. She said the only teachers who were working were the homeroom staff that had to prepare for the beginning of school the following week.

"Come back tomorrow and we'll go over a few things," she said.

The school custodian—called a *školník* in Czech—drove us to the edge of town where our housing was located. Driving onto one of the four-lane freeways that snake through Prague, he headed southeast through a number of suburbs: Vyšehrad, Kačerov, Roztyly.

The custodian owned a tiny, four-door, white Škoda, the state national car. Perhaps five out of six passenger cars in Czechoslovakia are Škodas. Before Western cars began to be sold in wide numbers in Czechoslovakia, the rest of the cars on the road were usually Trabants (East Germany), Ladas (Soviet Union), Zastavas (Yugoslavia), and Polish Fiats.

A typical joke about the Škoda: how do you double the value of a Škoda? Fill it with gas. A second joke, but completely true, is that in Czech, the word *škoda* means "pity." So if one says, "To je škoda," you are saying, "It's a pity."

In reality, Škodas aren't the worst cars you've ever driven—Trabants and Ladas are worse—but they are slow and sometimes hard to start. Since Volkswagen's 49 percent investment into Škoda in 1991, the rebuilt and modernized Škoda has become very much of a success story throughout Europe as a cheap but effective mode of transportation.

But the older Škodas, forget it. With luck, you might be able to accelerate from 0 to 60 mph by next month. Things rattle and bang and you have to talk loudly in order to be heard over the roar of the engine.

The country also makes Tatra vehicles, including trucks, tractors and heavy limousine-like sedans that sound like motorboats when they accelerate. Tatra cars apparently only came in two colors, black and silver, and looked vaguely sinister—like the black ZIL Soviet limousines that used to ferry members of the Party to functions around Moscow. Trabants are a mystery, with the gear shift on the steering wheel and most of the frame constructed literally out of plastic. Until U2 decided that Trabants were fun and popularized them via their

Achtung Baby album from 1991, the car was always the laughing-stock of the Warsaw Bloc car industry. As for the Soviet-made Lada, a Russian friend of mine used to say that the Soviet Government's praise for its cars was simply nothing more than a "Lada Shit."

The ride out to the housing gave me my first chance to see the housing projects thrown up by the Communists over the past forty years. If Faust's apartment had seemed tranquil and idyllic in all of its splendor and grace, this was an architectural side of the city that the tourist books generally didn't bother to dwell on.

Beginning in the early 1960s, the buildings were hastily thrown up by the government because the country faced a severe housing shortage. Usually square or rectangle blocks of battleship gray concrete and steel, the buildings are uniform and unaesthetic. Every room is exactly the same. Phony pinewood formica covers doors, some walls and the inside of bathrooms.

Years before, when we lived for a time in New York, I was shocked by the gross uniformity of the huge, ugly housing projects in the South Bronx and New Jersey. But those places had been but mere blips on the landscape, strange contusions that seemed out of place with my protective suburban world. Ugly buildings in Yonkers and the South Bronx were only ugly and you drove by them and everyone in the car rolled up their windows and locked their doors and said "Gee, I'm glad I don't live there" and then the buildings were gone and everything was hunky-dory again.

In the former Warsaw Bloc countries, from Prague to Vladivostok, these huge housing complexes are everywhere, normal reminders of socialism's failure to synthesize aesthetics with the need to properly house the masses. Some American visitors to Prague often remark the previous government should be commended for at least making an attempt to house its people. But at what a cost? The apartments are dehumanizing and grim, with each family being treated in the same ugly, offhanded way that defined socialism at its most gray and unappealing. While it is true that many governments around the world have experimented from time to time with these housing complexes. most have discovered that they often end up creating more problems than they solve.

The building in Prague where we would be living was one of these *paneláks,* except it had been painted brown and white. All around our building were literally kilometer after kilometer of more apartments.

Our building was appropriately named "Dům Učitelu"—The House of Teachers. "Dům" was pronounced "Doom." It had been just completed and was to be used for visiting students and teachers from other countries in the socialist brotherhood, including Cuba, Bulgaria, the Soviet Union, Libya and North Korea. Now that the socialist party was over, the halls were going to be filled with visiting students and teachers from all of Czechoslovakia's new friends, including England, the United States, Ireland, Canada, Australia and Germany. It was like a mini-United Nations.

The manager of the building went over the rules: no visitors after midnight, no mixed couples living together unless they could prove they were married, no parties, and no loud noise. I was assigned a room on the 16th floor—a distance too far to jump in case of fire, I noted as I poked my head out the window in the floor's communal kitchen. The kitchen had some white formica counters, cabinets and several hot plates. There was no oven, but I was told that one would be installed soon. A separate room contained two large pinewood dining-room tables with plastic red and white checkerboard tablecloths. Yet another room had a television and an array of chairs. Near the elevators was a room with a washing machine and a place to hang wet clothes out to dry.

My "apartment" actually consisted of two rooms, one for my roommate—who hadn't yet moved in—and one for me. In my room, there was a small daybed, a table that folded out to seat as many as six people, a cupboard with glass doors and a hideaway for the duvet, pillow and sheet. Two large closets neatly accommodated all of my hanging clothes, while the rest of my things I shoved in a smaller, wooden cabinet.

The view? Well, it was about the same from every window in the building: lots and lots of other grey buildings the same height receding into the horizon.

I sat down and bounced on the bed. Not too hard, not too soft. Spongy. In the entryway near the door was a small refrigerator and a large shelf that later became known as the "eating bar" as there wasn't a proper table: one simply stood in front of the refrigerator and stared dumbly at the blank white wall while eating. There was a separate bathroom and another small closet with a sink and a shower. I was most pleased to see the shower instead of a bathtub.

Everything in the room and the building was spanking new and clean. So much that the halls reeked of fresh paint and cut wood and electrical insulation. It took weeks before the lot of us had managed to overpower the new building scent with our own. I went back into my room and looked again at the bed and the cabinet and the book-shelf and thought of home in San Francisco. I felt like I had been assigned a room in a sanitarium.

Meeting up with Nikola and Dora again on the ground floor (they had been assigned to rooms on the third floor), we picked our way through the maze of buildings and found the local subway station, which thankfully was only about a five minute walk from the Dům. We were lucky, Dora said, because we wouldn't have to endure long bus rides or walk a kilometer every day just to reach the public trans-portation.

The subway's three different lines stretch out across Prague so that a good portion of the city is reachable in only a matter of minutes. Of all the mechanical systems in the country, the subway works very well and is effective, something President Havel had gone out of his way to note in his otherwise somber 1990 New Year's Day speech when he assumed control of the government.

Trains came about every five minutes and the riders didn't seem as impatient as in the United States. People waited quietly, staring forward and saying little.

When one of the long, gunmetal grey cars arrived, we took a space on seats fashioned from heavy red plastic along each side of the car. Signs in each car in Czech and Russian reminded everyone that the Soviet Union had been kind enough to build the subway for the Czech people. In addition, all of the stations were in the process of chang-ing their names from socialist monikers like "Gottwaldova" (after the first "Working Class" president of the country, Klement Gottwald) and "Kosmonatů" (after the Soviet cosmonauts) to local locales like

"Vyšehrad" and "Háje." These new names generally derived from a local landmark or part of town, not a famous Soviet war hero or member of the Politiburo.

It was a long way from the apartment to the center, and at each stop, a prerecorded voice blared out a Czech sentence. The doors slammed shut so hard it looked like they would sever limbs.

I asked Nikola what the recording said at each station. She smiled and said, "Ukončete výstup a nástup dveře se zavírají."

"What? What the hell does that mean?" I asked. I couldn't even begin to pronounce the first word.

"Please finish your getting on and getting off as the doors are closing," Nikola said in a rough translation. She tried to help me through the first few words but quickly gave up in frustration. The sentence was more than a mouthful. I really didn't know how I would ever learn to speak well enough to make anyone understand.

The ride was clean and stable. But no one talked at all. Instead, the riders just sat quietly and looked straight ahead. When the car came to a stop, the silence was literally deafening.

We arrived back at the apartment down by the river in time to eat a wonderful dinner of ham, cabbage and Czech dumplings—*knedlíky*—made from potatoes. This meal is perhaps the best known, traditional dinner one can have in Bohemia and Moravia. The ham was smoked, the cabbage like German sauerkraut, but much sweeter, and the dumplings heavy, sliced and shaped like small fifty-cent pieces. We drank wine and Nikola and Dora told Faust all about the housing and the schools. Nikola's school specialized in sports and Dora's in math and science. Both of them were literally bubbling over with anticipation.

In the interest of avoiding cultural faux-pas in Czechoslovakia, I asked Dora about various dos and don'ts in public. Some of the advice, like not pointing in public and covering one's mouth while yawning, made sense. But I was a bit mystified by the rule that one did not scratch (anything) in public, even if the itch is killing you.

While I was getting used to a few of the new ways of life, like sitting down to bathe and pulling a chain to flush the toilet, I was still having a hard time remembering to change into slippers every time I entered the apartment. When at work or at home, Czechs without fail wear slippers instead of regular shoes. While part of the reason behind the habit is rooted in Czech culture, a major reason for the slippers is practical: the slippers don't muddy up the home or wear down the carpets or rugs. Earlier in the day at the school, Dana had showed me a pair of the children's slippers—*bačkory*—which they were required to wear.

Many Czech workers, too, wear their slippers, especially women in food and liquor stores. Even though these slippers are admittedly a lot more comfortable than regular shoes, it still is an amusing thought to think of the country's high-level politicians making critical decisions about their nation's future while wandering around in their slippers.

After dinner, we watched a program on television that featured a high-strung British teacher encouraging his students to speak English with him. Both the class and the teacher seemed too overjoyed at the prospect of speaking English together and the whole thing came off as a tad unbelievable. Still, it was a useful thing to see the kind of phrases the teacher worked with. He started with the basics: *Good morning, What's your name? How old are you?*

As I watched all this, I was still doubting whether I would be able to make the children understand. Dana had told me earlier in the day that she was happy that I couldn't speak Czech, simply because the children would have to try harder with me in English and couldn't cheat.

Early the next morning, I dressed quickly and headed out the door with a map, a notebook and a camera. As we would be spending the afternoon moving our things to the Dům, I didn't want to lose much time. Nikola looked at me carefully as she handed me some money that Faust had loaned us until we got our first paychecks.

"Are you sure you're going to be OK?" she asked.

"Yes," I said, "I'm sure I'll get lost. Please don't worry."

I went down the stairs and onto the street. It was the first time I had been truly alone in several days and I had an odd, giddy feeling that seesawed back and forth between joy and trepidation. Nobody knew me. I was free to explore anywhere and that prospect excited me. However, I could just as easily be snatched off the street and sold into Soviet slavery for a dime and no one would know or care. That scared me.

I decided to walk along the river until I got tired and then head back. It was another hot, muggy day and the sky was overcast and grey. I immediately began to sweat through my shirt.

Upon reaching the river, I discovered that there was no sidewalk running along the water. There was only a major road used for carrying cars and trucks. After nearly getting squashed by several huge trucks belching noxious blue and black exhaust, I retreated back towards Faust's apartment. Checking my map again, I selected a different route that would take me to the American Embassy located squarely in Malá Strana or Lesser Town, one of the five sectors that make up the heart of Prague's downtown.

Nearby, the window of the state run record store called Supraphon was cluttered with records that were more than several years old. The previous government licensed only a few western records each year so locals had slim pickings when it came to imported music. There was a Duran Duran album from 1984, a handful of Czech records and a collection of "Negro Spirituals" sung by Paul Robeson, the black American actor and singer whose outspoken leftist political views made him popular in the Soviet Union and a pariah in the United States during the McCarthy era. Also in the window were several albums by David Peel, a singer-songwriter from the late 1960s who dreamily sang about the benefits of free love and the legalization of marijuana. By 1973, Peel's music had faded worse than his tie-dye t-shirts and his career was consigned to the "Where Are They Now?" file. Judging from the display, Peel's latest record, *Bring Back the 60s,* was either a big seller here or merely one of the few available records.

Faust had said the night before that people in Prague were still shaking their heads about the recent visit of the Rolling Stones to Prague. The Stones had posed for pictures on a balcony at the castle, ate fish with President Havel at a local restaurant and then played to over 300,000 people at the mammoth Strahov Stadium, a structure usually reserved for the most holy of Communist events, including a massive sports presentation called *Spartakiada* that was held only once every five years. For the first time in its history, Prague's subway ran beyond midnight to accommodate the thousands of people who needed to get home. The Stones had also allowed copies of their most recent album, *Steel Wheels,* to be licensed by Supraphon and sold at a low price. The album was snapped up faster than toilet paper in the markets.

I moved on from the record store to a nearby book store that had a selection of *samizdat*—forbidden—literature in the window. These clandestine volumes, including Havel's plays and essays, were now beginning to be properly printed and released to a large readership. Included amongst the books were new recordings by exiled Czech folksinger Karel Kryl and an older recording of Havel's play *Audience,* featuring Havel and a popular local actor, Pavel Landovský. There was also a new book, *Soudruh Agressor* (*Comrad Aggressor*) about the August, 1968 invasion. This was the real story of what the Soviets called the "Great Befriendment of Czechoslovakia," including how many citizens had been killed on the streets and which Czech and Slovak leaders had betrayed their own people by inviting the Soviets to invade. People could earlier have only gotten this information from a *samizdat,* or through word of mouth. Here it was, now freely discussed and able to be sold in a book store.

Goods varied little from shop to shop, as each market seemed to have the same paltry arrangement of foodstuffs sadly arranged in each window (peaches from Red China, bottles of wine, coffee, tea from Vietnam). A hardware store had an impressive array of wrenches and nails lined up in its window. By the looks of things, the display hadn't changed in recent years as most everything had rusted.

After about 45 minutes of meandering, I entered the Malá Strana portion of the city that features narrow, interlocking streets running slowly up the hill towards the giant Castle. With its cobblestone streets and aging, decaying baroque buildings and structures, the Malá Strana quarter is a perfect magnet for tourists who come to imagine themselves as 18th century subjects of the Castle. Malá Strana has played a vital role in Prague's artist community. The noted Czech writer Jan Neruda and the painter Alfons Mucha both lived in Malá Strana, thereby encouraging other artists to move to the neighborhood. Kafka and Rilke also lived for a time in various apartments there.

One paper store had a window piled high with nothing but toilet paper, all of it gray and with a violently rough surface. Several doors down, I stood in the shade of a meat store watching a woman cutting hunks of salami and huge pink fat sausages. There seemed to be at least ten different kids of sausages, everything from small hot dog sized links to long, coiled white sausages that looked like enormous tapeworms. The smell of the meat and the lateness of the hour reminded me that I was starving.

At a small stand-up snack bar called an *občerstevní,* I bought a bottle of pale lemonade soda and two *cheblíčky,* small open faced sandwiches that are quite popular all over portions of Germany, Poland and Czechoslovakia. Depending on the quality of the restaurant, the little sandwiches, which are made from small slices of white bread, come heaped with everything from a dollop of mayonnaise and a slice of ham and a pickle, to elaborate arrangements of egg and caviar. I ordered by saying "please" a lot in Czech and pointing (delicately) to what I wanted behind the glass counter. The shop assistant asked me if I wanted one or two sandwiches and I noticed that she used the more European style of counting by using her thumb to indicate "one."

My first *cheblíčky* weren't much—a spread of bland potato salad topped with a bit of hard boiled egg and a pickle. The major problem with eating a *chebičky* is that they tend to fall apart quite easily (unless, of course you're eating a day-old stale sandwich, which is often the case in many of the cheap restaurants) and collapse onto the plate or your lap in a soggy heap. Or, just as you raise the sandwich to your mouth, the pickle and egg drop off suddenly to the floor.

Refreshed, I went back onto the street and made my way up a narrow route lined with several buildings in various phases of reconstruction. As I reached the top of the street, I saw the American Embassy, which looks out over the city from a position not far from the Castle. It was strangely reassuring to see the American flag hanging above the entrance and a group of Marines on duty inside. I turned and headed back down the hill, narrowly avoiding being crushed by a small Škoda that came barreling down the street at the same moment.

As I walked along, I found myself ruminating about the weariness I had glimpsed in Faust's eyes. They had seemed so tired-looking. But he wasn't alone in this. People seemed to carry the weight of their years in their body. Everyone seemed tired: fatigue showed in Dana's eyes at the school, in the shop assistant's arms as she cut huge fat slices of white cheese for a customer and in an elderly woman's stoop as she waited in line for minutes before she could enter a store. Older men looked utterly beaten: the lines in their eyes were deep and chiseled over a canvas of dark blotches spreading upwards from the tops of their noses. They walked with hunched shoulders, their faces squashed down towards the pavement, their entire frames seemingly forced down by some giant, unseen hand.

When I arrived back at Faust's apartment, I asked Nikola whether she saw the same weariness in the people.

"Of course," she said. "Life isn't easy here. Many people don't have cars, they have to wait for everything, then they don't get what they want at the end of the day and they've worked very, very hard for nothing."

The fatigue I saw all around me was deepened by the poor quality, generic and shapeless clothes so many people were forced to wear, simply because there wasn't anything better available in the shops. When Havel and other dissidents entered the government, none of them generally owned Western-quality clothes fit for leaders of a major power. While Havel and the new Foreign Minister, Jiří Dienstbier (a close friend of Havel's and a fellow dissident) now had a good array of fine looking suits, the average person on the street was far from being able to afford or even find decent-looking clothes. Denim was available but looked cheap and faded. Too-dark brown polyester jackets and sad grey pants were abundant. There just weren't any vibrant colors to be seen; everything was devoid of color, rumpled and as fatigued as the faces. Old men peered like goldfish from behind thick glasses that must have weighed half a pound.

In the early afternoon, we took the metro back out to our new home on the edge of town. Faust wished us luck and said he would bring our luggage later in the day. Upon arriving back at the Dům, I found the 16th floor still fairly quiet, with only one person in the kitchen preparing an early dinner. I wandered along the hall listening for signs of life, but it seemed dead. Several people had put their names on the doors ("Hi! I'm Susan!") and even one girl had put up a special "Thought For the Day" on the door written in loopy handwriting on a pink notecard. It all seemed so much like college.

I spent the evening curled up in my little room with its bare, echoing white walls and found Voice of America on the shortwave. It was a comfort to hear some English and catch up on the news, all of which seemed to be grim: American troops were deploying by the thousands to Saudi Arabia and Stevie Ray Vaughan, one of my favorite blues guitarists, had been killed in a helicopter crash in Wisconsin. Depressed, I snapped the radio off and lay in the dark, listening to the occasional sounds of people shutting their doors or flushing their toilets.

Nikola and Dora woke me up early the next morning. They were nearly inseparable and usually charged with energy from the first moment of the day. While they busily discussed buying paper to make flash cards for their students and planning future lessons, I was struggling along behind them with more perfunctory needs like coffee and breakfast.

"Ah, I think you'll find that Czechs really don't eat much breakfast here," Dora said, while I got dressed. "They usually start with a roll and butter and some of the that strong coffee you had yesterday. People generally don't have the money for more. And besides, they all get up so early—like 5 A.M.—that they don't have time for more."

OK. So no breakfast today. I realized I had to get to a market soon so I could fix my own meals.

After a morning in our schools, we were all supposed to meet at 11:30 A.M. at the main school office to sign some work papers. While we were riding the metro, I tried to learn some of the station names and a few words from my phrase book. But after awhile, I found myself again drawn to the lack of emotion or words emanating from the people around me. It was like everyone was alone in his own sleepy

35

fog. People weren't robots *per se,* as they sneezed, wiped their noses, read papers and mumbled occasionally to their companions, but next to American society, the Prague metro had a funeral parlor atmosphere.

Although Nikola wanted to walk me down towards my school, I waved her off at the metro station.

"Have no fear," I said waving my hand dramatically. "I can find it. I remember where we were yesterday." Nikola watched me rather doubtfully as I wandered off down the hill towards what I believed was Prokopová. Although, it was a school, it wasn't *my* school. Sighing, I gamely went inside and asked the first person I saw where Prokopová was by just saying the name of the school over and over (Prokopová? Prokopová? Prokopová?) By now, I had also found in my phrase book how to say, "Where is?" in Czech. A teenage boy steered me back onto the street and gestured with his arm down towards another square that I immediately recognized as the right one. I thanked him very much in Czech and English and continued on my way.

Once inside Prokopová, Dana greeted me warmly and took me to see the school secretary, who slowly typed out my forms with two fingers. On her desk was a new recording of official and clandestine radio and television broadcasts from the 1968 invasion, including the famous words of encouragement repeated daily by the free radio stations: "We are with you; Be with us."

The secretary wrote out on a small piece of paper how much money I would be making each month: 2,987 crowns, or about $103. Dana whistled low through her teeth and clucked her tongue.

"I see they are paying you top rate here for a teacher even though you have never taught before!" she said, without sounding surprised or angry. "The average salary is about half that, and it can sometimes take up to ten years of teaching to get this kind of money. It must be because they want you to stay, you filthy rich American!" Seeing the look of concern on my face, Dana laughed and hit me slightly on the arm. "I'm only teasing of course! You must thank the principal for your money when you see her next."

While the secretary typed out yet another form, Dana explained that she wasn't the only teacher with whom I'd be working.

"There is another English teacher, and you will meet her when school begins. Her name is Jana. In fact, you will have the same office as her." Dana led me down the hall to a small narrow room with one window and a long table that would serve as a desk for us. There were two bookcases against the wall and a small hot plate for making coffee or tea.

Dana kept apologizing at every turn for either the condition of the building or the quality of the furnishings.

"I'm sorry that we haven't more to offer you and I think you'll find that the salary is quite low compared to how much you must have made in America but then. . . ."

"Gee, if you make it sound so bad, perhaps I'll leave," I interrupted, smiling. Dana turned and giggled.

"I'm sorry, Douglas, but you will come to see how terribly bad off we are this year and with everything in such a state!" She swept her hand around the building as if to show me the near collapse of her country.

I left the school with my papers and with plenty of time to reach our 11:30 A.M. appointment at the offices nearby. It was once I headed back out onto the street that I got confused.

Having somehow misplaced the address, I decided to try and follow Dana's vague instructions as to where I should be going. This, as I discovered after less than two minutes, was not a wise idea and I found myself zig-zagging from tree-lined street to tree-lined street in hopes of finding the correct building. "It's not far," I heard Dana saying as I left Prokopová. "Less than five minutes." An hour later, my forehead streaked with sweat, I somehow bumbled into the appropriate gray building.

Although I was only a few minutes late, I didn't see Nikola or Dora anywhere and the secretary in the office had no idea why I needed to give her any papers. We stared at each other, trapped inside our own languages until a tall, balding man in a white tennis shirt and khaki pants came along and helped me. He spoke English.

"I was supposed to bring these papers down here for some kind of meeting at 10 A.M." I explained. "I'm sorry I'm late."

"It's perfectly understandable. Prague is a big city," he said, not knowing it had taken me nearly an hour to stumble several blocks. "This is not the right office, but I have a car and I'll take you to where you want to go." We bounded down the stairs and into his Škoda. On the drive, he asked me questions about America and why I had come to teach. He was a "super principal" of sorts, responsible for several schools in the district.

"I will come to your school later next month to see you and the other teachers," he said. He smiled a lot as he drove, which was very fast. After less than five minutes, he pulled up in front of a building near the center of town. "It is here," he gestured, at the building. "On the fourth floor." He shook my hand and told me to call him if I had any problems. As he drove away I realized I hadn't gotten his name.

After climbing to the fourth floor, I went inside and talked to the secretary, who spoke some English. I told her I had my papers and that I had missed my meeting which was at 10 A.M. She replied that she didn't know anything about any papers but that the "meeting" was actually scheduled for 11:30. It was nearly 11:30. She told me to take a seat and I did so, feeling weary. I had a funny, sinking feeling that I still wasn't in the right office. Finally, when the meeting commenced, it turned out to be for a group of British teachers who had come as part of a holiday package to see what Prague's schools were like. There was one from London and another from Manchester and one from Wales. When they asked me to introduce myself, I didn't know what to say.

"I'm afraid I'm not supposed to be here!" I cried. "I was only supposed to deliver my working papers to Libuše Hravánková at 10 A.M.! I'm an American. Not with a group!" They looked stunned in a proper British sort of way and said I could stay for the meeting if I wanted. I left the office as quickly as I could bought a proper map with the few crowns I had left. Finding Prokopová on the map, I walked back to the school—a considerable distance that took me the better part of another hour to cover. I didn't care, mostly as I didn't trust anyone to give me a ride or myself enough to risk the bus system. Back at Prokopová, Dana was busily sorting through books in her classroom. She took one look at my sticky glasses and dirty shirt and nearly screamed.

"What happened to you?"

I explained as best I could and Dana laughed and told me to give her the papers. *She* would make sure they got to the office safely. "As we can see, you Americans need help with direction!" She advised me to go home and take a shower. I found my way back to the subway and returned to the Dům where I collapsed onto my bed in a sweaty heap. I hadn't been lying there very long before Nikola and Dora were knocking on my door.

"What the hell happened to you?" Nikola said. "You got lost, didn't you!" I told them all about my walking adventure and they laughed and suggested I buy myself a leash to protect myself. After their giggles had subsided, Nikola said we were all going downtown. I nearly groaned.

"Come on, at least you'll be with us. You won't get lost that way," Nikola said, tugging my arm.

We took the metro to Wenceslas Square (Václavské náměstí), Prague's central and widest boulevard. When we came up onto the street from the subway, I immediately recognized the huge statue of Saint Wenceslas on his horse at the top of the square from pictures I had seen from the revolution in 1989 and also from the Soviet invasion in 1968. The statue was built in 1912 to commemorate a Czech patron saint murdered by Boleslav I in 935.

Just behind the statue at one end of the square (as it's a half-mile long and 200 feet wide, it's more of a rectangle) is the large National Museum, which contains a large array of archeological and anthropological displays. Constructed during the Czech national revival during the mid 19th century, the museum at night is impressive, lit up dramatically by spotlights that show off the building's domed glass cupola and gilded stone facade. The building is covered in grime as it now sits over a freeway that cuts across the top of the square. And, if you look closely enough near the top of the museum front, you can still vaguely see the places where they patched the bullet holes left by Soviet tanks in 1968.

Immediately below the statue, a round planter box had become a memorial to the many people who suffered or whose memories had been suppressed by the Communists. The cement around the planter was covered with flowers and flickering votive candles. Dora pointed

39

out some of the people in the pictures including T. G. Masaryk, the first Czechoslovak president in 1918 and Jan Palach, a young Czech who, as "Torch no. 1," had immolated himself on Wenceslas Square in 1969 to protest the Warsaw Pact occupation of the country.

Many people were milling about enjoying the warm late afternoon air on the square. Walking away from the museum towards its far end, we discovered a huge tank that had been rolled onto its side and covered with peace slogans and candles. To this day, I don't know who put it there, but the tank was a stirring sight to see. It was covered in melted wax and bits of flowers amidst bits of verse like "All U need is Luv" and "Give Peace a Chance."

We went to one of the official photo studios in Prague to have passport pictures taken for our official documents. Like everything associated with socialism, I quickly came to see that there was a very rigid order to the process. First there were the forms and the payment of money and then the actual photo session, which was carried off with all the solemnity of a wedding portrait.

After the woman had clicked off several black and white shots, she sighed and spoke sharply to Nikola, who was waiting her turn.

"She says you can't smile. These are for the official documents and people can't smile."

Oh. So no smiling. I tried to look as serious as possible until the shutter clicked again and the photographer seemed satisfied. In the picture, which I received several weeks later, my expression looked almost like Mona Lisa's.

After about an hour of wandering, we went into a small bar off of the main square. Dusk turned to dark and on an empty stomach, I drank several glasses of wine while we listened to De La Soul on the stereo. Unwittingly, I was about to be initiated into the Czech way of drinking, which more often than not, leads to ruin.

A man sitting on a stool near us took a liking to me when he heard me speaking English with the girls, who were trying to coach me in a bit of Czech. The man had a dark, furry beard and was wearing a jaunty sailor's cap. He already had drunk a fair amount. He mumbled something in Czech to Nikola, who turned and looked at me and started laughing.

"He wants to know if you will give him permission to talk to me," she said.

"Sure, I said," waving a hand through the air. "Why not." The two of them talked for a moment and then she looked at me again.

"He wants to know if he could buy you a drink because you are an American," Nikola said.

"But only if I can buy him a drink afterwards," I said. This was not a smart idea. The man was drinking vodka, and it is a poor job ever to begin drinking with someone who clearly knows what he is doing—and this man had lots of prior experience. In addition to the ruddy, red complexion that one develops over years of drinking, he had what I later came to call "The Voice," a deep, scratchy, raspy vibrato that afflicts hardcore drinkers in Prague. Their speech betrays years of unfiltered cigarettes, lousy food, too much beer (and, judging by this man's looks, too much of everything) and hard living. He sounded like someone doing a poor imitation of Louis Armstrong.

After two or three rounds had come and gone, I was starting to feel good as the chatter around me was warm and congenial and my feet weren't hurting too badly. But soon The Voice was back again, pestering me to have another round of vodka, which was insanely cheap, even by Czech standards.

"He says that before the Russians came, Czechs didn't drink so much," Nikola translated. I hoped so. The sixth—or was it the seventh?—round of icy vodka came and went and by then, it was too late. The room started to spin like someone was twisting me around on my stool. Everyone was merry. The Voice was especially jolly, dancing a little jig as he threw back another short glass of the cold vodka. Everyone was laughing. I thought I would be sick.

Dora and Nikola were doing their best to keep up with me and The Voice, but wisely decided that it was time for us to leave. They dragged me out of the bar just as The Voice wanted us to have "just one more." The subway closes down at midnight, so if you live outside of town, you have to end your celebrating or be forced to endure a long ride on a night bus that seems to take hours just to reach the end of the city. We came to call the final run of the metro the "drunk tank" as half the people on board are usually loaded to the gills. As we climbed

41

out of the metro into the dark night near our apartments, a strong wind was blowing across the open field. The heat wave had broken.

I awoke late the next day—a Saturday—and felt relieved that I didn't have to do much of anything for the day. I spent the morning slowly putting things into the closet space I had been allotted and fussing over the few books and papers I had brought with me. Nikola and Dora had gone off to visit their grandfather who lived on the other side of Prague. I was happy that I wouldn't have to see Nikola that day, as we had gotten into one of our patented arguments on the long subway ride the night before.

I sat down at my little wooden table, groggy and wishing there was an easy way out of my entanglement with Nikola. To take my mind off her, I wrote a letter to my friend Dan DeLuce, who was working as a reporter in Sacramento. Like me, he too was tired of his routine as a general assignment reporter and interested in a change of scenery. Before I had left San Francisco, he had seriously considered coming to join me later in the fall. Now that I had a job and a place to live, I hoped I could convince him that it would be possible to survive here in Prague. I hoped so, as he was one of my closest friends.

Shortly after noon, I walked over to the local bistro, located in a Dům Ucitelů replica next to our building. To me, the word "bistro" brings to mind Hemingway, the Champs Elysees or a pretty Italian eatery located on the outskirts of Rome. Unfortunately, not all bistros are created equal, as this small restaurant was saddled with a view of the Dům and featured a disappointing array of leathery looking *řízeks* (schnitzel) and *pivo*—beer—in bottles. Groups of people, mostly men, were gathered around square, wooden tables. At the far end of the room were slot machines. Nearly everyone was smoking and depositing their ashes and butts into huge, soup bowl-like ashtrays.

A waitress approached in a white silk blouse and a tight black miniskirt. She was wearing little white workplace sandals that flicked off her heels as she crossed the room. Flick, flick, flick.

"Pivo?" I asked, tentatively. After sizing me up, she decided to opt for the German approach.

"Ein bier?" she asked, looking at me, her thumb up in the 'one' position.

"Ano," I said, responding with the Czech word for "yes."

"Ja, ja," the waitress answered and flick-flacked her way back to the bar. This was ridiculous. I had to start learning Czech quickly or soon I was going to be speaking in grunts and groans copped from a hodge-podge of different tongues. I settled into a table near the window and opened *Letters to Olga,* a series of letters written by Havel to his wife in the late 1970s while Havel served his longest prison stint. Suddenly, out of the corner of my eye, I noticed a number of people staring at me. It was a feeling I came to know well over the following months. My American-ness was written into my clothes, walk and look. My button-down striped shirt, khaki pants and wire-rim glasses all sent off shrieking flares. Five earrings in my left ear also accounted for some of the stares.

I pretended not to notice the staring and instead concentrated on reading my book. Somewhere during my second beer, which was excellent, the bartender switched the radio off and played a cassette instead. Within seconds, I knew what he had chosen: the Eurythmics' soundtrack for the film version of George Orwell's *1984.* All around me, people drank beer after beer and smoked endlessly and the casino machines jangled and whirred in the background.

A man came in and ordered a beer. In a process I would see repeated endlessly, he poured the liquid into a tall glass with a meticulous flourish and stroked his beard with a speculative gaze while he waited for the foam to settle. When it was ready, he tipped the glass back and let the beer slide into his throat. The liquid burbled out of the glass like a bathtub with a huge drain and within seconds the whole thing had vanished into his stomach. Wiping foam off his lips and beard, the man turned and exited the bistro. Total elapsed time: about one minute.

Once I heard a great story about how much booze Babe Ruth could consume in one swallow. Without a doubt, this guy could have given the Bambino a run for his money.

As I reached the end of my second beer, the edges of the room lost their sharpness, my book lost its focus and I began to drift among the smoke and the boozy drinkers and the haunting soundtrack.

43

Back at the Dům, I was slowly getting to know the few others that had moved in. Others, I was told, would be coming in the next few days. My floor was heavily dominated by Americans, most of whom had recently graduated from college. In the early evening, there was a general organizational meeting so everyone could get to know each other and arrange "house" rules. I had a vague sense I was traveling backwards in time and soon would be asked to rush a fraternity or "cop an allnighter."

Even after more than four years, I can still see them clearly and always only with their first names. There was Jenny, a wholesome looking girl from Alaska, and Linda, a serious, well-spoken graduate student from Georgetown and Leila, a recent graduate who had previously lived in Indonesia and Susan, a tall, striking woman with a huge head of frizzy black hair and an equally booming personality. There was a girl named Brigit, who had graduated from the University of Southern California not long after me. There were two older women in their mid-40s, Petra, a manic British woman who invariably wore only black and Carol, an American with sandy-gray hair and a bubbly personality who had been a teacher in New England before deciding to resign and head to Prague. Everybody seemed so enthusiastic, charged with emotion and plans for all their students.

A majority of the Americans had found their way to Prague via several different educational groups which were supplying local schools with English teachers. Few of us had any teaching experience, save for a retired couple living on the floor below us and several people who had taught in poor neighborhoods as part of fulfilling their college curriculum.

Despite the fact that I was nearly the only one who hadn't come as part of a "program" or "experiment" (it all sounded so clinical), I did note that all of us seemed to be drawn to Prague by a variety of common threads: namely, a desire to participate in something unique and interesting while avoiding the withering job market in the United States.

After my "test" beers from the early afternoon, I was keen to go and find a real pub in the maze of apartments surrounding the Dům. I believed that pub life would draw me closer to the real Czech world, whatever that was. Most of the others on the floor were still exhausted from jet jag, having only arrived in Prague the day before. Shortly after 8 P.M., Brigit and I found ourselves sitting with two very tired looking and drunken workers who were well into their seventh and eighth beers. Although the two men were as interested in us as we were in them, there simply wasn't any way to make conversation. We merely drank and smiled at each other. As pubs go, it wasn't much — wood walls and smoke — but they kept bringing us beer and didn't make much of the fact that we were blabbing away in English.

As we walked back to the Dům late that evening, I looked around at the scenery: aging cars with names I couldn't pronounce and empty fields dotted with scrub weeds and piled high with mouldering concrete and rusting steel.

The glow of so many TV stations switched to the same channel made the structures look like giant television displays in department stores, with the same eerie, repeating flashes emanating from each apartment every time there was a cut or scene change. There were only three stations and few programming options.

"I feel like Hansel and Gretel trying to remember how to get home," Brigit said as we picked our way back towards the apartment building.

3

School Days

I arrived at school Monday morning shortly before 7:45 A.M. The entryway of the school was a giant mass of children pushing and shoving their way inside. As I was sucked inside, Dana appeared behind me and welcomed me to my first day at Prokopová.

"Oh dear," she said. "What a mess. The first day of school is always like this." She took me upstairs back to the office where they had given me a desk with Jana Krupková, the Czech English teacher who would be sharing the room with me.

Jana had been teaching at Prokopová for many years. Her English was excellent and she spoke in very correct sentences with a strong British accent. Her light brown hair was bobbed into a conservative wave that reminded me of no-nonsense British matrons.

Jana showed me where to hang my coat and put water on to boil. While I drank a cup of the strong Turkish coffee, she pulled out several textbooks that we were going to use, including a series of books with different colors called *Angličtina* (English).

At 8 A.M., Jana led me down the hall to a small corner room shaped slightly like a pie wedge—my classroom for the year. I stood in a beam of sunlight and doubtfully considered the space. There were several rows of desks built to accommodate two pupils, one battered brown teacher's desk and a weathered blackboard on a stand. The walls were faded yellow. High ceilings and tile floors created an echo chamber whenever someone spoke, which unfortunately, in the case of languages, is often.

Jana left me alone in the classroom and went to gather the children for my first class who were still with their "form" or "homeroom" teacher. I poked my head out the window, and looked at the construction site next door where they were building a new five story building for the trade unions. "When that's completed," I told myself, "I'll go back to the United States."

I turned away from the window, looked in the desk and nervously sat in the hard, wooden chair behind the teacher's desk.

Presently, Jana came back with a group of third-graders. Average age: eight and nine. To this day, I'm not sure who was more bewildered—me or the students. Some of them looked like deer caught in the headlights. I felt like I had something caught in my throat.

Jana looked at me thoughtfully. I thought she was going to burst out laughing.

"Well," she said. "Good luck. I'll see you after the lesson. You'll do fine." She turned and spoke sharply to the children in Czech, who trembled slightly at her words.

Then she turned and left me alone with the kids standing somewhat rigidly behind their desks. Some of them fidgeted from side to side with their hands behind them. Fifteen pairs of eyes stared at me.

Nothing happened. They just stood there, waiting. Finally, I realized they were expecting me to sit down. So I sat.

"Good morning," I said in English. Then I tried it in Czech. "Dobrý Den."

"Dobrý Den! Pani učiteli!" the class chimed almost as one. *Good Morning, Mr. Teacher!*

I looked around the room at all the faces. Some of the children smiled. Others just stared. Dressed in school clothes—no nonsense shirts, tough denim, pretty dresses and plain slacks—they looked just the same as American school kids. Some of the girls had bangs, others had braids. Some of the boys had butch haircuts, while a few had hair almost to their collars.

I initially had a fear I wouldn't be able to remember all of my kids' names. But I was relieved to see the children had arrived with little cards indicating the special English names I was supposed to use instead of their real Czech names.

I got up from behind the desk and paced along the aisle, looking at the cards. There was a Mary and a Susan and a Betty, two Margarets, a Helen and a Sally, several Johns, a Bob, a Peter and a big tough nine-year-old named Steve. The names were so American Apple Pie and wholesome that for awhile I thought I had the cast of the Hardy Boys and several truck-stop waitresses and mechanics in class with me.

For a time in another class, I had what I called the Apostles sitting in the front row: John, Paul and Matthew.

Since the total number of Czech words that I knew didn't add up to ten fingers (one of the words being *pivo* for beer so that was definitely out), I was hopelessly at a loss to explain to them who I was.

So, with visions of those condescending British travel stories where the explorer meets a savage in the jungle, I tried just introducing myself. I wrote my name on the rickety blackboard that was essentially a piece of wood on a easel-like frame.

"My name," I said, patting my chest, "Is Doug." I tried it again. "My name is Doug." I gestured to a pretty blonde girl sitting in the front row, who had bangs and braids. "What's your name?" I asked.

The girl just looked at me dumbfounded, and then turned and looked at her friend. Some students giggled. Or was it snickering?

I turned to the blackboard and wrote, "Hello, my name is _____." Then I turned back around. Without having to ask, a student raised his hand in the back of the class and said, "Hello, my name is John." It broke the ice.

"Hello, John," I said, moving to the back of the classroom. "My name is Doug." I shook his hand enthusiastically. He laughed and the entire class laughed with him. Evidently little John, or Jan, as he was really called in Czech, had been taught some English before.

We went around the room, trying everyone's name and repeating, "Hello, my name is . . ." until I started to sense that the magic and wonder had been wrung out of that phrase. I wrote some other greetings on the board: "Good morning," "Good-bye," "Thank you." Next to "Good morning" I drew a little sun. Next to "Good night" I drew a moon. Then the bell rang. The 45 minutes had seemed to go by very quickly. The children ran almost as one out of the room and I headed back to my office, where Jana was waiting.

"Well, how was it?" she asked.

"It was fine," I answered, not knowing really how to sum up the experience. I put the kettle on the burner to make some coffee.

"Well, you'd better hurry, as I'm going to go fetch another class for you." Jesus, I thought. I'm supposed to do this every day for six hours?

At 9:40, we had a true "coffee break" where the teachers would gather to drink tea or coffee and smoke cigarettes while the children were herded into the hallways to walk in long circles around the building while they nibbled at snacks brought from home. The first day the school staff tried this "marching" in the hallways, there was complete pandemonium, with kids milling about, pushing and shoving. Dana was in the center of the students and saw me as I passed by.

"You see, we are trying to arrange such a kind of experiment," she said, laughing. "I don't think it's working." As the school didn't have an outdoor play area, the kids never got a chance to go outside and work off energy, and the idea was to keep the kids moving during the break in hopes of wearing them out a bit. But it didn't really work. Kids have so much natural energy that, if bottled up for too long, it just spills over into class. What they needed most was a place to kick out the jams for awhile.

Shortly after noon, after four different classes had surged in and out of my room like some kind of angry tide, I went back to the office and Jana saw panic in my eyes. She laughed, tossing her head back.

"Now you see why teachers are always so cross!" she said, pointing her finger in the air. "Noise, noise, noise! Always running! But you are finished for today. I'll show you where the school canteen is."

"Canteen?" I asked.

"The place where you and the children eat lunch," Jana said doubtfully, looking at me like she had said something wrong.

"Oh, you mean the school cafeteria!" I said, finally catching up with her thoughts. "A canteen is something you drink water from on a hike."

"Perhaps in American English," Jana said. "But not in British

50

English." She was very correct in her usage and doubted the veracity of diluted American English.

As she led me downstairs, we discussed American and British differences in English usage including: "windshield and windscreen," "truck and lorry," "trunk and boot" and "garbage can and dustbin."

"You'll find that most people in Czechoslovakia speak British English," Jana said, entering the lunchroom which was simply two rooms, holding rows of tables covered with vinyl tablecloths and wooden chairs. Kids came in from the far end of the room and lined up near a window leading to the kitchen. They came away with soup and a plate piled with meat and dumplings. They looked like little inmates lining up for chow. Several teachers wandered about trying to keep order and imploring the kids not to dawdle over their food.

"As you are a teacher, you can go to the head of the line and then eat with us over here at this table," Jana said, pointing at a table where a number of teachers were busily eating.

While the food certainly wasn't the height of culinary excellence, it wasn't awful either. The soup tasted vaguely of vegetables, the meat was sweet, overboiled and swimming in a pinkish, salmon-colored sauce. I used the dumplings to soak up the sauce like little sponges and then sat back, feeling bloated.

"How do you like the Czech food?" Jana asked, from behind her tray of food.

"As you can see, I ate it all," I said, gesturing to my overloaded stomach. "I guess I like it. I've never had these, these, *knedlíky.*"

"Oh, the dumplings!" Jana said, putting a hand over her mouth as she laughed. "They will make you very fat, like all of the Czech men I know! You can have more if you want." She gestured with her fork and knife over to the line where still more children were waiting with their trays.

"No, no!" I practically screamed. "Thank you!" I hastily changed the subject and asked her whether I would have other responsibilities at the school.

"Yes," she said. "But let me finish my lunch and then we'll go back upstairs. Help yourself to some tea." She pointed to two large water coolers on a table. I filled a glass and found that it wasn't really tea but heavily sugared water flavored with tea.

While the other teachers ate in a more European style, using both knife and fork at the same time to maneuver the food about on the plate, Jana looked at me and clucked.

"You Americans eat so quickly!" Jana said. "You never take time to properly enjoy a meal." I looked around at the other teachers who seemed to be engaged in some race to dispose of their food. There was no discussion, save for an occasional grunt for salt.

"What do you think of Czech people so far?" Jana asked suddenly.

"Well, from what I can see, I think they are generous, pleasant and sweet-tempered." Jana laughed and translated my words for the other teachers at the table. They all looked up from their food and smiled appreciably. Jana continued to laugh.

"You watch, Douglas, and learn Czech. Then you will see that we are not so nice to each other. In fact, we are sometimes rather nasty."

Upstairs, over what must have been my fourth cup of coffee for the day, Jana, Dana and I went over the daily schedule and assigned me several duties, including watching the children in the hallways and supervising the lunchroom. I didn't mind these duties and asked for them as I simply wanted to be included; Dana was more than happy to dole out jobs left and right.

"At some point, we will also probably send you to our camp in the mountains," Dana said. "We call it a 'school in nature,' and the children go there for two weeks every year to get some fresh air and have a rest from Prague."

I was fascinated by this program and asked if all the students participated. Yes, I was told, it was a government program. Children were provided with proper rooms, three meals and a snack each day and had special classrooms. Dana went out of her way to explain that it was more than rustic.

"We actually move everything up to the mountains: our books, playthings and work for two weeks."

After the meeting, I made copious notes about each of the classes and what we had accomplished. Dana and Jana hadn't really suggested any way of keeping score, so to say, in each of my classes, and I figured I better keep a journal of each class that would record progress and work assigned. I made out plans for the following day, including additional words and useful phrases that would help me communicate better with each of the kids.

I also had a peek through the English books I had been given, which were the old government-written readers for kids. To say that they were awful was an understatement. They were stupid, banal, dull, poorly written and aimed at the slow-witted.

Even worse, the books were either slyly or overtly lined with political jargon to ensure that the kids would receive a proper socialist education.

Submitted for your amusement, is a typical "poem" from the first-year book:

> *A Working Song*
> Left, right,
> Keep in Step
> The day is bright,
> Workers of the World, Unite!

So the child—probably at the age of eight or nine—learned the word "worker" before "ice cream." Later installments of the books included such riveting topics as "Lenin's boyhood" and "A Trip to an English Factory." Even if the students had found the topics selected for them interesting, chances are they wouldn't have been able to learn much from the text as many of the sentences were nearly impossible to read without getting crosseyed. From "Technical development":

> "Let us pick out one example: automation, under monopoly capitalism, strengthens the tendency to economic crises, while in the socialist countries it leads to the shortening of working hours and to a higher standard of living."

Or this gem from "A Chat With a Ghanaian":

> "Czech: I spoke to a number of students from Asian and African countries the other day. I wish you had been with us. You might

53

have found our discussion interesting.

Ghanaian: And what did you talk about?

Czech: Well, we discussed the relations between the socialist countries and the developing countries of Asia and Africa. We also discussed East-West relations and the role played by the neutral countries."

Sometime in the mid afternoon, I headed back home, exhausted from having seen so much. Some of the children were so small! With little button-sized noses, straight haircuts and small cherubic faces, they all looked so innocent. I bought a few small things for dinner in a store near the metro and went back to the Dům to discover that I had now had a roommate:

"James McLarsen," he said, stopping to shake my hand in the doorway of our rooms. "I'm part of the experiment. Are you?"

"Afraid not James," I said. "But I am teaching."

"Great!" he said, shouting over his shoulder as he began unpacking books and clothes from a duffel bag which was sitting on his bed. While he unloaded his gear, James proceeded to give me his life's story: he had recently graduated from Bennington College in Vermont and had joined the others in the teaching program. He liked jazz and admired the fact that I had a David Murray tape on one of my shelves.

"I hope you don't mind that I was looking through your cassettes. I love David Murray."

I said I didn't and watched him buzz around his room. He was fit, with short brown hair and looked like an extra from an L.L. Bean catalog: khaki pants, plaid shirts. Boat shoes. James went on: "Anyway, like I was telling that girl down the hall, nobody got drafted to do this teaching and so we're all in the same boat and should remember that. We chose this."

We *sure* did, I thought to myself, and wondered how Nikola and Dora had fared during this first day. A few minutes later, I found out, when Nikola barged through the door to my room. From the look in her eyes, I thought she had ingested a handful of amphetamines.

"It was so wonderful!" she said breathlessly, nearly running all the words together. "I got an office and the kids were *soooo* nice and they liked the Muppet books that I had brought with me!" Her eyes were wild and she couldn't stop grinning.

"They understood Miss Piggy and Kermit?" I asked.

"Yes! Isn't it so great? Even though they had never seen them before! And then we all went outside and played games—hopscotch, you know—and then we . . ." Her words faded into the background. I was too exhausted, drained, relieved and jet lagged to listen. Next door, James was telling someone else about whether he could find a mountain bike in Prague. I needed some air.

"Well," Nikola said suddenly standing up, "you look tired. How was your day?"

"Uh, fine. I'm sorry, but I think I'll have to tell you about it later. I think I really need a walk right now." My head was buzzing. I went outside and took a short walk through the tall buildings and found the local supermarket. A long line of shoppers snaked out the side entrance as people waited for carts. Apparently one had to have a cart to go inside, whether one wanted a stick of gum or food for a family of five.

Later, as I was passing the communal television room on our floor, I heard the sound of a baseball game and thought that I was losing my mind. Curious, I stuck my head in the room and found that, yes, there was a baseball game on television and it was in English! What's more, it was the San Francisco Giants against the New York Mets from Candlestick Park in San Francisco.

Even though the game was nearly a week old and the sight of baseball made me homesick, I was in heaven. One of the Czech television channels had arranged to carry several hours a day of Screensport, a British sports cable channel. While I was sitting there watching the game (predictably, the Giants lost), I got up and looked out the window at the dozens of apartment buildings stretching away into the horizon.

"Where am I? Just who are these people!" I shouted out the window. But I didn't get an answer.

4

The Czechs

J ust who were these people, anyway? Beyond the few books I had read by Havel, the news events from the previous fall and some articles I had found in magazines, there wasn't a whole lot of useable material in my local library back in California. In fact, the card catalogue didn't even have a good reference marker for the country. It simply said: "see listing under Eastern European countries and peoples."

Historically, I was not alone in my ignorance. As the Munich crisis was building to a head in 1938, British Prime Minister Neville Chamberlain was quoted as saying: "How horrible, fantastic, incredible it is that we should be digging trenches ... because of a quarrel in a far away country between people of whom we know nothing." Regardless of Chamberlain's naiveté, he was savvy enough to note that most Westerners didn't know much about Czechoslovakia or its people.

Chamberlain would have done well to read "At the Crossroads of Europe," an essay from the 1920s by Czech writer Karel Čapek. In it, Čapek described his country this way: "In these few contradictions ... it is a country old and yet new, great yet small, rich yet humble, highly cultivated and yet very primitive. Nature and history have imposed upon it the fate of being the heart of Europe, of being a crossroads and a link between nations and cultures."[1]

Despite Čapek's positive words, I quickly discovered that Czechs like to stereotype themselves as cynics. I saw it first in Jana and Dana, who shared a dry, self-deprecating sense of humor.

"I think you will find our jokes more bitter than you happy Americans would like," Dana said, when I asked her about Czech wit. She told me a typically Czech joke:

"A Czech goes into a meat store and says, 'I'd like to have three kilos of veal, please. And I'd like you to pack it up nicely for me.' And the butcher says, 'Great! Shall I play the flute as well?' The customer replies, 'Oh, you're kidding!' To which the butcher says, 'Well, you started it.'"

Not long after, I saw a translated version of Jiří Menzel's formerly suppressed film, *Larks on a String,* about Czechs in a work detail during the Stalinist Era.

"You're so Czech!" one of the characters announces to a friend who receives a promotion. "The minute you become somebody, you believe your shit doesn't stink!"

Their mordant humor reflects a historical lack of confidence in themselves and their nation, a belief that they will never be allowed to govern their own future—somebody else will always be doing it for them.

"They decided about us, without us," said Edward Beneš, who, as President of Czechoslovakia, was forced to watch helplessly as England, France, Italy and Hitler's Germany carved up his country at Munich so as to ensure Chamberlain's "peace in our time."[2]

Beneš' angry statement was prefigured by the legions of invaders who have ruled the Czechlands, sometimes for centuries: the Hapsburgs, the Germans and the Russians. Other nations have imposed their government, language and culture upon the tiny Slavic nation that unfortunately lay in the center of Europe. "Who rules, Bohemia, dominates Europe," Otto von Bismarck said in 1866, and for centuries, numerous invaders were happy enough to make themselves master of the true Bohemians, the Czechs. It is not surprising to discover an inferiority complex running like a muddy river through the Czech psyche.

Czechs sometimes speak cryptically of themselves as survivors who always give up when challenged. Either they were soundly defeated, as at the Battle of White Mountain in 1620, which ushered in the Hapsburg rule; they didn't fight back (the 1968 Warsaw Pact invasion); or weren't allowed to fight at all (the Munich pact of 1938).

Poles will fight and lose, Serbs will fight endlessly, Russians will attack, but the Czechs will lie back and have the crap kicked out of them, despite attempts by Czech leaders to promote a stronger national identity.

"Not to be afraid, that is the main issue," said T. G. Masaryk, the first Czechoslovak president, during a speech to Czechs and Slovaks in Chicago in 1918. "We Czechs seem not to know how strong we are. We are nine to ten million. Let us clench our teeth and let us say: We won't yield!—and that will be the end of pessimism."[3]

But there is a well-documented sense of doom stemming from their fear of history repeating itself, as their little country has spent much of the 20th century wobbling from one political extreme to another. As Czech historian Ivan Sviták notes in his book, *The Czechoslovak Experience,* the country endured Hapsburg submission (pre-1917), embraced democracy (1918), was slaughtered by fascism (1938), tentatively re-embraced capitalism and democracy (1946), and surrendered to Stalinism (1948), de-Stalinism (1967) and re-Stalinism (1969).[4]

Again, again and again, Europe's uneven journey from Versailles to Potsdam, Cold War détente and Warsaw Pact demise have trapped the Czechs and Slovaks in a frantic tug of war between East and West. Always they were forced to choose and always they came away feeling betrayed.

"For centuries, we—Czechs and Slovaks, whether in our own state or under foreign control—lived in a situation of constant menace from without," said the Czech President Václav Havel not long after assuming the powers of his office. "We are like a sponge that has gradually absorbed and digested all kinds of intellectual and cultural impulses and initiatives."[5]

Geographically, the Czech Republic and Slovakia lie between the 48th and 51st degree of northern latitude and between the 12th and the 22nd degree of eastern longitude. The location on the globe ensures mostly cold winters, with snow well across the country, and moderately warm summers.

However, this doesn't take into account the effect of pollution on the climate. Older residents of Prague wistfully recall winters when it used to regularly snow in the downtown; now, the carbon monoxide and other pollutants in the air has caused the city to heat up in exactly the kind of "greenhouse" effect scientists predict for the rest of the globe. So now snow in great abundance in the city is somewhat rare. As opposed to America, no one ever came along and "discovered" the area of Central Europe that today is the Czech Republic. There was little need for a boatload of Norsemen or a Columbus to blunder into the New World. Man's been there a long time, as archaeologists have dug up remnants of Neolithic hunting tribes near Dolní Věstonice in the southeastern portion of the Czech Republic.

Briefly, the Czech Republic is divided into three regions: Bohemia, Moravia and Silesia. Bohemia includes the major cities of Prague, Pilzen and also famous Karlovy Vary, which is also known to some Westerners as Carlsbad. This area, along with portions of Northern Bohemia, comprises what was more widely known to the world as the Sudetenland, the aforementioned region long coveted by Hitler because of its heavily German population.

Moravia, which forms the eastern part of the country, includes the major towns of Olomouc and Brno. Here, people speak in a slightly different dialect than in Prague and hold folk traditions and music that are as unique to the region as are its gentle, rolling countryside and acres of vineyards. Silesia is a tiny, generally unrecognized region in the north eastern country near the city of Ostrava.[6]

Slovakia, which until the split comprised the easternmost portion of Czechoslovakia, stretches through more mountainous land until it butts up against what was the Soviet Union and is now the Ukraine. Not only is the Slovak language different than Czech (although not so much that Czechs and Slovaks are prevented from understanding each other—think of it as extremely different British and American English), the people are different in culture and temperament. The country is also highly industrial, especially near its capital, Bratislava.

In addition, both the Czech Republic and Slovakia are crisscrossed by some of Europe's major rivers, including the Elbe, the Danube and the Oder.

OK, enough of the Rand McNally statistics. What do the two countries really look like? I pondered this question for a long time as I studied maps of the region. It doesn't look much like a carefully planned country, as borders run higgildly-piggildy every which way. But, then again, what country looks well-planned? Most national borders have been decided because of conflicts that ranged over centuries. While Czechoslovakia's borders have a certain historical *raison d'etre,* almost no one has agreed on where they should be. Hitler forced the Munich crisis because he believed the Sudetenland should be returned to Germany. To this day, there are still arguments over what compensation should be given to the thousands of Germans who were expelled from the country following the end of World War II by the Czechoslovak government in retaliation for the German atrocities in Czechoslovakia during the war. Through late 1945 and early 1946, Germans were given short notice and a maximum baggage weight of 65 pounds before being told to leave the country.

Abstractly, some have said the Czech Republic and Slovakia look like leaves floating in the center of Lake Europe. I would suggest that perhaps they are more like oblong clouds in the sky. When the country was still unified, I thought it looked vaguely like a bear crouching forward on its paws.

Regardless of however you choose to view the countries, they are small. Very small. If you travel west-east through the Czech Republic and Slovakia, you would traverse an area 767 kilometers long. Going north-south, the country you cross is less than 276 kilometers. That's barely more than an area the size of Pennsylvania or New York. Even with the poor roads, it's still possible to drive from one end to the other in little over 20 hours. A trip to Berlin, Nüremberg or Vienna from Prague takes only about 6 hours by train.

Czechs and Slovaks take great pride in their history and are well-schooled about the development of their cultures. With the exception of Prague, which has long been a bastion of intellectual ferment throughout Europe, much of the country is richly agrarian or industrial, with these roots stretching deeply into the soil, well back before the development of socialism. I am a child of suburbia and the big city, used to people in constant motion, skipping across the country like stones on a pond, and consequently, I am always deeply surprised to encounter people whose families have spent generations in the same town, the same village.

The region's long, tangled evolution makes for exciting history, something Czechs like to remind you of nearly every single time you head out to yet another ancient ruin or castle or something that is All Important.

"You know, this pile of stones was here before America was even discovered," they say, with a friendly, disarming smile.

"Oh, yes, that's true," I respond with my best piss-on-myself-and-America voice. "We have no real history, y'know."

While I am in the middle of denigrating my own country, I'm all the time wondering why, if they've had so much more time to get things squared away, why in hell can't they get fresh bread into the markets every day?

5

Kids! Kids! Kids!

Teaching quickly became complicated. With each passing day, I gradually gained more and more respect for what my former teachers in the United States had to endure. Standing alone in front of 20 children is difficult enough: one must find a way to be entertaining for 45 minutes (God forbid you are charged with leading a two-hour conversation class). The teacher discovers that he must be many things—leader, preacher, clown, dictator.

After awhile I began to feel like an actor doing a one-man show or a stand-up comic. On bad days, I felt like a unfunny comedian in a suburban Holiday Inn. When I lost the kids, it was just like getting no applause from the audience. And kids, God bless 'em, know no other condition than honesty. If teacher is stupid and boring, the kids will respond with bored expressions that just say, "Find another line of work, Mac." If teacher is brilliant, funny and engaging, chances are you'll catch their attention.

But teacher wasn't always brilliant, funny and exciting, especially when teacher had a hangover and had to sit down like some aging conductor trying to make it through one more performance of Richard Strauss' *Four Last Songs*. Or when teacher decided he wanted to have the kids write a dictation or some other terribly unpleasant exercise.

After more than a month, I began to recognize that the children, despite speaking a different language and coming from a different culture, were essentially the same on the face of things. There were sick children who coughed and sneezed, class clowns who pretended to eat their buggers and primadonnas who thought they were above learning. My classes had boneheads and future athletes and nerds who raised their hands to answer a question even if you merely glanced in their direction. And there were quiet children who learned everything you set for them and then faded away each afternoon.

To the kids, I was some kind of space alien dropped in from beyond Alfa Centauri. Officially, I was "Mr. Teacher," but to some of them I was "Mr. American" or "Dawglas" or "Pan Leetleeee." For the first few weeks, until the euphoria of having a non-Czech in the school wore off, I collected various "fan clubs" that would gather outside my office or classroom, hoping to talk or walk with me from one place to another.

"There hasn't been such a commotion since the year we had a colored teacher from Libya here at school with us," Jana said one afternoon after she saw me being followed by a pack of kids while I was on my way downstairs to the lunchroom.

And, my God, the amount of energy the children had was staggering. I couldn't keep up. The younger they were, the shorter their attention span. The older ones were often lazy and indifferent.

For the littlest children, trying to get everyone interested in what was transpiring at the front was like trying to get 20 dogs to watch television at the same time. The minute I thought everyone was in line was the moment little Jan or Markéta decided to glance away or drop something on the floor or begin fiddling with one of their dolls. The noise or motion caused everyone to look over to see what was going on and I was back to square one again.

Because of the high ceilings and tile floors in my classroom, the maximum amount of noise was created during my lessons. The kids' desks were made of rickety Formica and metal which reverberated as the uneven legs rocked back and forth. Rusty chairs banged and squeaked. Books thundered when dropped.

Originally, I tried seating everyone in a circle so that we could encourage conversation. But this didn't work well, as some of the kids couldn't see the blackboard. So then, I put everyone in rows, but that created an entirely new set of problems, with little cliques forming all over the place. The good girls would sit up front, average students in the middle, and the bad boys and dumbbells hidden in the back.

A class known as 5B was the worst. Long before I ever reached the classroom, I could hear them storming away, throwing books and making a merry racket. After I entered the classroom, it would quiet down a bit, but then somebody would start up in the back, playing one of numerous games, passing notes, pulling hair or mumbling quietly to a friend at the next table.

Believing (falsely) that I was smarter, I tried lot of tricks. I changed seating plans on a weekly basis. I gave unexpected pop quizzes and dictations and made everyone read aloud from the books, despite the fact that they were horribly boring. Regardless of whatever I tried, nothing really changed: the students remained boisterous, I tore my hair out, and perhaps only a few actually learned some English.

By the end of the first week, I managed to commit to memory about 87 percent of the various faces that passed in front of my eyes every day. The rest I—well—worked around with all of the precise fumbling that President Reagan used to display at his press conferences.

"Uh, uh, exercise number four. How about ... uh ... uh ... you? Ah, yes, you. Sweetheart?" Then I'd wave my hand nicely in their direction, thinking about all of the feminists in America who would burn me at the stake for addressing one of my young female students in such a sexist fashion.

Some days went well, with each class working their way through the old socialist books without a whimper. Other days were like pulling teeth.

Which leads to a more difficult, entirely more beguiling problem: when is a child goofing off or merely expressing himself? It's a tough question, but after teaching for several months, I could see why many of the teachers at Prokopová applied the most stringent rules in dealing with their classes: no talking, standing at attention when answering questions, excessive homework. Unfortunately, in a language class, one must speak, often frequently, and one often doesn't have a lot of homework to dole out, with the exception of strict verb texts, grammar exercises and word lists.

What's more, it gets tiresome merely repeating the same phrase over and over: "Is this your pen? 'Yes, it's my pen.'"

Regardless of whether you are trying to distinguish between pens or hands, these repetition methods quickly get stale. The kids hate it after ten minutes and so does the teacher, who gradually wishes more and more he could go get loaded in the teacher's lounge. So, why not a bit of variety here and there? Why not play a word game? Or how about singing a song? "The Alphabet Song" was good in a pinch. And "Old MacDonald" went over big as the kids loved to shriek out the "E-I-E-I-O!" refrain.

Of course, like everything else in life, getting all of the fun stuff in line with the work *de rigueur* took some fine tuning. When I quit teaching two years later I was only just beginning to get the hang of how kids function, and even then it seemed to be a fairly imprecise science.

Several well-intentioned teachers who lived with us in Dům Uči-telů sadly tried a number of tricks copped from the film *Dead Poets Society,* including ripping pages out of textbooks and dramatically standing on tables. The kids were shocked, aghast. Standing on the table! Damaging school property! This was unheard of! But, pretty soon, everyone wanted to do it, just to break the rules. The result after two weeks: absolute chaos.

One evening after dinner at the Dům, Suzi, a pretty, young woman fresh out of college, nearly broke down in tears in the kitchen as she recounted how the children had run amok in her class. Everyone listening to the story was very quiet, most probably thinking about the similar troubles they were encountering. Finally, one teacher who lived on a lower floor, set down his wine glass, and remarked, "Gee, I'm glad I only teach adults."

It was naiveté and inexperience, of course, that was hurting us. At the teachers' house, we had all happily trooped off the first week thinking we would right all of the wrongs that preceded us in school:

>—*Me? I wouldn't tell children to be quiet. They're only exercising their right to express themselves. Don't stifle creativity!*
>—*Me? I wouldn't run my class like a museum. I'm sharing with*

66

the students. NOT instructing! Hey, they have a lot to teach me too!

—Me? I'm hip! I'm cool! The students dig me! They think I'm the most! And they'll dig the tie-dye, too! I'm teaching them the lyrics to "Uncle John's Band!"

Less than a month after our foray into the New Generation of far-out American teachers bringing The Word, the tune had changed significantly as people came back to the Dům each night from work:

—Goddamn little brats! Teacher, teacher, teacher! I explained it three times, you little goddamn twerp! Shut yer trap.
—I tried to be nice. Why are you doing this to me?
—Hey, man, I was wild. YOU don't know how much. But this! This is, well, unusual. Hey, like it's outta my league. I fought authority. Know whatta I mean? These kids, well, they're like not the same!

In addition to the lack of proper training, there also seemed to be some sort of unspoken canyon between the Czech and American teachers, almost as if both sides were waiting for the other part to reach out first for help or give some direction in the classroom. At my school, Dana and Jana seemed willing and interested enough in keeping me operating, but only so far. Either they were so deeply wrapped up in keeping their own classes functioning (Dana especially) or perhaps they were afraid to challenge me lest I get upset and go home.

I, on the other hand, couldn't figure out why some parent hadn't stormed into the school demanding to know why the administration hadn't fired the incompetent American.

But like so much of the changing country, there was a sense of all-hands-on-deck urgency to our arrival in the country. For years, people had been goaded into learning Russian and now there was a critical need to learn useful languages like German and English. There was little time to question the rules of how people were taught; to get the country moving would require a massive effort at reeducating its children.

To remedy things a bit while I was still trying to gain a modicum of control and understanding, I tried to think back to all of the awful days when we were bad in school, made too much noise or got too hyperactive. The teacher would always have a "quiet time" and have us put our heads on our desks while she meandered about the room making soothing noises and clucking her tongue.

When I tried the same thing in my unruly classes, I got a variety of responses—kids making snoring noises, winking at each other, giggling; finally, one lad making farting noises by blowing onto his arm. Later that night, as I drowned my sorrows in Czech beer, I sadly recalled that, alas, I too had done the same things in school.

It was almost as if I had unwittingly lured myself into repenting for my sins as a child. All the horrors were coming back, except that now I was on the receiving end of the teacher jokes. One Friday afternoon, after a particularly difficult week attempting to keep order, teach and still preserve a sense of humor, I nearly fell to my knees and cried to my old elementary school teachers who must have been watching me with perverse glee. I wanted to beg their forgiveness: "I'm sorry for the time we hid all the chalk! I'm sorry for the time we taped the Playboy centerfold to the map of Egypt! I'm sorry for when we gave Harold Schmertz a wedgie!"

Such confessions aren't possible when you're deep in the middle of 6A, diligently working your way through Exercise 14 of "I am/was going" and there's still another 25 minutes left to go. Do kids know that teacher is silently hoping like they are that the bell would just hurry up and ring?

In the early months of the school year, I must have made every mistake, violated every rule and generally made a mess of just about everything that can be screwed up in a classroom. I am still amazed that the kids learned anything.

I finally pressed Dana and Jana about my difficulties in the classroom and they both gave me different suggestions.

"Go slowly. Speak carefully," Dana said. "Have the students work in pairs a bit more."

"As a teacher, you must know how to teach and when to be able to take a break and have the children work for you," Jana said. She was a big believer in breaks, as she liked to complain about how much she and the others had to work.

But when none of their suggestions worked, Dana arrived in one of my classes to deliver a lecture to the students that just about curdled their hair, tore paint off the wall and embarrassed me. For once, the children were quiet while they listened to her explode in Czech like an officer screaming at a group of cadets.

"There, Douglas," she said, adjusting her big, round glasses. "I hope it will be better now." And it was, for several days, until things slowly reverted back to mild chaos. Jana was perhaps a bit more practical. She took several hours off from her classes and watched me teach. She suggested making simple changes—I was making the little kids write too much.

"Have them draw little pictures instead. They can barely write Czech," she said. "They'll never handle English script very well." So instead of learning to write, I made large cards with pictures on them of cats and dogs and houses and trains. I would hold one up and ask a student to tell me what it was. Jana also suggested that I praise the students more.

"Tell them how good they are doing. Be more gentle with them. They're so young, remember. And don't try and speak so much Czech. They'll only get confused. You're going to be a very good teacher. Don't give up."

With the older children who were expected to handle more challenging material, I worked to keep a "happy balance" in my classes between rote exercises, dictation, and the lunatic fringe. One problem I was finding is that there weren't a lot of extra books and materials to use in the classroom. One had a blackboard, chalk and, if one was very lucky, a tape recorder and a few cassettes. Later I was given a television set and a VCR.

"You're so lucky, Douglas," Jana said as she watched two workmen in faded blue overalls slowly lug the video equipment into our office. "It's because you're an American, of course, and we want you to feel that you have all the tools you need. I myself don't have such equipment yet." Although Jana's thin smile told me she was ribbing me, I felt a hot flash of embarrassment crawl up my neck.

Unlike American schools with their overstuffed closets of equipment and computers, the Prokopová school was lurking somewhere in the 1950s. There was no copying machine for the first year and books were a valuable commodity, so students generally shared theirs, and often couldn't take theirs home at night. Much of the work was done by laboriously copying material into these small bluebooks of about 25–40 pages each. These notebooks are generally all the student will have to learn from, and they become more and more valuable as the year goes on. If a student loses one—poof!—out goes notes from the entire year.

I yearned to speak better Czech so I could control things a bit or just answer simple questions. I had already had a number of hilarious encounters because I couldn't understand what the students were saying.

Several weeks after I began teaching, two students confronted me after class and began pressing their little blue notebooks in my face. They were quite excited and babbled away at me in Czech. What I heard was something along the lines of: "My teacher, Mr. teacher, sayshit. Say shit."

What? My mind groped for an answer. Even though they had spoken Czech, I clearly had heard, "Say shit." Say what?

"Mr. teacher, say shit," they protested again, almost in a chorus. So I said it.

"Shit!" They stopped and considered me rather silently.

"Ne, ne. *Sayshit.*"

"Shit!" I said this time, a little more vigorously. While I was worried one of them would tell someone I was swearing in front of the kids, I was also curious about where two little nine-year-old Czech kids would have heard the word.

Our little interchange carried on for another 30 seconds or so, with me retorting "Shit" (I was now hopping up and down), while they kept saying "sayshit." Presently, Dana came along the hall and I was able to pull her aside.

"Uh, these kids keep asking me to say shit," I said, with a determined look in my eye. "Why?" Dana looked troubled and then questioned the children, who were glad to finally have a rational human being with whom to speak. Then Dana began to laugh.

"No, no, they're asking you to give them several more notebooks." She put a hand across her mouth to keep the laughter from spilling out. "A little notebook is called a *sešit* in Czech. It only sounds like your vulgar American word."

Oh.

Even with all of my troubles, I was discovering that when things went well, it gave me an immense amount of satisfaction. When a child that you have taught from the very first day, a child who earlier couldn't say "thank you" or "I live in Prague," stands up and says "I am 9 years old and I have a dog," you can stand back and admire your progress and revel in the fact that you have, at least for a short period of time, changed another person's life in a tremendously positive way. To teach a student how to count to 100 and then 200 and then 1,000, is exciting. Helping the student learn how to add, subtract and divide in English is even more rewarding.

And, with the exception of a couple of real stinkers, it was difficult to remain angry towards the children for very long. They were just too innocent and honest. I liked the youngest ones, especially, for their sweetness and desire to learn. They were all so young! I was somehow proud I could teach them English.

One afternoon, I was talking about something relating to the "To Be" verb and believing I was making a tremendous amount of sense. A hand went up in the back of the class. My God, I thought, a question! I have succeeded as a teacher!

"Teacher, what do you think of Rambo?" a little boy asked at the back of the class. It was the sincerity reflected in his eyes that made me laugh.

6

Havel: A President for the People

The more I read about Václav Havel, the more interested I became in the country's new president. An internationally known dissident and playwright before he was thrust into the more traditional world of politics following the November, 1989 collapse of the communist government, Havel is perhaps one of the most unique personalities to emerge on the world stage in decades.

The son of a bourgeois and important Prague family, he was prevented from advancing scholastically and professionally by the intimidating Stalinist government in the 1950s and later drifted into the theater, holding a number of jobs with a company in Prague. He began to write for the stage, and until the Warsaw Pact invasion in 1968 he had been reluctantly tolerated by the Czechoslovak government and was recognized as one of the country's more important young writers.

But in the period of so-called "normalization" that followed in the early 1970s—when opposition was soundly crushed—Havel became increasingly politically active. In an open letter to the Czechoslovak President Gustáv Husák in 1975, Havel warned the government that its continued harsh treatment of the citizens would only lead to failure. Sooner or later, Havel wrote, people "would demand punishment for the permanent humiliation of their human dignity."

Havel's words tap deeply into Czech history, as the struggle for national autonomy goes back well into the Middle Ages, when a Czech pastor, Master Jan Hus, first attempted to reform his corrupted church in Bohemia. Such action against the ruling Catholics was tantamount to revolution. "Faithful Christian, search for the truth, hear the truth, learn the truth, love the truth, speak the truth, hold the truth, defend the truth until death," was Hus' motto at the small Bethlehem Church in Prague where he was a pastor. On July 6, 1415, Hus was burned at the stake for being a heretic and his ashes dumped in a river running through Konstanz in Germany.[1]

Havel is photographed as a slight man, with thinning brown hair that he often parts with a brush of the hand in a seemingly nervous gesture. More often than not, his hair is mussy and this unkempt peculiarity lends him a slightly raffish air. A carefully trimmed mustache and precise physical gestures betray his European intellectual background. His smile cut lines deeply around his oval face and he wears his age plainly and openly. He smokes constantly, working each cigarette down to the filter before stubbing it out. Soon, his hand is reaching for the pack again.

His delivery is not polished, and he tends to look away from the questioner, fixing his gaze on some immovable object around him. Sentences from Havel's low, rumbling voice stop and start erratically, and he punctuates his phrases with various short, rapid clearings of the throat. His words come in gulps.

In *Disturbing The Peace,* a book-length interview with Havel that was published in 1990, he is asked whether he has ever considered suicide. "Is there anyone who has never thought of suicide?" he says. "Of course I've thought about it—many times—and in fact I still do, but probably only the way everyone who is capable of thought thinks about it."[2]

For the previous government, Havel had been the most dangerous of all criminals: a man with a conscience, a moral center and Job's patience. He spent more than three years in jail for dissident political acts including the drafting of Charter 77, a human-rights document that was prepared as a fundamental and comprehensive analysis of the overall situation in Czechoslovakia. Charter 77 urged the government to comply with the recently signed Helsinki Accords, to which Czechoslovakia was a signatory.

"Havel's writing is European, but it has a good American sense of humor," the late New York theater producer Joseph Papp said in 1991.

Papp recalled the first time he met Havel in 1968: "He was like a conservative hippie. His behavior was not hippie. But he loved the Beatles. He loved *Hair.*" According to others who met Havel while he was in the United States that one time, he expressed an interest in trying LSD (but didn't), attended an anti-war demonstration in Central Park and interviewed Czech exiles about their time abroad.[3]

Papp called Havel a conservative hippie, appropriately; Havel is intensely serious and highly philosophical. His essays on freedom and democracy are persuasive and thoughtful—albeit often bewilderingly complex, dripping in Heideggerian rationalizations and Ionescian absurdist philosophy. Very much a patriot, he chose to stay in Czechoslovakia even after many of his friends had emigrated to the West. Shortly before he was sentenced to his longest stint in prison in 1979 for "anti-government actions," the government told Havel they would give him a visa so he could travel to the United States and Joseph Papp offered him a job as playwright-in-residence at the Public Theater in New York City. But Havel rejected the visa, opting instead to go to jail. "The solution to the situation does not lie in leaving it," he has said. "Fourteen million people can't just go and leave Czechoslovakia."[4]

"I know what he was facing. I was there," says the noted Czech film director Miloš Forman. "I knew I would have to go to prison or collaborate with Communists, and I didn't have the guts or courage for either, so I left. He stayed and went to prison. He is my hero."[5]

I remembered reading the 144 letters Havel wrote to his wife, Olga, while he was in jail. They are long, soul-searching philosophical tracts about life and the Self. Complex, often maddeningly obscure and dense, they provide a picture of a man who is committed to his principles, but unsure of the path his life is taking. He writes her about his bad moods, the nature of "Being," the concept of death and the constant ache of his hemorrhoids.

On December 21, 1980, while less than half-way through the long stint in jail that would last until January 1983 he writes Olga:

"This letter will probably reach you sometime around the New Year and so some New Year's wishes would be in order. The more I think about it, the more I incline to the opinion that the most important thing of all is not to lose hope and faith in life itself. Anyone who does so is lost, regardless of what good fortune may befall him. On the other hand, those who do not lose it can never come to a bad end. This doesn't mean closing one's eyes to the horrors of the world—quite the contrary, in fact: only those who have not lost faith and hope can see the horrors of the world with genuine clarity."[6]

Havel is very hip, and counts among his friends Lou Reed, the late Frank Zappa and Paul Simon. One of his earliest acts as president was to invite the Rolling Stones to play in Prague as he saw the band's music as a major influence on dissidents and rock bands in Czechoslovakia. In *Letters To Olga,* he recommends that she buy Pink Floyd's *The Wall.* During his first visit to the United States as president in early 1990, he asked to see CBGB, the dark underground rock club in Manhattan where many of Havel's favorite musicians began their careers.

Although Havel was extremely well known in literary and political circles around the world, his rise from jailed dissident to President of Czechoslovakia came swiftly over little more than a month. Even though the entire country had been shaking quietly throughout 1989 as first Poland, and then East Germany and Hungary dissolved their governments, Prague's hard-line rulers led by Czechoslovak President Gustáv Husák and the Communist Party leader Miloš Jakeš, vowed that any disturbances would be swiftly crushed.

As late as July, 1989, the government was still rounding up various dissidents throughout the country. Havel had been arrested in January for attempting to leave flowers at the spot where Jan Palach had burned himself in 1969 to protest the Warsaw Pact invasion. On June 28, František Stárek, a dissident publisher, was sentenced to two-and-a-half years in prison for "incitement" against the state after he attempted to publish a journal called *Vokno* (Window).[7]

As the 21st anniversary of the Warsaw Pact invasion loomed in August, dissidents urged people to avoid confrontation with the government and wait for the right moment. "The authorities are waiting exactly for this type of action to be thus able to strike hard to paralyze people's democratization for a long time to come," Havel said.[8]

But by October, many commentators believed the end of the Communist Party in Czechoslovakia was drawing near. In mid-November, just days before a student demonstration in Prague would set the stage for the revolution, Jiří Dienstbier, a noted dissident, was optimistic about the future:

"The next step? I hope it's Czechoslovakia," he told *The New York Times*. "I think it could be. The leadership here is dead, only waiting to be carried away. Jakeš is completely discredited. The party's only alternative to the status quo is to open up the system, but they know that once they open it up, they are doomed."[9]

On November 17, 1989, Prague police brutally and violently suppressed a student demonstration in Prague that was being held to celebrate "International Day of Students" and a Czech student named Jan Opetal, who had been executed by the Nazis during World War II. The students responded with a nationwide strike at colleges and universities, as well as many high schools. As word of the protests traveled, intellectuals and dissidents began organizing their own meetings at theaters in major cities.

Sensing they had received the opening they needed, Havel and other actors, writers and dissidents hastily organized against the government in the next few days, calling for bigger mass demonstrations and general strikes.

As opposed to previous times when the government remained in control with the aid of the police and the army, this time, fortune was on the side of the demonstrators. As so much of the Warsaw Pact was crumbling, the opposition—many of whom were students—knew that this was their best moment to try and bring the Czechoslovak government to its knees.

"If the government continues to reject this extended hand and to spit on it, it is risking that increasing tensions in society will grow into a social confrontation," Havel said, in announcing plans for a general strike.[10]

Within a week of the initial demonstration, Havel found himself leading an umbrella opposition group called Občanské Forum (Civic Forum) into negotiations with the Husák government on reforming the government. One of the major keys to the success of the revolution was that the government lost control of the media during the week preceding the fall of the government. Support for political change intensified outside Prague when the huge protests in the center of the city were broadcast on national television. Students fanned out like evangelists across the countryside into the small villages and towns to bring the news to a usually skeptical populace.

Initially, the government agreed to remove key hardline Stalinist members of the Politburo and form a new coalition government composed of Communists, members of Civic Forum and other political parties. The government also agreed to change the provisions in the Czechoslovak constitution giving the Czechoslovak Communist Party (Komunistická Strana Československa) the leading role in society. It appeared a new government might resemble neighboring Poland's, where Communists and reformers shared power.

On November 26, when Havel and Alexander Dubček, the leader of 1968's "Prague Spring," addressed more than 300,000 people in Prague's main square, the leadership of the Communist Party resigned. It was Dubček's first appearance in public since he had been kicked out of the Communist Party in 1970. Although Dubček had somehow managed to avoid prosecution by the hardline regime, he had been banished to his house near Bratislava in Slovakia.

Havel, Dubček and the others celebrated when they learned of the resignations, believing they had won a great victory. But when a new government was announced on Dec. 3, Civic Forum was barely included, and most of the changes in the government were cosmetic. The issue was clear: the hardliners were not going to give up power easily.

Following yet more strikes and demonstrations, and with the army and police sitting on the sidelines, the government's power slowly ebbed. More changes in the government and cabinet were announced. And, for the first time, Havel's name was mentioned as a successor to Husák, who had announced that he would be resigning.

The temporary government to be formed would hold the country over until elections the following June. While there were some who wished to see Dubček as president, he simply carried too much political baggage from the past and was not perhaps the right person to create the "clean slate" the majority was seeking. Instead, Dubček became Chairman of the Federal Parliament.

In his resignation speech on Dec. 10, Husák thanked the nation for "cooperation and support" during his 60 years in politics. "If there were some mistakes," Husák said, "these were the mistakes of people, not the mistakes of ideas."[11] Here was absurdity at its most dramatic, as Husák was jailed for a number of years during one of the famous political purges in the early 1950s. In 1969, he rose again, only this time to send many innocent people to jail for their roles in the infamous 1968 Prague Spring reforms.

While there have been allegations from some news organizations, including the BBC, that the changes were set in motion with help from the Soviet KGB and the Czech state security who wanted to see the hardliners ousted, two independent commissions were never able to clearly establish what had sparked the various incidents.

Travel restrictions were relaxed on the borders in mid-December and more than 100,000 Czechs and Slovaks crossed the border the first weekend into Austria to spend the day "shopping" (they were only allowed to change a small amount of currency at the banks) and gawking at life in their neighboring country.

On December 31, Havel—reluctantly, he said—assumed the presidency, bringing with him a huge number of former dissidents (including Dienstbier, who became Foreign Minister) to run the government. The period came to be known as the "Velvet Revolution" because no lives we lost. It had all transpired so quickly, yet it seemed a perfect summation to the brilliance of one of Havel's central themes: "Love and truth will triumph over lies and hate."

Despite the outpouring of affection for the country's new president, the economic mess was daunting. Although conditions were difficult, the country wasn't as bad off economically as in Bulgaria, Romania or the Soviet Union.

Dana and Jana told me that they usually had most of the important goods, including milk, bread, butter, cheese and meat. They'd still have to wait in line, of course, to get these staples, but they were available. Some have said the longevity of the government was preserved by the fact that prices were held artificially low, stores were kept relatively full and basic provisions were available across the board. However, the distribution process seemed to be a bit haywire, as some products, like rice, potatoes or sugar, would simply vanish from time to time.[12]

Many of the shortages were often due to rumors spreading that something would be in short supply soon, or that prices would go up. People then panicked and started buying tons of the particular product.

"Some people did make very good money," Dana said. "People like waiters and cabdrivers and moneychangers. They often got their hands on a lot of hard currency." Ironically, dissidents also sometimes made better salaries, if they were lucky enough to receive money from works published or performed abroad.

While the country still was facing a major undertaking to move from one system to another, there were a number of favorable conditions that would help them, including Czechoslovakia's highly skilled workforce with several generations of industrial experience and a capitalist past which, despite the Great Depression, produced relatively high living standards. Moreover, the government's foreign debt was relatively low compared to the huge imbalances run up by neighboring Poland. This was in part due to the government's use of a strict import substitution policy, which kept them from borrowing from banks.[13]

"Objectively, it's a wealthy, but badly managed economy," said Valtr Komárek, an economist who was working to create a new economic plan for the country.[14]

Havel was extraordinarily blunt in a long and gripping New Year's Day address to the country in 1990 that neatly laid out the various problems.

"Our country is not flourishing," he said. "The enormous creative and spiritual potential of our nations is not being used sensibly. Entire branches of industry are producing goods which are of no interest to anyone, while we are lacking the things we need. A state which calls itself a workers' state humiliates and exploits workers.

"Masaryk based his politics on morality. Let us try in a new time and in a new way to restore this concept of politics. Let us teach ourselves and others that politics should be an expression of a desire to contribute to the happiness of the community rather than of a need to cheat or rape the community."[15]

He ended his address with a flourish borrowed from Czech history: "People, your government has returned to you!"

In the early spring, the new government had removed the most dangerous Communists from positions of power throughout the country, including the parliament. Mayors were replaced, members of the National Committees (which acted like town councils) turned out and new people were brought into the government. While many citizens would probably have liked more of the top leadership in major companies and local government to be replaced, the government had announced that there would be no large scale firings, as such removals required a five month notice and also because there was a lack of quality replacements.

While a full description of how the former government was organized would fill too much space and is about as interesting as reading the legal notices in the newspaper, the system operated along these general lines:

True power sprang, not from the federal government, or the President and Prime Minister's offices, but from within the Communist Party itself. While there was a Parliament and various lower level chambers across the country, it was those in the Party that really controlled what occurred.

The Communist Party structure, from the highest offices to the lowest rural council, was organized along Soviet lines, with a main Central Committee, Secretariat and Presidium (also known as the Politburo) and various National Committees spread out across the country. In addition, the trade unions and various parties loosely organized under the so-called National Front played a huge role in running day to day life. A third, and most insidious network of power obviously revolved around the security apparatus in the police, army and the internal spy networks.

Every sector of the economy was organized under a five-year plan that generally emphasized heavy industries like steel and coal mining. Farms were collectivized.[16] Almost everyone belonged to trade unions. There were numerous women's organizations and children's work groups and "Pioneer" groups where children would supposedly receive a proper socialist education. Either an organization was official or it was clandestine.

The government's first task was to prepare the country for elections, begin work on a new constitution and an orderly economic transformation.

During the spring of 1990, the government approved what was known as a "minimal plan" for restructuring of the economy by allowing for joint-stock companies, private enterprise and reducing the government's role in planning the economy.

After elections in June brought a new Parliament heavily comprised of members from the reformist Civic Forum and its Slovak counterpart, Public Against Violence (VPN) into power for two years, the government headed quickly towards endorsing a plan for radical economic reform. More than 30,000 prices in the economy were slightly liberalized.

But development of an economic plan was hampered slightly by differences of opinion at the very highest levels of the government, especially between several of the chief economists who had been selected to oversee the economic transformation.

Komárek, the Deputy Prime Minister, and Václav Klaus, the Minister of Finance, disagreed on the question of how rapidly the transition from one economic model to the other would be made. Dubbed by many "shock therapy" or "big bang," one proposal involved ending subsidies, throwing businesses and companies into privatization and restructuring the market around joint-stock companies.

Komárek argued shock therapy would hurt the average citizen and create high unemployment, a massive collapse of the GNP and inflation. He advocated a go-slow approach that would move towards a

Swedish model of centralized planning. Klaus disagreed, saying that the only way out of the mess was to move forward quickly. Klaus' economic plan was approved in September. Komárek's star in the young government slowly ebbed and he eventually became an opposition figure.

Klaus' conversion plan called for several major programs to be implemented over a period of several years including:

- Liberalization of domestic prices.

- "Internal convertibility" of the crown.

- Provision of an adequate social safety net, which ostensibly would protect pensioners and low-income families from the coming inflation.

- Encouragement of foreign investments and more freedom and responsibility given to managers of state-owned enterprises.

Directive planning from the government was abolished in the spring of 1990, and stores, restaurants and other small businesses were to be sold off in auctions starting in January, 1991. The so-called "big privatization" was still several years off and although plans were still being formulated, the general idea centered around having each company evaluated by the new Ministry of Privatization before being converted into a joint-stock company. In addition, there was a discussion of having citizens invest in the new companies through a voucher system that would allow people to purchase stock. In theory, the vouchers would encourage people to believe in the new market and get capital circulating to create a viable stock exchange and mutual fund market.[17]

The really Draconian measures, including development of a bankruptcy process, demonopolization of state industries and major reduction of subsidies, would be kicked in gradually over several years so as to not upset the country's already failing economy even more. As it was, state subsidies amounted to an incredible 16 percent of the GDP in 1990 alone.[18] Some of the money went to prop up the ridiculously large companies that were producing nothing of value and some went to individual households, schools and small businesses.

Klaus, like Komárek, had spent several years working in a strange, quirky office called the Institute of Forecasting in the Department for Macroeconomic Policy. The Forecasting Institute was a sort of think-tank where various economists, traded theories about different economic plans, including possible restructuring from central planning to a market economy.

In addition to the economic restructuring, another important bridge was crossed in late 1990 when the Soviets agreed to remove their troops from the country. Shortly before the elections, the Pope visited Prague and Slovakia and said Mass before hundreds of thousands of people. In addition, Havel had been persuaded to carry on as President after the June elections as the country simply hadn't anyone else who seemed a likely candidate.

There was some anger that the government hadn't done enough during its first year. A number of high profile stories dogged the Parliament through the year, most notably the so-called "hyphen" question and internal disputes within Civic Forum and Public Against Violence.

Almost immediately after the revolution, Czechs and Slovak ministers had begun bickering over what to call the country, now that it was no longer the Czechoslovak Socialist Republic. Slovak parliamentarians wanted to recognize their country separately and rejected a proposal to call the country the Czechoslovak Federal Republic in Bohemia and Moravia and the Czecho-Slovak Federal Republic in Slovakia. Finally, after more than a month of wrangling, the Parliament agreed on "The Czech and Slovak Federal Republic." A lot of Slovak nationalists, however, were still not satisfied and continued to rail against the new name.

Indeed, Slovak calls for more independence and even an outright split with Bohemia and Moravia were increasing every week. While it still seemed unlikely that the country would split—public opinion polls did not favor such a division—the conflicts between Czech and Slovak deputies in Parliament continued unabated.

Ivan Čarnogurský, the brother of the Deputy Prime Minister of

Czechoslovakia and a member of the Slovakian party called the Christian Democratic Union, said in an interview shortly before the June elections: "We think we have to continue in a federation. We want to come to a broader European union, and to this union we calculate to come separately, as two republics, Czech and Slovak. But it's not so simple, it needs time and we can't just cry independence right away without knowing how to bring it about."[19]

The seeds of the Czech and Slovak disagreements lay in conflicts running back to before the founding of the country in 1918. Slow to develop and always under the heel of the Hungarians, Slovak literature and language did not develop until after the 18th century. The Slovaks believed Prague and Czechs in general dictated far too much to the Slovaks in an regal and superior fashion. Slovaks contended that their end of the country was saddled with far too much heavy industry and poor land for crops.

In return, many Czechs thought Slovaks to be stupid, ignorant, poorly educated Slavs. Before World War II, Slovaks had complained the Czechs hadn't kept their end of the bargain regarding creation of a federal republic including a wide representation of Slovaks.

During the war, Slovaks had done little to help relations with the Czechs as Slovakia became a Nazi puppet state and was ruled by a Catholic priest named Josef Tiso, who was responsible for sending more than 66,000 Jews to Auschwitz (Tiso was hanged after the war). The Communist government after 1948 had managed to generally keep a lid on nationalist tendencies throughout the country, especially as several important leaders, including Dubček and Husák, were Slovak. In 1968, the Czechoslovak constitution was redrafted to create a truly federal nation in which Czechs and Slovaks had equal representation in Prague.

Now, in the fall of 1990, with the Communists gone, the Slovak nationalists were again calling for greater autonomy. "The new, non-Communist government is naive about the Slovaks," thundered Ján Budaj, a leader of Public Against Violence. "Most of them have not the slightest experience of Slovak problems, and have lived all their lives in the Prague Ghetto. No generation of Czechs has known Slovakia as little as this one."[20]

Police and Health Care

One morning, Dana took me to the police station where I was to receive my identification card and final visa. As we waded through various lines and offices searching for the correct department, Dana gradually grew more and more agitated. Finally spying the correct office, she steered me towards a long line.

"Now we can do some waiting, Douglas," Dana said, looking at me from over the top of her glasses. "This is something we do a lot of."

On the door to the office, there was a thick door with a small sign that read, "Don't knock. Wait until you are called." While it looked like a simple enough request, a problem quickly revealed itself.

Because you weren't supposed to knock, the officials on the other side of the door had no idea that you were waiting. Even more frustratingly, they rarely opened the door to see if anyone needed service.

The solution? Knock on the door, of course. Everyone did, and the employees then proceeded to help you. What's more, the employees didn't really seem to care one way or the other.

If experiences like these bring to mind the expression, "Kafka-esque," don't be surprised to discover that Franz Kafka lived for years in Prague's German speaking community and today is buried in a poorly kept Jewish cemetery in Prague.

While there are equally absurd situations in many American bureaucratic offices (visit your local Department of Motor Vehicles for a quick primer in what socialist bureaucracy would be like if it was implemented everywhere), there was nothing like a visit to an old fashioned socialist-styled office still ruled by *apparatchiks*—in other words, low-level Communist functionaries.

Consider some of the following choice rules and regulations from the local immigration office (italics mine):

- You must have your form. If you don't have the form, you won't be served. Please take a number and be seated. *(what if the ticket machine is empty and all the seats are full?)*
- Please don't ask for the form. They may be found at office #_____. *(usually in a different building in a different part of the city)*
- Please fill out the forms in black ink. Other colors will not be accepted. *(they also don't lend pens)*
- If the form doesn't have the official stamp, you won't be served. The stamp must be procured from office #_____. *(again, always somewhere else)*

And so on. The official stamps, the seal of bureaucratic approval, were the bane of everyone's existence. Once they were deemed necessary and valid, office staffs wielded the stamps like gavels at a political convention, thudding them down onto every single possible page of a document.

Just getting the necessary papers for a visa became a fraternity-styled scavenger hunt, as one was charged with collecting forms from different offices all over town, little tax stamps, photos and other bits and pieces of paper. Even visiting the immigration office during working hours could take several attempts until one had meticulously recorded the bizarre operating hours for future reference: Mondays, 2–4 P.M.; Tuesdays, closed; Wednesdays, 8–10 A.M.; Thursdays 4–5 P.M., etc.

In a few weeks, Dana and I returned to the police station and I was solemnly presented with a simple, white card that had my picture and information about myself and identified me as a "temporary working resident of the Czechoslovak Socialist Republic."

"Look at that," Dana said, "they still haven't changed the cards yet. So now you are a socialist, Douglas."

When we arrived back at the school several hours later, Dana groaned and headed for a little green bottle that was kept near the sink.

"That was terrible! I don't usually do this, but will you please join me in a drink?" She poured out two small glasses of rum and then relaxed. "I hate those police stations with those people being just awful to each other and always asking questions." She lit a cigarette and angrily tossed the match into a nearby ashtray. "They are all such nasty people, you know."

Just as I was still trying to adjust and keep everyone's name in order, my good health was showing severe signs of giving out. One of my biggest worries when I arrived had been that I might get diarrhea or some kind of intestinal bug from the change in continents. While I suspect that I have a stomach made of cement, and can eat everything put in front of me, the other end of my body didn't react quite as well. I quickly came down with sinusitis, an infection of the sinus area that has bothered me for several years. It's a bastard of an infection to kill and produces dizzy spells, nasty headaches and a temperature. It's also somewhat dangerous and should be treated with antibiotics without delay.

One afternoon when I began to feel lightheaded and dizzy, I asked Jana where I might go see a doctor. She looked at me with horror and said, "I hope it's not where *we* have to go! The doctors there are so awful!" I hoped her reaction was dramatics on her part, and I said that I really didn't care who I went to see, just as long as the doctor didn't fumble for a cranial drill and express a sudden desire to "take a quick peek inside."

Jana promised to do a bit of research about what to do with me and suggested that I go home immediately.

"It's really not that bad," I protested. "I just should go sometime soon, I think." But despite my reasoning, she still sent me packing back to the Dům in the early afternoon.

"Remember what we say Douglas," she said, nearly pushing me out the door. "Lékař léčí, Panbůh uzdravuje—a doctor treats you, but

89

only God makes you healthy. It's an old Czech saying."

Early the next morning, Jana left her classes in the care of a substitute and took me to the outskirts of the city where there was a new hospital only for foreigners. As we rode the tram, Jana told me she was quite excited to see what the hospital looked like, as it had recently been completed.

"It was supposed to be only for members of the KSČ, the Communist Party," she said. "Now it is just for the foreigners. So you can see, Douglas, just who is running the country now!" She shook a finger at me and laughed, but I suspected there was something buried deeper behind her comment.

When we arrived, we discovered the doctor who spoke English had gone off somewhere to a meeting. I would be examined by his assistant, a cheerful fellow in a big white doctor's suit who spoke almost no English ("only leeetle") and seemed to have only a vague notion of what was wrong with me, despite Jana's best efforts to translate descriptions of my past bouts with sinusitis. He took my temperature by sticking a thermometer under my arm and then looked in my throat.

"You are sick," he said, after listening to my lungs. "Very sick." He spoke with Jana for a moment and she translated.

"He's going to give you some pills and you will have to stay at home for a least a week and rest," she said.

"What!" I screeched. "A week! I feel generally fine and I have plenty of energy. I just don't want this to get much worse." I explained about the kind of antibiotics that I usually took.

"He says he will give you better pills to take, and that you have to stay home," Jana said, while the doctor smiled at me and wrote a prescription for me on a pad. Then he ushered us out of his room. While we were waiting in the hallway for the nurse to finish typing some papers, Jana explained to me about the Czechoslovak health care system. Everyone—the rich, middle class and the poor—received care for free, but the quality of care was sometimes lackluster and dangerously inattentive.

"If you need special care or want to have a special operation, you can always give something extra to the doctor who can move you up

90

the surgery list or pay better attention to you," Jana said. "A doctor in the family or one as a close friend is a very good thing."

"But what about this staying home for a week? In the United States, we stay home when we are ill and then go back to work when we feel we are ready," I explained.

"If you are sick, you must stay home," she said. "They give you a note and you must be at home. We have people—*kontrol*—who go around and check on people or call them at home. If you are not sick you must be at work. You should feel lucky. I wish I had those notes every week." She produced a giggle that was half snort and a chuckle.

"But a week!" I said. "Why so long?"

"That's usually how long the average sick time lasts. He may tell you to stay out even longer when you come back next week."

"So I have to stay at the Dům for a week?" I looked at her with pleading eyes while thinking about how far the leap was from the 16th floor.

"Yes," she said firmly. "Someone may come visit you there to check. We'll get another teacher to sit in on your classes."

The doctor came out with some pills in his hand. I was to take some Czechoslovak antibiotics and five aspirin a day. I didn't have to pay anything, except a small fee for services and the pills. Jana snorted again as we walked out through the clean, well-lit hallways. Although it was a fully functioning hospital, it seemed to be totally deserted. It reminded me of the hospital in the movie *Coma*.

"Look at how nice everything is!" she said, pointing at the new lighting and the newly painted brown and yellow walls. "We would never have had such nice places with clean rooms and comfortable chairs. So you can see about how terrible our society is, Douglas."

I went back to the Dům (the name kept ringing in my ears: Doom, Doom, Doom) and began a week-long stretch of forced solitude that was broken only when I dashed outside to the local market to buy groceries. I wondered if I should wear a disguise in case whatever bogeymen who checked up on people saw me and reported me to the authorities for breaking out of the Dům. Luckily, I had gotten paid by the school for my first month of work. We had all lined up one after-noon outside the accounting office where the school secretary carefully counted out each paycheck in cash. There were no checks, no direct deposit, no reduction of your salary into IRAs and Christmas Clubs and 12-month car leasing programs. One was given his salary in cash and you either put it in the bank or simply went home and stuffed it in a jar. And, if you lost it or were robbed, it was gone. I put mine in my closet under some socks. Even though it wasn't worth much in American dollars, it was a fairly good amount by Czech standards, especially since I didn't have to pay rent at the Dům.

The sweet children from some of my younger classes sent me an envelope full of drawings wishing me greetings and expressing the fervent desire that I recover quickly, as if I were prone in some sickroom with nurses attending to my sweat-clad body.

Mostly, I sat in the TV room watching an endless parade of mind-numbing Czech programs and CNN and reading the few books I had left. One of the three television channels, OK3, was a former propaganda channel for the Soviets. Every night they showed *Vrejma,* the news from Moscow. There wasn't much of value on the program. On Nov. 7, when someone tried to shoot Gorbachev in Red Square on the anniversary of the formation of the USSR in 1917, *Vrejma* devoted its entire broadcast to footage from celebration, including hundreds of smiling, waving happy "pioneer youth" and tanks, missiles and trucks, but said nothing about the shooting.

As the week wore on, I discovered that the antibiotics weren't helping and the huge amount of aspirin was giving me stomach aches. On the third day of lockup, I called my grandmother, who used to be Chief Nurse at a major Bay Area hospital.

"For God's sake," she said. "Quit taking the aspirin. You'll blow your stomach apart." I did and my stomach quit hurting. The next week I went back to the doctor and told him I felt fine (I was stretching the truth, but figured it was better than another week in the Dům). He told me in broken English that he was glad the pills had worked and that I should go back to school.

Not long after, my father had my doctor in San Francisco send me antibiotics I was used to and I tried to treat myself as best I could by taking vitamins and drinking enough water and liquids. I didn't bother to go back to the foreigner's hospital again, opting instead to go to the local clinic where all of the Czechs went. There certainly seemed to plenty of people still alive, so all the doctors couldn't be complete quacks.

Still, a visit to the clinic is one of the more demeaning experiences a person can have. There is no schedule: one simply waits in line as though it were an American Jiffy Lube or Fotomat Drive-In. The waiting room is almost always dark and crowded with ill people. The environment makes you feel worse. When your turn comes, you don little plastic white boots like you are going to be wandering through plutonium. The doctor, you discover, has all the bedside manner and charm of an overworked accountant. The female physician assigned to handle cases from the Dům showed no sense of humor until one day when I went to put several books on the floor next to the chair where I sat in her examining room.

"Ježiš a Maria! (Jesus and Mary!)" she said, "the floor is so dirty! Put your books on my instrument table here."

Despite being told not to by several Czechs, I was drinking the tap water at the Dům and at school. Although one of my guide books warned that the water could contain mercury and lead, I figured there was no way around the water source, especially since my attempts to find bottled water had failed. One evening, I had bought several bottles of what I thought was drinking water at the local grocery store. I found it rather thick and bitter. Curious, I gave it to one of the Czechs who lived on our floor. He looked at the green bottle with its faded label.

"Are you having difficulties with diarrhea these days?" I shook my head. "Well, this is something that old people generally drink to make sure they always go to the toilet."

I poured the bottle into the sink.

8

Into the Golden City

Between getting school into a routine and being sick, I barely had any time to develop much of a private life. I hadn't met many Czechs and was generally keeping to myself in the Dům during the first few weeks. Several of us Americans from the building had ventured out one night for dinner in a small restaurant in Malá Strana where the waiter told us he had only "one dinner, one dinner, ein, *one*." What he meant to say is that he was only going to serve one item from the menu and so eat it or don't.

Faced with a gross linguistic imbalance, we opted to accept his generosity and pretty soon the kitchen produced plates of pork, dumplings and the expected cabbage. And beer. Then they overcharged us and got extraordinarily huffy when we wanted to see a menu with prices.

"*Nein,* no," the waiter said, adjusting his clip on bow-tie and picking at his little mustache. "Here is the bill. You now please me to pay." One of the others at the table persuaded us to just drop some cash and forget about returning in the future.

"That way," he said, "eventually no one will come here again and they'll go out of business." Not a bad idea, except in a state-run economy, there was no such thing as an individual restaurant: all their profits went into one big vat and it didn't really matter whether they served one meal or 400 a night.

Restaurants really showed the negative effects of state-owned businesses. Waiters couldn't give a damn whether you wanted a drink, a meal, wanted to pay or had a dumpling lodged in your throat. If it took 45 minutes to get your soup, who cares? It's cold? So sorry. Successful restaurants were rare. Often waiters would simply make up false orders so they could get more meat deliveries which the restaurant then sold on the black market.[1]

Overcharging was rampant. A number of unique tricks ensured you would get ripped off, including the assessment of obscene amounts for *couvert* or plates of little almonds or "first drinks." Usually these offerings were brought out early in the meal when everyone was still arranging themselves and was gaily distracted by early dinner chatter. Once the diners would start complaining, the waiters would whip out menus showing the actual prices.

The night of our initial rip-off, we wandered around the Malá Strana area for some time until somebody suggested that we go the bar at the American Embassy. I didn't know what to think about the American government being in the business of selling booze to its citizens, but I trooped along anyway. Several others in the group were looking forward to having a Diet Coke and speaking English, which we had been doing all night.

We discovered that the "Dobry Den" (a play on the Czech and English uses of the word Den, English meaning "family room" and Czech meaning "day" viz: "good family room") was actually a short, stubby room located in the bowels of the embassy that featured a half-bar, a pool table framed by the flag of Texas and weight machines used by the Marines. Men were welcome, but it was women who were prey, as the Marines stationed at the embassy used the bar as a launching pad for alleviating their hard-up desires.

While several of these rather large gents circled around the women in our group, I nibbled some Cheetos and drank a Budweiser while talking to the American Vice Counsel Robert Shipley, who was tending bar that night. A polite fellow, Shipley had wavy hair past his collar, a droopy mustache and little round granny glasses that made him look a bit like a hippie.

Shipley said most people who worked there were bored because they generally couldn't leave the compound without permission or escorts. The compound was still subject to pre-revolutionary strict security. Once a week, two of the Marines drove a truck to Frankfurt and loaded up with supplies for the personnel at the American Army base. The government also sent over videotapes of television programming from the United States, including old basketball and baseball games.

Shipley told me that the Czechs liked the American ambassador Shirley Temple Black, who had been appointed to the position by Bush shortly before the revolution in 1989.

"They know her from the movies and also she's very personable. She makes quite an impression on people," he said, while pouring a Budweiser from a can into a short glass. "Lately, I've been busy because everyone wants to get visas so they can travel to the United States on vacations. There's a long line out the front door every day."

"Where is the ambassador tonight?" I asked, hoping Black might come in and buy us all a beer. I had met her several times in San Francisco, and would have enjoyed talking with her again.

"Tonight, she's at home," Shipley said. "She doesn't have a party or function for the first time in weeks. She's invited out almost every night for some function or another."

I was finding that I had a lot of free time in ways that I never expected. Freed from the usual rituals of American culture, *Sally Jesse Raphael, Arsenio, thirtysomething* and the like, I started to read more than I every had before. I read at breakfast, in the metro, during breaks, in the afternoon and after dinner. Chapters flew by, stories were dispatched at great haste—entire books consumed at one sitting. Luckily, the American Embassy had a large library of American books. Once or twice a week, I'd troop up the hill in Malá Strana through the narrow, cobblestone streets and go to the small embassy library.

As September elapsed, I began to see less and less of Nikola and Dora, who were just as overwhelmed at their schools as I was at mine. One afternoon I watched Nikola try and control a large and wild class of eleven-year-olds. Despite the fact that she could communicate with them, she was unable to impose any kind of order. Kids talked in groups, threw bits of paper across the room and carried on like it was a lunch break.

"I know it was chaos," Nikola wearily said later that evening. "I've tried to reason with them in every possible way. First, I said I'd let them play a game if they'd be good. Then I offered to let them read or do special exercises. Finally, I just got mad and said 'why are you doing this to me? Why can't you be nice?'"

"What did they say?" I asked.

"Nothing really," she said. "They really didn't have an answer. The worst thing is they all cheat so much. It seems like none of them ever do legitimate work!"

I had already noticed when I gave quizzes and dictation to my older students that there was a lot of blatant cheating: kids shared information, copied answers on crib sheets and acted like I was clueless to their intentions. While I wasn't surprised by the fraud, I was amazed at the number of students who seemed to care little about doing honest work.

Curious, I asked Dana whether or not she had encountered similar problems.

"I think it's hard to say whether there is more cheating this year or not, Douglas. But I must say that cheating is — or was — something quite common in our schools," Dana said. "Well, in the past, most teachers were afraid to give honest grades to many of the students whose parents were members of the Communist Party," she said. "We kept their files separate and made sure the students always received enough praise and good marks. Oh, it was often so complex and difficult because you couldn't say that a student wasn't studying. The parents were quite powerful and could always say that it was the teacher's fault!"

Dana went on to tell me that many of the law students at the university in Prague had failed their exams earlier in the year. "They were the first honest and open exams in many years and the teachers actually gave them real marks. The students all did very poorly!"

When I wasn't grading papers, I spent the late afternoons after school prowling through the narrow streets in the center of Prague, trying to orient myself and gain an idea of how the really city really felt.

My friends and I used to say that the city existed in two levels: *Prague* or *Praha*. *Prague,* as foreigners pronounce and spell the city, was where one was able to glide effortlessly through the streets, absorbing the city's hushed beauty and feeling the mystical presence of the many famous personalities who haunt the buildings: Beethoven, Mozart, Goethe, Rilke, Gogol, Chopin, Werfel, Smetana, Dvořák, Kafka and Goncharov. Prague was the city of golden spires arching up into a clear blue sky, of European graces and the twin gothic towers of the Charles Bridge, which has spanned the Vltava since 1357. Prague was fairy tales and long-forgotten kingdoms and dappled sunlight through murky coffee houses and the bittersweet taste of good beer.

And then there was *Praha,* as it is pronounced and spelled by Czechs, a city where cars choked the roads and old women in the trams were liable to whack you in the shins with their canes for seats. The difficulty of getting things accomplished made life exceedingly sluggish and often maddeningly complicated beyond all necessity. Praha was not a fairy tale; rather, it was a place of bad restaurants and smelly restrooms and sinister *vrátnice*—"house security"—who watched your every move in and out of a building with undisguised disgust. Praha was the city of waiting in endless lines and people who didn't protest when things should be outraged. Praha was decaying buildings with cracked windows and yellowed plaster. This world was socialism incarnate, the mother country of gross indignities that made one feel like an animal being rudely herded from place to place.

It was the gap between the two cities—Prague and Praha—that I longed to discover and knew must exist. Just as life in America is paradoxical, I knew that, in time, I could find slices of each world that were reasonable, which could knit together as an understood whole.

I explored the various sections of town: the Nové Město—"New Town" located off the river (new because it was built after the 14th century as opposed to other older sections), the Staré Město—"Old Town"—which dates back to the 13th century and today contains the most tourist shops, and the Malá Strana quarter where I had taken my first long walk. More than other European cities I have seen, Prague does not wear its modern architecture well. Many of the new buildings were designed by state committees and non-architects who didn't know anything about integrating architecture; the sheer number of historic buildings packed end to end throughout the town causes the modern structures to clash hideously with everything around them.

I didn't have a route during these weeks; I merely bumbled my way through the streets and lanes, often narrowly avoiding being flattened by speeding cars. I traced the crumbling walls and moss-covered facades with their ornate stucco moldings and elaborate balconies with black-rod iron fixtures.

Unless one climbs to the short hills that rise behind one bank of the Vltava, or rides to the top of a nearby television tower, it is hard to get a wide view of the city. Most of the structures are simply short. Perhaps a clear view of the metropolis isn't necessary more than once; Prague is best absorbed slowly, cobbled together in a series of still-life images: the narrow streets, the lovingly restored buildings, the beer pubs and odor of cooking cabbage and brewing coffee. All of these things define the city at its best, just as the view from a fourth-story window across aging rooftops and smoking chimneys scarred by pollution and neglect is more revealing than a panoramic view from on high.

One afternoon, I climbed to the top of the city hall tower in the center of Old Town. From there, I gained a better view of life as it unfolded: old women leaning on their windowsills while they scanned the street life below; an elderly couple propped up on uncomfortable-looking day beds while they watched endless amounts of television; a solitary wife preparing goulash and boiled potatoes in a kitchen the size of a closet; cracked and faded facades with their once elegant goblins, baroque decorations and pigeons nesting in broken water spouts.

When I came home in the evenings, my feet sore from tramping about, I took a long shower and washed the grime from my hair and the backs of my ears and off my face. Prague is beautifully filthy. It is not a city for cars, but still there are too many of them screeching and roaring through streets that were laid in the Middle Ages.

A friend of mine calls the country "a nation of 16-year-olds behind the wheel" and he is right: while not as arrogant as Italians or dangerous as the French, bad drivers make the roads between Prague and Bratislava in Slovakia downright dangerous. The drivers speed while fussing over innumerable cigarettes, scratching their beards, checking the map, making poor judgments about when to pass on tiny, two-lane roads. Men able to afford faster, Western cars become terrors as they bellow down the streets, unaccustomed to the power and unpredictable speed beneath the hood of their cars.

The exhaust from all these automobiles mingles with the coal smoke, soaking everything in a fine layer of dust and gritty soot. In an hour, a white shirt becomes dotted with little black flecks and socks turn gray. Everything feels soiled.

One of the first questions Westerners usually ask Czechs upon arriving in Prague is "how could the Communists have screwed up so much? Didn't they know what was happening?"

The answer is complex. Many Communists did know that the infrastructure was sliding downhill, especially the state of the environment. An official 1983 government report, *Analysis of the Environmental Situation in the ČSSR,* reported a shocking one third of the forests were critically damaged. Farm production was plummeting. Life expectancy was decreasing. Eighty percent of the country's butterflies had died. The report was suppressed and never released to the public.[2]

The country today has a clean air act that requires for industry to conform to international emission standards by 1998. Overhaul and diligent work by the government to push reform will need to occur for this to happen.

I don't know how many times I've heard well meaning Americans puff up their chests and bellow in righteous indignation: "Geeze, how could you have let Communism happen? If it'd been me, I *woulda* throttled those nasty commie bastards. I *woulda* armed myself to the teeth. I *woulda* stood up to them, for God's sake. I *woulda* (blah, blah, blah)."

Well, sorry, but I don't think you *woulda* done much of anything. Certainly not after the authorities started questioning you, harassing you and threatening to take away your job. How unpleasant do you want to make your life, anyway? So sorry, comrade, but you're outta line.

Chances are you would have simply shut up and gotten on with your life, however difficult it was. It takes courage to challenge a truly dangerous government—a lot more than raising your fist at a *save-the-gay-whales-of-color* rally before heading home in time to catch *Roseanne* on the boob tube.

Czech friends have told me that they generally find foreigners and aging Czech and Slovak exiles the quickest to be angered by the specter of communism. They say there is a tremendous amount of false superiority present among these people. One dissident in the early days put it plainly: "What you have not lived, you will never understand." Not surprisingly, a lot of Czechs simply hunkered down, didn't complain and followed every rule and regulation, regardless of how ridiculous they became.

Although I was—and am more and more as each year passes—impressed by the grandeur and transcendent beauty of the mixture of Baroque, Gothic and Renaissance architecture, I seem to be someone who is more drawn to the present. Consequently, it took me a long time to develop a love affair with the city. I would look at a building, read about why it was important and say "Humph!" to myself with my mouth open, my head tilted back, my hands in my pockets, and then move on down the street and discover I was more interested in the way an elderly woman had fixed the bandanna on her head and was dragging a cart loaded with groceries over the cobblestones.

Clearly, I was having the same trouble emotionally connecting with the architecture in the same way that I never really liked the Reubens I had seen at the Louvre in Paris or the Greek and Roman statues in the British Museum in London. To me, there was something too dead, too clinical and too removed about these treasures.

Old Town Square (Staroměstké náměstí) in the heart of the downtown has been sumptuously renovated so most of the buildings on the square look the same as they did several centuries ago. Regardless of how many tourists clog the square each day, the battering events of history the square has seen helps to bring the buildings alive in a dramatic way. Protestant Czechs were executed here by Emperor Ferdinand II in 1621 following the Battle of White Mountain, Nazis burned part of the Old Town Hall before abandoning Prague in 1945. Gottwald used the square to proclaim the socialist future of the country.

As I sat in a cafe stirring a cup of the thick Turkish-styled coffee, it occurred to me just how much I had to learn about the eternal scope of history. I recalled what one of my students had said to me in a discussion class several days earlier when I asked her what she thought of when she heard the word "America."

"Mmmmn," she said. "I think Mickey Mouse."

"Something else?" I asked.

"Mmmmn, Reagan? And Disneyland. Sun. Big cities," she said, listing the items off on her fingers. "Oh, and television," she added.

Oh dear, I thought. Even though she was only fourteen, she was echoing what other people seemed to think about the United States. Martin Walker, the British journalist who writes for *The Guardian,* says American export culture is dominated by a sort of "softpower."—from the records and the films, to food, jeans and cars. So much of the world is attracted to America's "soft" consumables that give a quick pleasure and then fade. Other cultures—especially the French—are simply piqued by the constant assault of movies and music flooding out of the United States.

Conversely, if Europeans had a hard time figuring out America and our habits, I was fairly disgusted by how much Czech men liked to spit. Often and everywhere. Sometimes the spit was just a quiet dribble from the mouth; other times it was accompanied with a great snort and nasal clearing.

When the weather is cold and slows the evaporation process, Prague's streets are littered with tiny blobs of saliva and other unmentionable gunk. It is a more earthy attention to life. Old women and men honk their noses cheerfully, doing what we in high school used to call "nature blows," in which the viscous contents of the sinus cavity are violently ejected (usually with great skill and accuracy) through the nose where they land with a splat on the street.

During my first month in Prague, I visited other well-known land-marks, including U Fleků, a brewery that dates back to 1499 and still produces gallons of its own special black beer. One afternoon, Nikola, Dora and I sat in the restaurant's sunny garden for several hours drink-ing several mugs of the pub's frothy dark beer and listening to the babble of German voices all around us. We learned soon that U Fleků is a tourist hangout we wouldn't want to regularly visit.

In the evenings, I often stopped for dinner at the Automat Koruna near the bottom of the Wenceslas Square. New in Prague, with little Czech, it wasn't apparent to me that I was eating in a restaurant that had all the charm of an Automat in Times Square. The Koruna was a huge stand-up cafeteria. Several kiosks sold different bits of food: sausages from one stand, hot meals from another, little sandwiches at a third, desserts at a fourth and drinks at a fifth. If you wanted a variety of things, you had to stand in five different lines. The first time I went in I didn't see the trays and spent half my time feeling paranoid as I rushed about trying to assemble everything, all the while looking nervously over my shoulder hoping that my food wouldn't get stolen. One of the elderly cleaning women in the cafeteria finally noticed me and came up and presented me with a sympathetic look and a tray.

The Koruna was a Prague institution, but an abysmal mess: dirty, grimy floors; the perpetual smell of sausages and stale beer lingered in every faded crack. Under poor lighting, people stood at stainless steel tables the kind you'd find in an autopsy room, hunched over their food, eating quickly with smacking gums and little delight. The food was bland and ridiculously unhealthy (huge globs of mayon-naise, fatty pork, salt) but the milieu was fascinating.

As the food was cheap and the beer even more so, old men with weathered faces like Popeye stood around for hours, smoking unfil-tered cigarettes called *Start* (Start what? To die?) and drinking beer from chipped and cracked mugs.

Over the top of a paperback book, I watched them for minutes. They were all so unique in character and each one hiding a different story. I watched as they wiped the beer foam from their beards and rubbed their high cheeked faces which narrowed to a finer, more pronounced jaw than the oval-shaped American face.

The Koruna was a swirl of dark-skinned Gypsies, Czech workers in dirty blue jumpsuits and little canvas tennis hats, men sporting flat depression-style caps, and old, stooped *babkys*—women from rural villages—wearing bandannas and carrying huge shopping bags or dragging grocery carts behind them. Their teeth or jawlines cut forward in odd angles, mostly because they hadn't had the luxuries of corrective dental procedures like braces and retainers. I was reminded of Kafka's description of people around him in *The Castle:* "They looked as if they had been beaten flat on top and their on their features as if the pain of the beating had twisted them to the present shape."

The Koruna was my domain for several weeks until I wised up and found other places to eat. I would cheerfully kill several hours drinking lemonade from the oddly shaped socialist mugs and glasses, each with an oblong trademark set off by a socialist star and an obligatory line for the half-liter or .3 liter liquid.

I was terribly sad when they closed the Koruna about a year later. It seemed as though a bygone product of the socialist era had been silenced; I would have closed it off and made it a museum to how truly demeaning and uninspired life under socialism had become. Today the space where the Koruna stood is being prepared for a huge American-styled mall.

Several days after the beginning of school, I was on my way from the tram towards the school when I noticed one of the teachers from school walking beside me. She looked over and said in a thick accent, "Good morning." I was quite surprised. I had seen her in the hallways before, but had never spoken with her. She was very attractive, with long, straight brown hair and a beautiful, sympathetic looking face that was set off by the weary eyes.

"I didn't know you could speak English," I said.

"Oh, I don't speak very well," she said. "Hardly at all."

"It sounds like you speak very well to me," I said, as we reached the front of the school.

"My name is Jarka," she said, shaking my hand. Then she turned and headed up the stairs. It was several days before I spoke with her again.

I was watching the kids in the school cafeteria when Jarka came over to me and asked, in a tentative way, whether I would like to meet one of her friends.

"She is from England and is interested in moving here. I thought since maybe you seem to like it here you could try and keep her here."

"You mean convince her to be here?" I said.

"Yes. Can you go with us for coffee?" I agreed and returned to minding the cafeteria. Before she left she asked me what "convince" meant.

Later that afternoon, I met Jarka's friend, Anna, in a dark coffee bar in the center of town. Anna was a history professor at a university near Brighton who had managed to do the impossible: learn Czech abroad without ever having set foot in the country. It was a pleasure to speak English again—in fact, I think I must have jabbered for a half an hour—and we spent several hours comparing notes about Czechoslovakia.

Several days later, I met Anna and Jarka again after school and Jarka led us back to her apartment near the castle. She and her husband, Viktor, were temporarily subletting a flat of a friend currently in the army. As it is nearly impossible to receive a flat from the city, many homeless young people live in flats while the owners are away. Lots of friends in the army can be a good thing as you can secure their flats for long stretches of time.

In Czechoslovakia, one does not hold traditional "title" to an apartment. Rather, one receives the right to live in an apartment, modify it and adapt it. The apartment may be passed on to children or other relatives; inheritance is one of the most common ways of getting a flat. Sometimes newlyweds have to live with their parents or grandparents until someone in their family dies and leaves them a flat.

In fact, it is so difficult to get hold of a flat in Prague that many families put their children on a waiting list at birth in hopes they will be assigned a flat when they are about to be married.

Jarka and Viktor's temporary flat was up a long, picturesque road winding up to the Castle in the Malá Strana section of town. The steep street was dotted with pubs and small stores selling souvenirs and glass and it was a fair climb to their door, which was a large wooden entryway that accepted a huge, old metal key the kind you see in a Sherlock Holmes movie. The entrances to the apartments faced into an open courtyard that had stabled horses when the house was constructed more than 150 years before. After another long climb up creaking wooden stairs, we reached their apartment, a small studio with hardwood floors that looked out over a green valley. The sun was just coming down over the valley as we arrived and the light was shining broadly through the small windows, giving the room a bright and airy feeling. Against one wall, their friend had assembled a huge collage of pictures from the revolution, including a poster of Havel and Lech Walesa at a recent meeting. There was no formal bed, just a mattress on the hardwood floor.

I leaned out the window for more than ten minutes, admiring the view and wishing I could live there amongst the trees and cobblestones.

Viktor was an out-of-work engineer who wasn't completely sure whether he really wanted to spend the rest of his life working in a laboratory. Viktor's greatest joy was to be surrounded by friends in a happy environment (preferably a pub or someone's home) drinking good beer, smoking, listening to music and being happy.

"I think life is too short to work all the time," he said, his blue eyes meeting mine. He rested one arm on his chin while the other held a cigarette. Viktor had a kind, sincere face and looked directly at you while you were talking. With his short brown hair, close-cut beard and well figured body neatly tucked into jeans and a denim work shirt, Viktor was perhaps the first handsome Czech man I had met. Up to that point, I thought many Czech men looked overgrown, with wide, flat faces and soft, fat frames and crew-cuts that made them look too heavy.

I was also put off by the swaggering, overdone braggadocio of some Czech males who strutted about the streets looking like extras from *On The Waterfront* with their collars up, a perpetual cigarette dangling from their lips and a Billy Idolish-sneer as they gaped at passing females. After visits to Serbia and the Ukraine, I later discovered that the Czech cockwalk was, like so much of Czech culture, rather tame compared to the real meanness exuded by males in other Eastern European cities.

The Czech colloquial expression, "vole" (pronounced VO-LEH), is perhaps the chief spacing expression in the Czech language for many men, used as an American might say, "you know" or "dude" or another word meant to tie two loose thoughts together. "Vole," which literally means, "bull," can mean many things, like the American use of "dude." Consequently, "vole" appears in a lot of lower Czech like a mantra, as in this fictitious conversation:

"Hele, vole, musíme jít ."(Hey, look here, you bull, we've got to go.)

"Ale, hele vole, já mám ještě pivo ." (But hey, look here bull, I've still got beer). Of course, it looks strange when translated, but it sounds completely natural. Besides, American slang is equally ridiculous, especially when one considers our use of strange expressions like "word-up," "dude," "bitchin" and the all-time best, "like, um, you know?"

After I started tuning my ear to average conversations on the street and in pubs, I couldn't get away from "vole vole vole."

Although the men often looked shambolic, if not just sloppy, Czech women were stunningly attractive, graced by beautiful, arching cheekbones and delicate, sallow arms that looked soft and silky. They were simply gorgeous to look at, whether they were dressed in simple cotton dresses or low-cut, black mini-skirts (a popular fashion trend). As would be expected in a European country, Czech women don't often shave their armpits, and often don't shave their legs as well.

Whether it was something to do with the Czech diet or heredity, Czech women seemed to keep their figure into their forties (when they begin to expand like inflatable life-rafts), whereas almost immediately Czech men started to show the effects of mass consumption of beer, pork products, still more beer and the ubiquitous dumplings.

While I was silently ruminating on the differences between Czech men and women, Viktor asked if I wanted to accompany him to buy some beer at a local pub. Viktor grabbed a large ceramic jug, and he and I walked down the street, our shoes clicking on the stones, past other medieval buildings with huge barn doors and elegant and delicate stone trim, to the local *hospoda*—beer pub. It was warm and the late afternoon shadows cut across the faded paint like sundials. I was stunned by the beauty of everything around me: the castle above our heads, the cracks in the street, the gas lamps and perfect beer pubs. It all seemed so charming and mysterious, yet had endured for so many hundreds of years. Viktor gave the jug to the bartender who filled it slowly with eight glasses of beer. While we waited for the beer to settle in the huge jug, Viktor and I stood, hands in pockets and shyly looked at each other.

"I'm sorry that I don't speak English very well," he said, without looking at me.

"I think it sounds wonderful. You should hear how bad my Czech is." Viktor laughed and picked up the jug. We again walked back up the hill, this time more carefully, with the container oozing white foam. The beer was as fresh as the day it was made.

Back in the apartment, we drank and talked about music. Viktor and Jarka knew a lot about Western pop music and we spent much of the evening playing their favorite records.

"As I don't often understand the lyrics, I listen to the music," Viktor said. Consequently, he and his friends liked a variety of bands and singers who had strong melodies, including Phil Collins, Dire Straits and Whitesnake. Later, he and Jarka asked me about how American Football was played and I spent the better part of an hour babbling away, making little diagrams on paper and happily explaining the plays. Suddenly, I glanced up and realized by the looks on their faces that they hadn't grasped much of what I had said. I felt embarrassed and realized I was talking too quickly.

In the early evening, some of their other friends came over to the flat, and I soon discovered that these little get-togethers were a regular and major part of their lives. Jarka and Viktor had both attended the same *gymnázium*—the Czech equivalent of high school—and so had many of their common friends. Despite the fact that most everyone was in their late twenties, they all still were together. Most of my friends from high school were now spread out across the United States like raggedy carpetbaggers.

Given Czechoslovakia's relative tininess, it simply wasn't possible to move far away and be that far apart, especially in Prague, where one didn't need a car to travel around the city. We're often so isolated in America; one can't hang out with numerous groups of friends at once, except on carefully pre-arranged occasions.

Viktor and Jarka had a lot of friends. They seemed to flit in and out of their lives at regular intervals.

Jarda was a heavy-set, large man with a furry beard, long hair, and a large personality to match. A cameraman and stage director for Czech television, Jarda was given to wild mood swings and unpredictable behavior. He could be Jarda the Refined, capable of reciting poetry and jokes, or he could be Jarda the Pig, capable of consuming hectoliters of beer in one sitting and growing obnoxious beyond recognition. Jarda liked to sing Czech songs, many of which he had written himself and talk about his favorite bands, which included Whitesnake and Ozzy Osborne.

His girlfriend, Milena, was a small, delicate and quiet woman of inestimable patience. She had a dry sense of humor and a very warm personality that was matched by her sweet, sympathetic face. As Milena had a 12-year-old son from a previous boyfriend, she had a variety of part-time jobs, including checking coats at local theaters in the winter season.

And then there was Slávek and his ex-wife Hana. Although their marriage was on the rocks, they still continued to see each other almost every week by socializing with Viktor and Jarka. Slávek, who worked repairing and building elevators in Prague, was especially tortured by his ongoing attachment to his wife and was often morose during the first year that I knew him. Hana, who was a hairdresser at a shop in Prague, was wild and flirtatious with lots of boyfriends and didn't really seem to care one way or another what her ex-husband thought about it.

Finally, there was Pavel, a tall, well-built photographer for the Czech News Agency. Pavel spoke fine English and was, as opposed to the others, very focused about his work. Pavel actually liked his job working long hours as a photo editor, sorting through the hundreds of pictures that came along as part of each day's news. He was very keen on journalism and the news business in general.

For months, these people were my primary life blood and my true connection to the country. They were exceedingly kind and went out of their way to include me, even when I probably didn't fit in well. They made no judgments and were concerned that I be comfortable and happy. Jarka and Viktor seemed to be the glue that bound the group together.

Over time, I came to discover that Jarka had a rather mischievous sense of humor and unpredictable moods. Viktor was more placid and tranquil, content to talk quietly at the table while chaos raged around him.

On the last day of September it was clear the warm weather was drawing to a close. I put on shorts for the last time and Nikola, Dora and I climbed to the top of the tower at the end of the Charles Bridge to get a good view of the red rooftops and golden spires soaring into the sky from buildings in the Nové Město and Staré Město. Prague is nicknamed the city of one hundred spires and while it sounds like an advertising slogan, it really is true. There are actually more than four hundred. We enjoyed the fading sun and took a boat ride up the Vltava, the green water shimmering in the sunlight. By the time we came back to the dock, clouds had moved across the sky and it was too cold for shorts. The darker days of fall and winter would come quickly now.

I was excited as we rode home on the metro. Dan would be arriving the following day to begin teaching with me. Although he had considered trying to find work as a reporter in South Africa, I had lured him to Prague with promises of a place to live and a job teaching while he got organized as a reporter.

"There are plenty of news stories and the beer's great!" I added. After thinking about it for a few weeks, Dan had also quit his job as a reporter and sold off most of his possessions.

Dan was a perfect companion. We are both passionate and confident about our work but remain perpetually convinced we are always on the verge of failure. We both love Coltrane and old soul and lack the inner-strength for confrontation, preferring instead to vent our anger from behind the safety of a coffee cup, pen or word processor.

I left school early the next day and collected Dan at the train station. He looked as tired and bewildered as I had on my first day in Prague. He had just as much baggage with him. After a short visit to school, the school custodian drove him out to the Dům. Seven hours later when I returned home, Dan was still in a coma-like sleep.

9

Covering Up the Past

Despite feeling as though I wasn't learning much about teaching from Dana or Jana, they both proved to be excellent companions at work as we shared stories from our respective lives on a daily basis. Jana regularly brought various plates of tomatoes and cucumber from her garden at their cottage outside of Prague—it was still producing despite the chill—and Dan and I would sit about on breaks eating the wonderfully fresh vegetables. When vegetables or fruit are in season, one has to eat them quickly or else they shall be gone.

"You must imagine, Douglas," Dana said one afternoon while we were walking in the hallway, "how strange this year is for us, how different we are becoming. In the past we lived such a double life, you know, with one life in public and the other we reserved for our homes and children." She went on to explain how she and others would blithely mouth Marxist banalities while mocking the government at home.

"Of course, we had to be very careful about the children and always make sure they understood that what we said at home couldn't be repeated in school or anywhere."

Dana had traveled some through Europe and had spent a short period studying English and literature at a university in England.

"I always have loved London," she said one afternoon while we were standing in my office. "It is so beautiful."

"Yes, but I still think Prague is the most beautiful city anywhere,"

Jana said quickly, making sure I didn't forget about the Czech capital. Jana was far less sure of the changes going on around her, and often went out of her way to remark about how difficult life would probably become and how everyone would be poor. She worried about how they would have money to go to their *chata*—their summer home—and whether they could buy seeds for the garden. There are few things as sacred to Czechs as the summer home and the garden.

I asked Dana where she had been able to read some of her favorite western books, and she said she had gotten them in *samizdat* —the sometimes individually printed books that were furtively passed from hand to hand.

The first time I saw a *samizdat* book, I was surprised by the time and effort that had gone into producing the slim text that was the size of a school notebook. Each page had been cranked out on a typewriter using carbon paper and then pasted together into a bound volume. There was no name on the blue cover, no indication where it might have come from. But on the first page, there was a photocopied picture of Allen Ginsburg and several other people at William Burroughs' home in Tangiers. I had seen the picture before, at City Lights Bookstore in San Francisco. As I read the first line of the text, "Viděl jsem nejlepší hlavy své generace zničené šílenstvím, hystericky obnažené a o hladu ..." I slowly came to realize what it was: Ginsberg's epic poem, "Howl.": "I have seen the best minds of my generation destroyed by madness, starving hysterical naked ...."

Making the books was a labor of love and took hours of tedious work. As there were few copy machines available to normal people, the books had to be mass-produced using carbon paper and even that was sometimes hard to find and highly noticeable ("Say, comrade, why are you using so much carbon paper these days, eh?") One man, Vladimir Pistorious, worked for years at home producing samizadt books.

"I typed some of the books myself and sometimes I paid a typist out of my own pocket," he told *The New York Times* in 1990. "I count that the time we spent on these copies came to 10,000 hours, meaning five years of work. I lived by certain rules. I never spoke on the telephone. My colleagues did not know each other. Nobody knew anybody else. We did not use state office machines but worked at home. I tried to minimize my contacts. And my wife and I cautioned our son never to talk about what we did at home to any of the other children at school. We were proud that he never did."[1]

Dana never kept a *samizdat* at home.

"I read them at a friend's home or somewhere else, and then just gave them back as I didn't want to have them with us," she said.

After the revolution, people couldn't get enough of the various dissident writers, including Ivan Kíma, Ludvík Vaculík and, of course, Havel. But by 1991, publishers were reporting a great drop in sales of previously banned works. This was due to slackening interest in the revolution, the ever increasing variety of new books appearing each month and the fact that everything now cost so much more.[2]

Dana could also be extraordinarily frank, which surprised me. Once she told me that her 13-year-old son was not doing well in school and that she and her husband were very concerned that he would not be able to go to a good *gymnázium*. As opposed to schools in the United States, students were able to go on to higher education only if they passed tests at various stages. "He's been extremely disrespectful and also a problem in school. My husband even threatened him with such physical punishment, but it didn't seem to help." Not knowing what to say, I merely said I thought her son would turn out all right.

In exchange for these tidbits about their previous lives, I told her about the life I had had as a reporter, what my college was like and what kind of housing we had in the United States.

One morning I came along the hallway and found Dana and several children cleaning out the CD—civil defense—closet. The space was heaped with gas masks and books about surviving a nuclear attack.

"Every year we used to train with these things and parade about in the hallways," she said as the children poked about in the bin with all of the devices looking like giant rubber snakes and death masks. "They were to help us if we were attacked by you Americans." She laughed, but there seemed to be something more murky and angry buried beneath her statement. In fact, I was finding that it was hard for a lot of people to talk about the past in the way I was hoping. Certainly it wasn't a subject easily related, especially to someone who had never experienced their discomfort firsthand.

Jarka and Viktor were particularly set against rehashing their past, partly out of an intense dislike for all things political and partly because the past often conjured up unpleasant associations and memories. As they were both children of parents who were members of the Communist Party (something I learned independently of them having told me), they seemed reticent to engage in easy conversation about communism, except in passing.

Pavel, whose parents also had ties to the party, was more forthcoming, especially in relating bits and pieces of his short stint as a band member in the army. As he worked as a photographer for the Czech News Agency, he tended to see the entire mess through the eyes of a journalist and he seemed more comfortable with talking about the recent history.

Occasionally, anger would surface while people described life under socialism. One afternoon, while I was having coffee with Aleš, a Czech friend from the dormitory, we began to talk about an upcoming trial for one of the main Communist bosses in Prague.

"You know, when I read about these people in the newspaper," he said, hitting his fist against the table, "I wonder why they aren't all in jail." But then his mood cleared and he seemed to put his anger behind him again.

Ironically, it was Jarka who provided us with one of the strongest windows into their life under socialism when she warned me and Dan not to be so chatty with Jana.

It was a pleasant Friday evening and Dan and I had been rounded up for a trip to Borát, a formerly underground rock club that often featured many of the city's best bands and singers in a setting that, while certainly didn't meet fire safety standards, provided plenty of raw, electric atmosphere. Dan had only been in the country a few weeks, and like me, was still adjusting to the new culture.

I don't quite recall how the conversation developed, but it had to do with our crazy reputations at the school. Dan was already beginning to have his share of problems with the students and our exploits were well known amongst the teachers. One afternoon I encountered him dragging a student down the hall. "What do you do if a student spits on another one?" he asked.

Our lives were so well known, in fact, that Dan and I had funny feelings that somebody was spreading information around about what we did in our private time and what we said to the students in class.

"There is a reason for that," Jarka said. "It's Jana. I do not like Jana," Jarka said. "She is not a good woman, as she is very close friends with the principal." Jarka went on to explain how Jana in the past had made a lot of enemies in the school by informing on other teachers and students in the school.

"She gets a better salary, a better office this way," Jarka said. "Sure, she speaks English and that is one reason that she is in your office. But she has another office, too. It's upstairs."

I was flabbergasted; Dan was not surprised.

"What does she do to us?" Dan asked.

"Maybe nothing, maybe everything," Jarka said. "She may only just listen and tell people a few of the things you are doing. Or perhaps she is telling the principal everything. I don't know. I know that in the last few years she was very mean to me and reported on things I was doing with the children."

"Like what was that?" I asked.

"Making fun of Husák's (the former President) picture in the classroom. Making fun of the Communist way of saying things like 'Comrade' and stupid political things we had to do."

Jana wasn't a spy *per se,* just one of the thousands upon thousands of *kádrový pracovník* — workers csadres — who helped keep the flow of secrets going into the right hands.

Jarka's suggestion to us was that we should perhaps keep our more wild thoughts and experiences to ourselves.

"Anyway, this is enough about Jana. Let's go downstairs and see the music," she said, quickly changing the subject. Jarka led us downstairs to the main room where a band was thrashing out its angst with great blasts of feedback and angry screaming. The crowd sat on the floor, listening, smoking cigarettes and passing bottles of wine around.

"I think, if you wanted, you could have any woman here that you wanted," Jarka said, gesturing around the room. I thought she was in her frisky, pestering mood when she was only trying to provoke.

"Why?" I asked.

"Because you are an American and Americans are a new thing here. Every girl would like to have one to see what they are like." She was serious. I didn't take her up on the offer.

10

Had Enough Beer?

Dan and I left the Dům more and more frequently and began to discover Czech culture. With them, we ate not only the traditional meal of pork, cabbage and dumplings, we also tried *bramborák* (potato pancakes), which were brought to the table hot and bubbling from the massive amount of lard used to prepare them. They were delicious but the grease must have clogged half my arteries. In fact, 99 percent of Czech food is unhealthy, containing every no-no from smoked meat to high levels of salt, lard or sugar. Among my favorite of Czech foods is *smažený sýr,* which is little more than a block of hard white cheese which is first dipped in egg batter and breaded and then cooked in lard or oil until brown and crispy on the outside and soft and gooey on the inside. The fried cheese is usually served with tartar sauce and a side order of french fries. An elaborate *smažený sýr* is sometimes prepared with a slice of ham buried in the cheese. Once I ran across a really wild *smažený sýr,* which was encased inside a fried potato pancake. You might as well take a cardiac needle and inject cholesterol directly into your veins.

Newcomers are often disgusted by this meal, but usually end up succumbing to the pleasures of *smažený sýr.* Well washed down with beer, of course.

Despite being willing to try most new foods, I drew the line at consuming a few dishes, including a foul concoction called *tlačenka,* which is basically head cheese suspended in a gelatin base, and also *jazyk* (pig's tongue).

One night on the way to a concert, we stopped in at a pub for a quick bite to eat and some beer. Pavel ordered a traditional pub offering of sliced processed salami and onions drenched in vinegar. The food looked like the village idiot had been given a chef's hat and the keys to the refrigerator. Offering me a knife and fork, Pavel looked at me and smiled. "Now we will see if you are really Czech," he said.

Like everything else I was consuming with an omnivorous delight, I wolfed down the salami. Then several of us went to a small club where we saw an array of industrial-rock bands do what industrial rock bands in Prague usually do: sever a pig's head in half with a chainsaw, destroy old guitars and make an excessive amount of noise by letting off pyrotechnics. All supported by a wedge of sonic feedback. Meanwhile, my stomach was caught in the crossfire of what became an increasingly violent confrontation between the salami, vinegar and beer.

Czech cuisine is extremely limiting and bland. Poorly cooked Czech food has all of the zest and appeal of meals taken in a boardinghouse in Brixton. Until recently, restaurants were the biggest offenders, as the staff simply couldn't be bothered to put together anything that would leave the customer with a memorable culinary experience. For a *New Yorker* story about Czechoslovakia the reporter Janet Malcom once chose the Czech word *upatlaný*—when something has been handled too much—to describe the manner in which food is prepared. Plate after plate of soggy french fries, over-boiled meat and a paltry array of canned, pickled vegetables (usually peas, beets, diced carrots and sliced cabbage) emerged too often from the kitchen.

During the years under socialism, the government robbed the culture of any passion for cooking, washed it out and cleansed it of offending influences. Hence, chefs don't prepare meals with the heartiness of the Germans or with the tangy spice (unless salt counts) of the Hungarians. There was an approved "cook book" for every restaurant that the staff could only work from. There could be no specials unless it was approved by the central restaurant authority and there could be no diverting from the menu. The best meals I have eaten in the country, save for a few selected occasions, have been in people's homes where people can still muster traces of individuality.

The government didn't mess with the country's beer, mostly as it is impossible to understate the importance of the beer pub in Czech culture. These traditionally Czech environments still depend on the quality and reputation of each individual establishment. Several pubs in Prague are literally hundreds of years old, and dozens others date back to the 19th century. Dan used to call the most serious pubs "Czech mosques" as they are the holiest of all Czech places: partly a communal psychiatric ward, living room, dining room and church extension as the same faces gather every night to discuss their lives and troubles.

We have nothing in America that compares to the atmosphere of a Czechoslovak pub. *Cheers* doesn't cut it. Bars in America generally lack the range of experiences that can be found inside a Czech drinking establishment.

Czech pubs are usually brightly lit and terribly loud. After drinking in Czechoslovak pubs for several months, I came to realize how dark and secluded the American bar can be. Unless you go to a swinging, college-age bar, very often, the places tend to be somber. People drink in pairs, or alone. In Prague, pubs are raucous, filled with laughter, hearty talk and the sound of people letting go. And man, can they let go.

Everything in the pub evolves from some small ritual. After seating yourself at a table covered with a dirty, cigarette-burned tablecloth, everyone arranges their packages of cigarettes and lighters in preparation for what may be a long haul. Ashtrays are adjusted and beer coasters handed around. Depending on the quality of the pub, a waiter may actually ask the new arrivals whether they want beer ("Hey man, is the Pope Catholic?") or another beverage.

Not long after, beers in tall, half-liter glasses brimming over with white foamy suds are brought to the table by a waiter who seems to have ten more on his tray or wedged into his hands.

Boom! The waiter sets down beers and departs, leaving behind a small piece of paper with individual marks on it, indicating how many beers have been served. Unless the pub is highly unusual, you don't pay as you go but collect a tab covered with scribbles that slowly begins to look like a homage to Jackson Pollock.

While meditations about Czech beer could probably fill an entire book, suffice it to say that the makers of American commercial beer should hang their heads in shame. Take away that watery swill you call beer and give me more of the true Pilzner! Here is heaven, something sweet and delicate, a veritable nectar from the Gods! Some of the beer produced in Bohemia and Moravia is aged for more than three months, as opposed to the short maturation process used by the huge American breweries. A lot of Czech beer is brewed under the so-called German *Reinheitsgebot*—"purity command"—in which only yeast, hops, malt and water can be used in the brewing process.

The first draught from the cold glass goes down so smoothly you hardly notice you've quaffed a good third of the glass. Geeze, you tell yourself, I must be really thirsty. Then you sheepishly look around and see that everyone else has absorbed the same amount. There is a pause while everyone wipes the white moustache off their upper lip and collects their thoughts. The second and third swallows don't go quite as fast, but sooner than you realize, a second beer has been set in front of you and trouble is lurking.

Czech beer is commonly brewed in 10 "degree" and 12 "degree" versions. The degree marks refer to the amount of sugar added during the brewing process.[1] Unlike Bavarian beer, Pilsner is served in half-liter glasses instead of huge one-liter tankards. All sorts of superstitions relate to beer drinking: don't pour from glass into another. Always bang the glass down on the table after toasting.

Planning a lost weekend? The alluring, seductive properties contained in several glasses of Czech beer easily can enable one to stuff a lost weekend into a Tuesday night.

With the waiter and his beer-laden tray circling about like a hungry shark, the only way to stop the torrential flow of beer is to make like boxer Roberto Duran and say, "no mas." Otherwise, a fresh beer is automatically set in front of you whether you say "yes," "more" or merely burble into your glass.

While you are on your way to becoming merrily tanked, people all around are cheerfully doing the same. The pub rings with the sound of fresh beers being thudded down onto tables, empty glasses clinking and people talking or sometimes playing cards. Drinking isn't limited to beer, as often the hearty drinker will accompany their beer—or beers—with a shot of rum, vodka, or *slivovice,* a strong Slovak brandy made from plums and other fruits.

Over at the beer taps, the head tavern waiter is lining up glasses of beer under the spigots. Because Czech beer has such a strong head often the beers have to settle for minutes so they can be filled all the way. A good beermaster pours his beers slowly and carefully, if he has the time, and there is quite definitely an art to the process.

One night, while I was at a pub in Hradec Králové, a town about two hours east of Prague, the waiter let me pour a round of beers shortly before the pub closed for the night. I quickly discovered that it's not an easy feat to get all the beer to the half-liter mark in one try.

With the waiter standing behind me, I was shown how to tilt the glass to just the right level so the beer can fill the glass without creating a mammoth head. He also showed me the key trick of filling the glass to just about one-half centimeter below the half-liter mark—to save beer.

"That's extra money for the pub," the waiter said, patting me on the shoulder and whisking the beers away. "The customer will never notice he got less because he'll be too busy drinking."

Later, he took me downstairs and showed me how to turn off the generator and hoses which pump the oceans of beer up to the spigots. Down below the pub, in cold, low-ceiling rooms with whitewashed walls and dirt floors, were dozens and dozens of beer kegs, all waiting to be tapped.

Everyone has a favorite beer, and there are more than several to choose from. The most popular—*Staropramen, Budvar, Velkopopovický Kozel, Gambrinus* and *Pilzner Urquell*—can usually be found in pubs and stores all over the country. Several of them are now being exported to the United States, and several other major Czech breweries want to get in on the action soon.

Just as the original Pilsner beer comes from the town of Pilzen, the original Budweiser comes from the large town of České Budějovice (in German, *Budweis*) in southern Bohemia, which began producing beer in the 13th century. Adolphus Busch, creator of the United States brewing company, selected the Budweiser moniker when he was ready to market a new beer in the United States, assuming the name would appeal to people who were familiar with European beer-producing regions. The beer produced in České Budějovice called Budvar is simply outstanding and very popular all over Europe. A 1939 agreement bars Anheuser-Busch from selling Budweiser in Europe and Budvar from selling to the United States.

After the revolution in 1989, representatives from Anheuser-Busch went to České Budějovice in hopes of acquiring the brewery, which produces about 350,000 barrels a year. Immediately the possible sale of one of the Czech's most valuable treasures to an American company blossomed into a major controversy. Czech politicians and beer traditionalists worried the American company would force the little brewery to change its manufacturing process and ruin the final product. Others complained about American hegemony over the world beer market and suggested the Czech government exercise tight control over any sale. At stake was not only the brewing process but the right to use the name Budweiser in Europe. Up until that point, the American beer company had been unable to expand sales outside of its domestic market because the Czech brewery held the trademark of "Budweiser."[2]

In the end Anheuser-Busch settled into the town of Ceské Budějovice, built a new cultural center for the people there and inaugurated a waiting game. Whether they ever are able to buy all or a part of the brewery remains to be seen, but they are the only international brewery still negotiating with Budvar.

The first time I went into a Czech supermarket and entered the liquor aisle, I was astounded by the range of potions and spirits one could ingest. While there is a stereotype that Poles and Russians drink Vodka, Czechs seem to drink ... well ... *everything*. It took me the better part of a month with my dictionary to figure out what a lot of the various bottles contained, including an ominous looking flask that was filled with a pinkish liquid simply labeled *liker.*

If you're looking for a more refined experience, you can always go to a *vinárna* (wine bar), which generally serves hard liquor and wine and is quieter and darker than a pub.

Either way, if you don't smoke, you're in for a rough ride. Even by European standards, Czechs and Slovaks seem to smoke endlessly. According to a 1992 study by the National Center for Health Support in Prague, 38 percent of Czechs and Slovaks were smokers, including an astonishing 50 percent of the men and 28 percent of women. On average, people smoked more than 16 cigarettes a day.[3]

With all of the cigarettes blazing merrily away, one feels encamped in a smoldering fire. The air has a slight smoggy, grey Los Angeles-basin look to it. If you smell your clothes after several trips to a vinárna or pub, you'll swear you were once near a burning building.

One quiet evening in mid winter, I was appointed by others to go looking for a pub that had a television, as there was a good hockey game on that evening between the Czechs and Canada. Televisions in pubs are a bit rare and are often packed whenever there's something interesting on TV. After finding a pub that did indeed have a television, I asked the waiter if it would be possible to reserve a table for that evening.

"No, we're all booked," he said, as he straightened mugs behind the bar. I looked over at a table located squarely in front of the television. The table was empty except for one man, who was in what I can only describe as the "finished" position: head face down on the table, arms splayed out like an extra in a Western who has been gunned down in a barroom brawl. I pointed at the table.

"What about there?" I asked, gesturing towards the drunk, who looked like he might drool on the tablecloth. "It looks like he doesn't need the table any more."

"He reserved it," the waiter said with a shrug. "Until he leaves, it's his to do with as he pleases. Besides, his friends may come back."

On a more somber level, the excessive amount of drinking isn't funny, it's disturbing. One can't drink so much in the United States, as one is usually leashed to a car and bars are just so much more expensive than in Prague. Perhaps Americans have a puritan, work ethic which isn't a part of Czech culture. Beer at lunch is common and taken as a tradition and a right. At the Škoda factory works in Pilzen, the local brewery makes a low alcohol beer that is served to the car workers at lunchtime. But drinking, along with sex, was the one thing

125

that wasn't regulated under socialism, which probably explains both the high amount of alcoholism and extramarital affairs in Czech and Slovak relationships.

On one level, I liked the food and the good beer; night after night, however, it became repetitive and fattening. It wasn't surprising to discover after several months on the dumplings, pork and beer treadmill that my pants were getting a wee bit too snug when I put them on in the morning. When I lived in San Francisco, I was able to keep in good shape by joyfully running along the water at night or going to one of many good fitness clubs in the Bay Area.

I had initially ruled out running immediately after arriving in the city and receiving a lungfull of the foul, polluted air that hangs over the city. But as we lived on the outskirts of town with little more than cornfields all around us, I figured the air couldn't be too spoiled. So for awhile I tried running through the maze of buildings all around the Dům. I had little success: I felt like a mouse trapped in a scientific experiment and was habitually attacked by the numerous dogs that wandered freely during the day. Czechs love dogs and they love to walk them a lot, as their apartments are usually pretty small. But they don't like walking them on a leash. The rare sight of a jogger happily prancing by often stirred the dogs into thinking I was a potential meal and they'd tear off after me. I first took to carrying a stick with me while running, and then, after the onset of winter made the roads and walkways slick with ice, gave up running all together.

OK, so, if jogging was out, how about hitting a fitness club? Great idea, except there weren't many and the few I could find were often located in difficult to reach places that required a lot of travel time.

"I don't know what the problem is," Viktor said sympathetically several nights later. "It's much easier to exercise at the pub."

11

Our Wild Life

The days quickly filled with so many adventures that I am now sorry I didn't pay more attention to my diary. There simply just wasn't time. In the evenings, or during the day, I stole away to make little notes on scraps of paper or on the back of napkins. As the evenings grew later and the beer flowed, the notes would became less and less cogent. Often, the morning after, I was hard pressed to decipher my hieroglyphics or remember just why something the night before had been so interesting. As I puzzle over these slips of paper, I can only wonder what happened the night I went to a restaurant and witnessed: "man yelling at wife, who seems to be having birthday. She receives ice skates as present and then stands up on table in ice skates and begins to sing. Man barks like a dog."

There were a number of great adventures during the first several weeks after Dan's arrival, including a trip to the *Slavnosti piva* (Beer festival), an amalgamation of a country fair and a berserk Hades-like wedding that would have made Caligula nervous. Hundreds of people milled about drinking beer in the cold air or inside huge halls where different bands played polkas and jazz at frenetic speed. In another part of the fair, outrageously drunken people were mounting thrill rides of all kinds only to stumble off on the verge of nausea or well past the threshold.

Through the blur of the evening, I recall dancing madly to a polka while the hall's art nouveau framework swirled around overhead like a kaleidoscope and then staggering outside in search of a toilet only to find that there weren't any and that people had appropriated the side of a beer truck to use as a temporary urinal. One hundred men pissing at the same time sounds like sheets of water running off a tin roof in a heavy storm. Later, we drove bumper cars around a small track, slamming them so hard into the walls I thought beer would leak from my ears.

■

Manic evenings like the beer festival were tempered by the quiet and lovely weekends we spent outside of Prague with different people from the Dům. One of the most traditional of all Czech activities is visiting someone's summer house on the weekend. To get away from the Prague air, the hustle and bustle and relax—that is the Czech spirit! Many Czechs have their own cottages and spend hours working on them, and in their gardens in the summer.

One Saturday morning in late October, Dan and I and several others from the Dům headed southeast to a small town near the castle of Konopiště, which was occupied by Franz Ferdinand until he was killed in Sarajevo in 1914. Alena, a Czech who taught English and lived in the Dům with us, would be our guide and host at her family's small cottage. I hadn't been out of Prague before, and felt somehow I was losing my sense of direction as the bus left the confines of the city and roared through acres of green fields and tall waving trees.

More than any city I have ever seen in America, with the possible exception of Reno and Las Vegas, towns in Czechoslovakia end with a sharp abruptness. Even in Prague, where the intense, mass construction of apartment buildings has pushed the city limits farther and farther out each year, the rolling, green fields sweep up quickly once the town ends.

After an hour we were dropped off at a tiny village with a pub and a meat store around a square. It was quiet, as all the stores were already closed for the weekend. An elderly man rode a bicycle through the square. After more than two months of noise in Prague, the stillness was refreshing.

"This is very nice," Alena said as we walked out of the village

128

along a small country road. "This is a better place to be than in dirty Prague."

Many Czechs would agree.

"According to the census I am a city dweller," Minister of the Environment Bedřich Moldan told a Western reporter in 1991. "But my family realized the national dream of having an old farmhouse in southern Moravia. Psychologically, most of our people live in the countryside. The rest is something we just put up with."[1]

We stopped at a small grocery that was still open and bought a handful of *párky*—small sausage links—and some bread. Then we headed down the road to Alena's summer house. Along the way, she pointed out a dilapidated farm house and shuttered pub that had once belonged to her family but had been taken away by the Communists when the country had been nationalized in 1948. Now, under the terms of the recently passed "restitution laws," the government was going to give title to the buildings back to Alena's family.

"We are thinking about renovating the pub and leasing it. Or maybe my parents will sell it," she said. "They haven't decided."

Their country home was a big rambling house with two floors and several rooms stuffed with old antique furniture. It all smelled wonderfully musty and slightly damp.

In the afternoon, we went on a long walk through rolling hills covered with trees and springy, grassy fields. We encountered a wide brook flowing at the base of a hill, and walked down a relatively steep slope to its base. As the sun cut through the trees, we split up and wandered our separate ways. I hopped out along a series of large boulders into the center of the stream and knelt, looking down into the water. The trees enveloped me and appeared to sag under the weight of their colors, for it was fall and the leaves had dissolved into flaming bursts of burnt orange, red and rust.

I looked back at Dan sitting by the edge of the stream, and he smiled, squinting at me through the sunlight. We shared the peacefulness of the moment and the natural serenity of it all: the gurgling of the water, the wind through the trees and the sound of our own hearts beating.

Later, on the walk back, Alena picked some mushrooms that had popped up in the darker parts of the forest and showed us how to properly identify poisonous from good ones. Despite her instructions, I didn't bother sampling any of my choices. I have trouble remembering where I put the car keys in the morning, let alone which mushroom is safe to eat. Nevertheless, mushrooming is a popular fall activity. On Sunday evenings the trams and subway cars in Prague are filled with people carrying little baskets of tall brown mushrooms on their way back from an afternoon in the countryside.

By the time we reached the farm house, it was beginning to get dark. The house had no running water, so Dan and I were instructed to go to the local pump and fill several buckets with well water. In the evening, we built a fire outside using wads of old *Rudé Právo* newspapers from before the revolution ("President Husák Welcomes Bulgarian Farm Union"). We sat in the dark under the stars tearing off hunks of fresh brown bread while the sausages slowly blackened and oozed oil into the fire. We drank some home-made wine that Alena had found in the cellar and sang songs around the fire. Finally, I sank into a musty feather bed that sagged in the center and fell into an exhausted and happy sleep.

I awoke the next morning, not to the sound of cows gently mooing or a farm breakfast cooking on an open hearth, but to the sound of a four-alarm fire in my stomach. It was shortly after seven o'clock and a yellow sun was just peeking over the green fields that surrounded the farmhouse. I know this because I was hopping around in those green fields in my underwear and t-shirt trying to find a comfortable place in which to be sick. Whether it was the well water or the home-made wine or the sausages or some dastardly combination of all three, my body had decided to purge itself.

With no vegetables or fruit, my digestive system was reduced to a shadow of its robust self. The fried cheese, sausages and mystery meat from the school cafeteria were constructing an immense sea wall in my stomach, preventing most cargo to pass through. My family air-mailed me some vegetable laxative powder, and I tried taking massive doses in hopes of loosening things up, so to speak. No such luck.

When matched against an army of hard salamis, thick dumplings, fried potatoes and other gluey foods, the natural fiber retreated like a routed army.

Occasionally, there were sudden, unexpected and embarrassing changes. Once, while heading home from school, my body was suddenly seized with the urge to relieve itself.

"Like now," it sang. "Like here."

Scampering across a park, I ducked into the main train station, and hunted around until I found the men's room. To my great dismay, a sign informed me that it was closed. By the time I found another toilet, I didn't care what horrific smells awaited me on the inside.

Entering the men's room, I was greeted by a sleepy looking washroom attendant collecting money at the door.

"What do you want to do?" he mumbled through a cigarette.

"Aaaah, errrr," I stumbled, madly fumbling through my mental Czech dictionary. Unable to think of the polite way of expressing myself, I finally blurted out the first thing I could think of. It was something Viktor had taught me.

"I'm going to shit out really quickly!" I nearly screamed in Czech.

With that, the power of Czech slang took hold and the attendant went into quick action, tossing a handful of toilet paper at me.

"Pay me after," he said, grinning like a bastard and directing me towards the stalls with a sweep of his hand.

The final break with Nikola came suddenly and was irrevocable. Another one of our pathetic arguments, a lot of screaming, useless words. I was disappointed and somewhat depressed, but Dan urged me to move on as quickly as possible.

"I don't like to watch someone else suffering over a relationship, friendship or whatever the hell this is," he said after I arrived back at our rooms like an enraged rhinoceros. "If there's this much pain, let it go."

And I did, resolving to avoid contact with Nikola and Dora and make my own way through the country. It wasn't hard, as we barely ever seemed to be home. The alarm clock went off seemingly before

I had set it; it often was still dark when we rose. We'd shower quickly and eat a hurried breakfast in front of the "eating bar"—the refrigerator—and then run (usually late) to the metro station. There was the long ride to school through the metro, passing stations I had trouble remembering the names of, let along properly pronounce. I usually pronounced one of the more phonetically difficult stations, "Jiřího z Poděbrad," like I had a lisp and marbles in my mouth.

Once out of the metro, we'd almost have to run past the old women sweeping the street with brooms fashioned out of a bundle of long sticks, past the meat stores with their windows of sausages and smoked meat, past housewives doing the shopping for the day by waiting in lines at first the bread store and then the milk store and finally, the vegetable stands. Our breaths rose in the cold air that stung your nose, not only from the chill, but from the coal-filled air. Then there was the blast of noise from the children, the endless ringing of the bells and suddenly, it was lunchtime and I was back downstairs in the cafeteria eating or watching after the kids.

And there were so many errands! Which meant, naturally, more lines. By now, we had gotten used to waiting in line at the post office to pay various bills to the government. As everything was nationalized, one simply paid the bills at the post office—very few businesses then handled money. I still hadn't gotten the hang of properly filling out the complex payment form—*složenka*—which had to be filled out in triplicate. We had also developed a strange relationship with several older women in a laundry across from school where we took our shirts to be properly washed and ironed.

One of the teachers from school explained one afternoon that it was highly unusual for the laundry to handle such small things as shirts ("always the women do this at home, Douglas"). After several months of schlepping our bags of dress shirts to the laundry, one afternoon the woman there told me that they couldn't accept them anymore. After a few minutes of simple Czech sentences back and forth and hunting through my dictionary, I realized why: the woman who had agreed to do our shirts had died!

"You should get a Czech woman to do these," the shop clerk said sweetly as I gathered up my dirty shirts and turned to leave. We ended

132

up washing the clothes in our bathtub and drying them on the backs of chairs in our rooms. Occasionally, Dan and I borrowed an iron from a Czech teacher who lived down the hall. Other days, we went to work with wrinkled shirts.

At the end of the day, I'd find myself falling asleep on the subway, dog tired from kids or staying out too late or running about like a madman trying to collect enough fresh vegetables to assemble a decent dinner. Or merely I'd find myself "ear tired" from trying to listen to too many conversations or concentrating on putting together a correct sentence in Czech. All around me on the subway, people sat with English or German textbooks; it seemed everyone was studying a different language. Dana told me she thought many of the Czechs were just trying to show off to others on the subway that they were smart enough to learn another language.

Although I made some progress learning to speak Czech during the first month, I still had absolutely no structure, no clear understanding of the language and no real feeling of progress. Jarka's friend, Anna, who had nearly achieved fluency, kindly lent me her copy of James Naughton's *Colloquial Czech,* which, more than any other book I ever came across, made good sense of what is a very difficult language.

It was not long after receiving *Colloquial Czech* that Jarka and I were having coffee one afternoon after going to an art exhibition. Although she could speak English very well, she liked to push me into speaking Czech and often wouldn't respond if I asked her a question in English. After I stumbled over some rudimentary Czech sentence, Jarka asked me if I had been studying.

"Yes," I said, bowing my head slightly in shame. "Some."

"Where is your Czech book?" she asked. After I produced the textbook from my bag, she lit a cigarette and said, "Give it to me."

And so, my formal education of Czech began on a grey Wednesday October afternoon in a dark wine bar. Jarka guided me through several chapters and had me read passages aloud. Then she started to explain how the Czech language works.

If you want to learn Czech, you'd better have a good teacher and a lot of patience, the minimum tools needed to achieve any kind of average fluency. Simply put, Czech is not a "user friendly" language.

Although it uses the same "Roman" alphabet as English, there are a number of extra letters, including š, ě, č, ž, and the dreaded ř, that require different sounds.

Of all the letters, ř is the worst, because there is simply no sound like it in English, or, for that matter, any other language. To this day, I've never seen a written description that does the letter any justice; some things have to be heard to be believed. Roughly put, ř sounds like a cross between a buzzing rasp with an slightly vague *r* sound mixed in. For foreigners, it is a bastard to get around, and it appears everywhere. There is a lot of joking about the letter ř as even more than a handful of Czechs simply cannot pronounce it properly.

Obviously, I had difficulties getting the ř down, especially since I couldn't even r-r-r-roll my tongue properly to make repeated sounds. So the letter ř became a kind of mantra for me. I practiced it everywhere; in buses, trams and the metro, between classes and at home before I went to bed. Over and over, I kept repeating the strange noise that, like free jazz, simply sounds wrong until you do it correctly. I worried about what I was going to do if I didn't manage to eek out at least a passable ř. I would have to spend the rest of my time avoiding numbers like four (written čtyři: note the ř), instead telling cab drivers to "Please take me to the building next to number three." But even that's out, because three has the ř: tři.

Slovak, which bears more than a passing resemblance to Czech, doesn't have ř, but they do have several other characters that don't appear in Czech.

While I was trying to master pronunciation, I also picked up a habit of repeating names and words of everything I saw. I'm sure I drew more than a few stares as I walked down the street happily mumbling to myself everything I saw printed in windows and on posters.

Czech is a Slavic language, with more than a few passing similarities to Russian, Bulgarian, Polish and Serbo-Croatian. Like Latin, sentences all "decline" in that the endings of nouns, pronouns, numbers and adjectives all change according to their usage in the sentence.

134

For example, if you were to say, "Do you have a book?," you would not say "kniha"—the Czech word for book—the same way you would say "kniha" if you say, "I have heard about a great book."

Now, of course, there are male, female and neuter nouns, each with their own special endings, depending on their usage in the sentence. As if that wasn't enough, within each gender are several kinds of male nouns, several kinds of female and several kinds of neuter. Of course, they all too have their own endings in singular and plural.

Got it so far? Great. Just remember all the pronouns change according to their usage. Adjectives do too, and, sigh, so do numbers.

People who have studied Latin will find the Czech language easier to grasp. But as Latin went out of most high schools along with high-button shoes, many Americans (especially myself) were thoroughly befuddled.

As if the business with the nouns wasn't bad enough, those crazy Slavs had to go and screw up their verbs, too. Instead of having just one set of verbs, the Czech language has two for each action. One is to indicate an action done once, and the other to indicate something done over and over. So, if you learn the verb "mávat"—which means "To wave"—you must also learn "zamávat," which also means "To wave" (only once). Learning 100 verbs really means you must learn 200.

"Speak Czech slowly and clearly," a Czech told me one night while I was trying to communicate some huge thought. "Don't rush it. Pronounce each syllable carefully. They're all meant to be spoken equally." The advice made me think of Czech as ragtime music, as Scott Joplin used to write on all of his sheet music: "Do not play quickly—ragtime must never be played quickly."

After a year, I had only begun to see the complete picture of the Czech language, even with the help of five different Czech textbooks. I kept flipping back and forth between them, as they all had various strengths and weaknesses.

To help bolster my knowledge, I bought armloads of the various Czech newspapers that came out in the mornings and evenings. Before the fall of the government, the main newspaper had been the broadsheet *Rudé Právo* (Red Justice), which was the mouthpiece for the Communist Party. After November, 1989, *Rudé Právo* and the several other officially sanctioned newspapers, including *Mladá Fronta* (Young Front), *Svobodné Slovo* (Freedom's Word) and *Práce* (Work or Labor), had reorganized their staffs and attempted to move to various points on the political spectrum.

Czechoslovakia was the only country in Eastern and Central Europe that enjoyed a continuous period of press freedom before World War II. Before 1948, there were 41 daily newspapers printed throughout the country. After 1948, that number was halved during the first year as printing facilities were nationalized and editors and journalists were driven out of the business by the Communist Party.[2]

Of course, the Communists did allow freedom of the press. This is from their first constitution: "Freedom of the press is guaranteed. Thus in principal it is forbidden to subject the press to pre-publication censorship. The law decides who has the right to publish newspapers and reviews and under what conditions, particularly in order to ensure that profit should not be the aim of publishers."

In an analysis of the Czechoslovak press, a Yugoslavian journalist wrote: "From the middle of 1947 till the middle of 1948, 80 percent of the news on foreign affairs came from national reporters either reporting from abroad or doing their own research at home. Three percent was acquired from TASS, the Soviet news agency. After June, 1951, that percentage had been increased to 46.4 percent from TASS."[3]

A 1990 Gannett Foundation Report on Czechoslovakia ranked the country's broadcast and print technology near the bottom of the Iron Curtain countries, well behind Poland and Hungary. One major printing press in Prague dated back to 1936. New technology, like offset printing facilities were rare.[4]

Curious about how changes were proceeding at the various newspapers, I went over to *Svobodné Slovo* to see their editor in chief, Miroslav Kovařík. Like all newspaper offices, the Slovo office was a jumble of magazines and newspapers, cluttered desks and half-full cups of cold coffee. The biggest difference, however, between their office and American newspapers was that there were no computers to be seen anywhere. The staff sat hunched over old manual typewriters, busily picking out their stories. The atmosphere was something out of the 1950s as people shared telephones and typewriters and ran back and forth delivering copy to various production people.

Kovařík, a thin, gray-haired man who appeared to be in his mid-50s, was very interested in the fact that I was an American in Prague. He had me sit down for a chat in his office.

"We are still getting used to doing things for ourselves," he said, playing with a pencil. "We don't have much in the way of materials as you can see, but we do what we can." He asked me if I wanted to teach English at the newspaper, and I declined, saying that I had too much to do. Lately I had been getting more offers to teach English than I knew what to do with. A woman had even approached me on the subway after overhearing my English.

Kovařík said I was welcome to come and talk to the staff anytime. "If you need to write something, you may come here too."

As I dug through the newspapers, I generally found that it was extraordinarily difficult to make sense of the articles because of the level of the Czech, especially if the articles appeared in the "new dissident" press, including the daily *Lidové noviny* and *Respekt,* a weekly political commentary newspaper. So after awhile, I generally restricted myself to purchasing only *Večerný Praha* (Evening Prague), a working-class newspaper that generally featured easy-to-read headlines and short articles.

I soon discovered that learning another language is like getting a pair of glasses that only come in focus several months later. I would be quietly sitting on a tram looking out the window when suddenly I would see a sign and realize for the first time what it meant. Or I would catch a glimpse of a headline in a newspaper and discover that someone in the government "protested a new law."

After a few months, I even discovered the meaning behind the numerous cryptic comments I had seen painted on walls all over Prague: "Neparkovat!" I wondered if this was some political exhortation for the masses to rise up. It meant, "Don't park here."

12

Americans in Retreat

"You watch," one of the women said one night while we were cleaning up the kitchen at the Dům. "In a few more weeks, people won't be so cheerful and friendly like in the kitchen. People will start withdrawing and keeping to themselves. Some will probably go home." Although her comments were harsh, they were accurate. It was only late October but the winter was coming into bloom. Teaching had long since become a job. It was natural to expect that there would be a few casualties. But I wasn't prepared for the sheer number of people who packed up and left in the first three months. James McLarsen, my former roommate, who had been a ghost since moving in, was one of them. Although he had arrived with a professed goal of finding the "soul of the Czech people," he was now headed home with a different attitude.

"I can't eat any more of their goddamn crappy food!" he said one evening when he came to the apartment to tell me he was leaving. "I want a bagel, see my girlfriend and watch TV when I want to! I want to read the Sunday *New York Times!*" He left us to contemplate the evening shadows that fell so gracefully over the endless buildings near the teachers' house.

It seemed only too natural that the curiosity about life in a socialist country would begin to wear thin for some.

When I first arrived, I watched and listened and tried to keep my opinions to myself, especially when pressed about "whether I thought America or Czechoslovakia was better." I didn't want to wind up as one of those rambling, imbecilic Americans who seem set on lecturing everyone about everything while talking with their mouths full.

But Lord, did we babble amongst ourselves. We droned on and on about the *pesto con funghi* we would eat, the movies we would rent on video, the money we would withdraw from our ATM's, the clothes we would order off of the Home Shopping Network. Remembering this, I am ashamed, wishing that someone could have stopped us, saying: "QUIT WHINING AND GO OUT THERE AND JUST EXPERIENCE THIS. THEN GO HOME."

It was a curious thing, being removed from the culture that we at once disdained and also relished. Little things, like washing your clothes in the bathroom and hanging them out to dry soon became a chore and the bitching started.

Americans sometimes made complete asses out of themselves. One evening several of us sat cringing while a a young Italian *New Yawker,* fresh faced, clean, well fed and swaddled in REI and L. L. Bean clothing, sat holding court over beer with us. He was drunk on Prague's high-octane beer and was raving about how cheap everything is. "This means nothin' to me," he said, leering, waving a 500 crown Czech banknote about (worth about $17 USD). "This means nothin' to me. Nothin'." To a Czech it was a serious amount of money. The Czechs at the table gawked in amazement.

I discovered later Czechoslovakia was a paradise, compared the hellish experiences one found as one proceeded gradually East through the Ukraine, the Baltic States and Russia itself. In countries like Estonia and cities like Minsk, overcrowded trams made Prague's seem luxurious by comparison. The lines were longer and just plain meaner, sub-zero temperatures whistled through every crack of your teeth and the consumer shortages were greater. Belgrade at the peak of the Yugoslav war was a scary hellhole, with runaway inflation on a par with the Weimar Republic and massive shortages. Encounters like these made me hang my head in shame for ever bad-mouthing Prague.

But that doesn't mean Czechs liked waiting in lines any more than the overbred domesticated Americans. After the revolution in 1989,

Czechs began to refer to situations that harkened back to the grim socialist days as being *stará structurá* (old structure).

I once spent the better part of a month gathering all the necessary forms for a visa only to discover each time that I was somehow still short a document or two. On perhaps my fourth visit to the office, the woman sitting behind the desk noticed my crestfallen expression as I turned and headed wearily back out the door.

"*Chudáčku* (poor boy)," she said sweetly in Czech. I was enraged. The next time I returned to the office, I found a different employee sitting behind the desk. This time, I was sure I had everything I needed. I laid out my forms like a Las Vegas gambler who knew he had a winning hand. The man gazed over the assembled array of forms, notes, photos and tax stamps. Then he looked at me.

"What do you have all this for?" he said, sweeping his hand across the table. "I only need these three." And with that, he signed my visa into my passport and returned it to me. I headed back onto the street, successful at last, but still completely frustrated—a sensation I had come to know well after spending time in the country. My friends and I would tango for months with little, insane, nagging problems like visas or getting something repaired. Problems didn't grow old, they became hoary; the issue would drag on and on for days, weeks and sometimes months until by the time whatever it was that you were trying to solve either went away of its own accord or stumbled to some ignominious end. Either way, no joy was allowed in the moment of completion; one only had a dull rage and a feeling of exasperation.

Often, after encountering said situations, my Czech friends smiled and shrugged their shoulders. "Itzzz normal," they would say in their heavily accented English. Actually, what they were really saying was: get used to this way of life, you pampered American. You're not at *Lucky's* or *Safeway* or *A&P* anymore where they have 24-hour nonstop service and Automated Teller Machines and if there are more than three people in the checkout line ("Three's a crowd!") somebody comes running from the back room wearing a pained expression and acting like they would be willing to walk across hot coals just for you, the vaunted customer.

Or, if they didn't say "It's normal," often they said, "Be happy you

141

were able to get something." This phrase usually came after one had spent more than an hour waiting in line for bus tickets to some dreary, godforsaken town only to find out that the bus had been oversold and you'd have to stand for the three-hour journey.

Still, rarely did I see a Czech grumble or cause a disturbance because of a delay. There is an almost Buddhist-like tolerance to accept a given situation and wait. One afternoon Dan went to make reservations at Café Slávia, a popular and fashionable restaurant and coffee house in Prague. Upon arriving at the restaurant, the maitre d' approached him frantically, waving his arms. "Go away, go away," he said. "There's been a bomb threat and everyone must leave." Dan surveyed the restaurant and saw a fair number of people sitting at tables.

"Why are all these people still sitting here then?" Dan asked.

"Because they're waiting to pay," the maitre d' said and turned to implore some other people to leave the building.

Many of the country's pastimes, like so much of its working and living conditions, recalled simpler, less technological days that have vanished from the middle-class in America.

People still entertain themselves. At parties, there is rarely someone there who doesn't know how to play the guitar well enough to produce numerous Czech, Slovak and Gypsy songs. Children, from the earliest days at school, learn songs that generations have spent their whole lives singing. And, because sheet music is rare and expensive, the children copy the songs into books with the chord changes marked above the words.

Card games, including bridge, canasta and a Czech game called *mariash* are very popular. All girls in late elementary school are required to take sewing, knitting and other stitchery classes. Thus many women still spend their time making new clothes and expertly fixing those that are worn. Whether or not boys will ever included in these classes seems doubtful; this is Europe and these are much more ingrained traditions.

This is hardly to suggest that we Americans are incapable of tying our shoelaces without help, but with our huge and rapidly homogenizing society, the ability to do things the "old fashioned way" is, in many cases, not being passed on.

Although life is changing rapidly for Czechs and Slovaks, life revolves heavily around the home in a way that has greatly vanished in many parts of America. There are no late-night coffee shops, few fast-food restaurants in which to dawdle and no cavernous malls where one can waste endless hours of time. People stay home or visit friends in their homes. Before World War II, there was a huge cafe society in Prague. But after the war, the cafes never really revived and what few establishments managed to survive were smashed by the arrival of the Communists in 1948. Only today are there hints of a revival.

One night in mid-October, a Scottish friend of mine from another floor in the Dům came to our kitchen to inquire whether any of the men on our floor would like to accompany a young Czech teacher to dinner with some visiting Americans. As I happened to be the only man in the room, I accepted.

"What's she like?" I asked. I preferred to avoid more bad emotional attachments.

"Go and see for yourself," my friend replied. "Anyway, I'm busy and can't go. She asked me first."

After dinner I went downstairs and knocked on the "young woman's" door. Her name was Renáta Nováková and she was hardly young—she was my age. The minute she opened the door, I was entranced. She had long blond hair and her slim figure was defined by a black t-shirt and black tights. Thankfully, she spoke English. I sat down and immediately went into my hyper-babble mode in which English floods from my mouth like a broken fire hydrant. Even after a month in Prague, I still hadn't learned how to slow down my conversation speed. After a few moments, Renáta lit a cigarette and regarded me seriously.

"I'm sorry, I don't think I've understood half of what you've said. I should write some of this down," she said, reaching for a pad of paper. "Otherwise I forget new words."

She explained why she needed an escort. An American lawyer and his wife from Oklahoma had arrived in town bearing several cartons of English-language books and had presented themselves at her school, where she was an art teacher. In return for the free books, the school's principal was going to take the American couple out to dinner.

"What's your principal like?" I asked.

"She's a cow and doesn't speak English," Renáta said coolly, stubbing out her cigarette. "So she asked me to bring someone. You look fine." I couldn't tell if her serious expression was masking a sense of humor.

"Have you noticed that a lot of Communists are stupid?" Renáta asked me. I shook my head. "Well, my principal is just this type—all smiles and nothing to say. She's done some terrible things to people."

The next evening we met the principal, whose name was Marta. She had brought her husband—grey, swept back hair, dark, square glasses, imposing jaw—and went to the restaurant where William and Barbara Briggs were waiting. William was an anti-trust lawyer in Oklahoma City, fighting the big oil companies and his wife was involved in a number of different causes. They were keen to learn everything they could about Prague and the country. They gave Renáta a "Greetings from Oklahoma City" t-shirt and kept up a steady stream of conversation. To me, the Briggs were very typical liberal Americans: talkative, bouncy and full of wonder. They assumed everyone thought like themselves. But to Renáta, the principal and her husband, the Briggs were acting like visitors to a zoo.

While we ate a visually uninspiring meal of fried beef, french fries and canned vegetables, William asked the inevitable questions about why Czechs and Slovaks hadn't tried to overthrow communism earlier. He also wondered how difficult life was under communism.

What William didn't realize was that the principal and her husband were angry Communists who were most unhappy about the changes. So, in responding to all of William's questions (he was a lawyer, after all), they did the best thing possible: they lied.

"No, yes, it was terrible," Renáta translated. "We just survived. We lived as we could with the government." The only hint the couple ever gave of their past during the entire dinner was at the end when William

144

asked how it was that the Communists came to power in 1948.

Renáta explained that there had been an election in 1946 in which the Communists had gained a healthy percentage of the the vote (over 30%) and had taken the lion's share of places in the cabinet. As there were numerous Communists working in the Ministry of Information and Interior, they were only too glad to help undermine, manipulate and distort what was going on in the country before Gottwald took power in 1948.

In 1948, the remaining democratic ministers resigned from the cabinet, complaining that the Communists were priming the country for a coup. They expected President Beneš to call new elections. Beneš didn't and instead caved in to extreme pressure from the Communists and the *lidové milice* (people's militia) organizing in the various factories. He appointed Communists to fill the vacant slots on the cabinet and the government was delivered into Communist hands without a single shot being fired.

"So who did you vote for in 1946?" William wanted to know.

"I voted in the National Socialists," the principal's husband said, squinting at William through his thick lenses. The National Socialists, while not being Communists, were able to give their seats in a coalition with the Communists that help bring about the demise of the multi-party system.

After coffee, we parted at the subway and came home: Mr and Mrs. Briggs to their hotel and the principal and her husband back to their lie. Renáta and I went home and spent the rest of the evening drinking coffee and wine and laughing about the evening.

Renáta taught art and art history. Her room was filled with reproductions of pictures by Picasso and Klee and Adolf Born, a noted Czech artist. Although she had gone to see the Rolling Stones in Prague, she said she didn't know much about American pop music.

"Why should I care?" she said. "It wasn't on the radio much here. So how should I have learned all these songs? Do you know Adolf Born?" I shook my head.

"See? You have something to learn, too. Do you know Kandinsky?" She pulled out an art history textbook and started to show me paintings from the 20th century.

145

When I got back to my room later that evening, I told Dan how much I had enjoyed meeting Renáta.

"She's got a great sense of humor. It's dry," I said. "She can't figure out why so many Americans want to come to Czechoslovakia."

"Isn't it good when things work out well with a woman?" Dan said. He was so right.

Understanding how an entire country can be co-opted by an authoritarian state is a mind-boggling exercise in frustration. In the Czechoslovak experience, so much of their recent history is tied to World War II; in many ways, they are still fighting a war that ended early 50 years ago. In the years directly after the end of the war, many people truly believed in socialism and that a close link to the Soviet Union was their best protection from the Germans.

After World War II, the Czechs fell into the Soviet Union's sphere of influence, partly because of decisions made at Yalta, but also out of a genuine desire to coexist; England and France simply couldn't be trusted any more to protect Czechoslovakia, the Czechoslovak President Eduard Beneš reasoned, and a defensive bridge was needed to the East.

"The Czechs spend their best energies for the defense of European humanistic values," Ivan Sviták writes in *The Unbearable Burden of History: the Sovietization of Czechoslovakia,* "but when they see that Westerners do not care much about them, they throw themselves into the open arms of the Slavs with the bitterness of a betrayed lover."

The orientation towards Moscow and the rise of Czech nationalism of the late 1940s ensured that, once again, a terrible amount of cruelty would be inflicted on their nation—this time internally through the aid of a repressive government and externally at the hands of Stalin and the Russians deciding, once again, about them, without them.

In addition, many of the Czech and Slovak Communist leaders stated in the 1940s that Socialism in Czechoslovakia would be different—a sort of Humanitarian Marxism. After 1948, when the country had switched leadership, a majority of the country still tried to support the government as best it could.

The Czech writer Josef Škvorecký recalls that in 1948, "The desire to serve the people or the Party (this was synonymous) was not just an empty expression; the big axes had not yet struck and the radical youth still believed that the revolution was made of poetry, flowers and an evening of love in a communal dormitory."[1]

Otakar Vávra, a noted Czech film director from the pre-war era, points to World War II as the antecedent behind the rise of communism: "No other explanation can help us to imagine and to understand how educated people, with a tradition of international political and cultural knowledge, could voluntarily submit to the authoritarian leadership and manipulation that they accepted after 1948. They believed that at such a time even democratic thinking must be temporarily suspended."[2]

Dan and I had several other encounters with people who didn't tell the whole story about their past. For about a month Dan had been tutoring the teen-age daughter of one of our teachers at school. Despite the fact that the girl spoke only passable English and the family none at all, we were soon invited over to their home for dinner, which was a Roman feast. Rarely have I consumed so much food or drank so much at one sitting. There was pork and potatoes and ice cream and champagne and coffee and shots of vodka. Pretty soon I was having trouble sitting upright on their sofa because my stomach hurt. We watched one of Havel's plays on television, a particularly cruel and biting one-act satire called *Audience,* and the entire family laughed. The mother, whose name was Hanna, told us how they were all working for the future now and how it was good to have Americans in Prague. The father worked in construction and traveled often to Germany on business. By the looks of their large home, they clearly had a comfortable life. They made no mention of the past, even when Dan asked the father what he had done before.

"I was in the trade unions," he said and then changed the subject. One of the nice things about not being able to speak the language is that the temptation to press a point is less.

Several days later, Jarka asked Dan and me how the evening had gone. After hearing about how we were wined and dined, she kind of sniffed and said, "Well, they were both members of the Party and lived off it well. They didn't tell you that?"

Later, I asked Dana whether this was true, and she nodded her head.

"I would say Hanna was one of the more powerful teachers here, simply because of her standing in the Party. However, this year, well, she hasn't got quite as much to do."

The following weekend, just as the weather was beginning to turn severely cold, Dan and I spent a lovely weekend outside of Prague working with the youngest children from school at the "school in nature" located near a castle in the town of Orlík, about an hour and half south from Prague.

All the way on the bus, I tried to imagine what the school would look like. I still pictured camps with wood bunks and outdoor toilets and strange, multi-legged insects that bit you or nestled happily in your sleeping bag until you got in and they were unhappily roused from their slumber. Upon arriving at the school, I was surprised to find that it was more like a pension or hotel than some rustic shack. All of the kids were housed four to a room with proper feather beds and white sheets and pillows. There were little desks and little chairs in each room and a little sink. The hallways were carpeted and there was a big roaring fire in the downstairs hall where the classes ate and met together at night. In the mornings, the students retired to various classrooms to work for a few hours before heading out for walks in the woods or to play games outside.

As we wandered up and down the hallways greeting the students who had already been there for a week, I was impressed. It was the first Socialist innovation that I believed was worth their time and effort. I tried imagining the same quality program in the United States and couldn't, mostly because it would have been horrifically expensive. Still, I think it would be a wonderful experiment for inner-city schools, as students might benefit tremendously from several weeks out of the ghetto to see that one can have more out of life than a trail of crack, gangs and misery.

In the afternoon, we played soccer on an uneven field. I played terribly and failed to score even when I was positioned in front of an empty net, a condition known by soccer fans as "missing a sitter."

One of the students asked one of the teachers as we huffed along across the dirt, "How is it possible that a big strong American can't score a goal?" To which I replied, in English, "because I suck at soccer."

At the end of the game, one side lost in the final seconds and their young 11-year-old captain spent minutes sitting on the ground crying and screaming at the other players. "I'm afraid this may be something in our national character," one of the teachers explained as we watched another teacher trying to console the student. "There's always a lot of finger pointing and blaming others when things go wrong. But in the end nobody does anything."

The shouting, noise, banging and crashing spilled out of my classroom and into the hallways. Teachers that generally didn't like me or my style of education complained about my lack of discipline.

"Douglas, they want to know why there's so much noise every day," Dana told me as we were packing up one afternoon. Although she said it with a giggle, I suspected that trouble was brewing amongst some of the staff.

Some of the anger had to do with the fact that I was an untrained teacher who was better paid than many teachers who had been working for years. And, whether I wanted it or not, I was also the focus of attention. There weren't a lot of non-Czech teachers in the school and everyone was interested in what Americans were like.

Some of my problems began when I was interviewed for a local magazine. The father of one of my students had approached me one afternoon wondering whether he could write a story about me for a local weekly newsmagazine called *Signal*. I said that it would be fine, and several days later the reporter and a photographer showed up in school. They photographed some of my classes and then in the afternoon, conducted a short interview with me in my office. Jana translated. The reporter asked me all of the usual questions, including whether I was happy, why and how I had come to Czechoslovakia and whether I liked one country more than another. Attempting to be diplomatic, I told him that I didn't prefer one country or the other and thought they were both very different places and that they both had their strengths and weaknesses." The reporter took all the information down and promised to show me the article before it appeared.

Several weeks later Jana produced a typewritten copy of the article, which she proceeded to translate in a breezy manner. If she had gone over it a little more carefully, I might have called the reporter to have him change a few "embellishments," including saying I had arrived at the airport with my "California sunglasses" around my neck looking for beautiful women. In places, he did manage to quote me fairly accurately and had ended the article by saying he believed his daughter had received the best possible Christmas present of all: an American English teacher.

As it was, the article caused a storm of protest from Dana and the headmistress, who were both extremely displeased with the article.

A copy of the magazine under her arm, Dana came into our office and stormed past me. "I am not unhappy with you Douglas, but this seems to be all Jana's fault, as she has brought a reporter in here and exposed our school. I do not think this was a good idea." Luckily, Jana was not in the office. Later, I heard them arguing noisily in the hallway. Jana looked most sad and close to tears when she came back to the office some minutes later.

"You see, I try and do something nice here and still people are mad at me. Don't worry, Douglas, this isn't about you. This is . . ." she didn't finish the conversation. Whether it really was the article or the publicity given the school that made Dana unhappy, I never learned.

But the other teachers laughed loudly when they read about my long search for a little glass coffee maker similar to a French Press that filters out the grounds. Called a *kavovar,* Dan and I had seen one at a student's home when we were invited there for dinner one night. Several days later, I had ventured out to the various large department stores, only to find that they didn't have any.

"Do you know where I could find one?" I would ask, only to be told that the "other" department store had them. It was like searching for the Holy Grail. I shuffled back and forth between several stores for the better part of a week, only to be told each time that I should try somewhere else. I eventually bought one several months later when a new shipment arrived in Prague.

"Now you know what it's like to want something and not be able to find it," Viktor said, when I showed him my treasured purchase. "Imagine waiting for a car or a washing machine like this! We used to wait in line for days just to get something very important. Be happy that you have what it is that you want."

Although my teaching left something to be desired, some of my traits were beginning to rub off on some of my students. One of my most advanced sections, 6A, was filled with eleven year olds who could speak and write fairly good English. Thus, we usually had a fairly jolly time each day. In fact, I rather looked forward to their sessions, as the kids were rowdy but also interested in speaking English. Three of the boys—Peter, Rusty and George—tried to outdo each other making up jokes in English.

"What do you like to eat for dinner?" I would ask, always expecting the same answer.

"Big beef," Rusty ventured.

"Animals!" George said.

"T-Bone Steak!" Peter finished. Peter had lived for a time with his parents in Mexico and seemingly always had his hands full with some project or hobby. One minute it was English, the next hour he had math lessons and in the afternoons he played endless amounts of tennis. For awhile, I tutored him in English because his mother, a serious looking woman with dark hair and a tired face, believed he wasn't learning quickly enough. I didn't mind tutoring Peter, as he was fun to talk with.

Once we discussed dreams, and he said his dreams were always the same.

"I don't know," Peter said, speaking quickly with almost no breath. He always rushed. "I never talk in my dreams. I open my mouth and no sound comes out. I can't talk."

151

If poor Peter was on the verge of burnout at the age of eleven, he wasn't showing it. He tried hard and usually didn't fool around too much.

One day, George came into class smiling broadly. Rusty and Peter were right behind him, chattering excitedly in Czech. From what I could make of their disbelief, they didn't actually believe that George had done what he had gone and did.

I looked at George. Underneath his straight blond hair, his ear was pierced with a gold stud. He pointed at me and said in English: "Now, I'm as you are."

Although the fact that I have five earrings in my left ear had been a point of great amusement and fascination in school, I never thought the students would go out and do something like this as well. I complimented George on his taste (the earring seemed to suit him) and went on with the class.

Several days later, George's mother arrived at my class, dragging poor George by the elbow. She was agitated, if not downright upset. As she spoke English quite well, she had little trouble coming to the point:

"Look at what you did to my son!" she said, pointing to his earring. "He will be, you know, maybe homosexual!"

"Actually, I'm sorry if you think I did this to your son," I said as calmly as I could, as I suddenly had visions of being sacked in an hour's time. "But I didn't know until he had it done. I've never said a thing about it to him before. I certainly didn't encourage him."

She seemed to relax a moment and fiddled with her hair that was arranged into a bun on the top of her head.

"Well, I think he is too young for this," she said, pointing at the earring. George didn't say anything and looked down.

"I don't think it looks too bad," I said. "In fact, it has some character and style." Then I added quickly: "But you are his mother. This isn't for me to decide."

"I see," she said, looking me up and down. "I see." She was thinking. She thanked me and led her son out of the room.

George kept the earring.

In early October, we received a number of new textbooks, including a reader for small children called *Come and Play*. Written by the Czech Pedagogical Faculty, it detailed the ongoing adventures of a group of small children and their pets namely: Paul, Rob, Jane, Blackie the dog and Pussy the cat. There was also a strange transsexual-like character named Pixie-Dixie who did strange things like fly to the moon and alight on Earth in a space ship. Try as we might, we never could quite figure out whether Pixie-Dixie was a girl, boy or merely a hermaphrodite.

Teachers worked with the book by having the children read little sentences like: "A ball for Paul." "A car for Rob." "Blackie is black." Some of the sentences were in English and some were in Czech so the children could get the idea of what was being taught.

But the authors of *Come and Play,* in their quest to make the book as exciting as possible, had also unwittingly introduced a number of cultural faux-pas into the text that made some of the American teachers blush while working with the book.

> ME: (trying to keep a straight face) "Jan, what color is Pussy?"
> JAN: "Pussy is black."
> ME: (now on the verge of spluttering laughter) "Good. And Susan, does Blackie like Pussy?"
> SUSAN: "Yes, Blackie likes Pussy."
> ME: "Excellent. And Robert, where is Pussy?"
> ROBERT: "Pussy is in the tree."
> ME: "Usually. And, Karen, does Blackie love Pussy? In fact, can you tell me, what is Pussy?"

This subtle innuendo sometimes went on for minutes. In the end, a number of the female American teachers refused to work with the book, even though it was the only new text and was free of Communist ideology.

The other new book was called *Project English* and was written in a breezy, modern style by an obviously well-to-do British teacher. Ranging from pictorials to comic-book pictures and short text, *Pro-*

ject English's goal was to make teaching fun by making the kids interested through stories about astronauts and silly characters and real-life adventures. And *Project English* did look fairly smart, with loads of full-color pages and stories about disasters and home computers and fun sports.

A group of upper-class English schoolchildren were "guides" through the various chapters that stressed attention to basic concepts like "Have you got?" and "What's he doing?" and "Where's she going?"

Trouble was, as good as the book may have been, we simply didn't have enough copies to use the text properly, the kids couldn't take them home and some of the fun concepts detailed in the text were far beyond the normal expectations of my students. It was a little hard explaining such new-fangled concepts as kids having a lot of material possessions ("I've got my own computer. It's great! I bought a new record!) to children who were happy to receive a book and some sweaters for Christmas.

Usually my students would scream to watch a video and scream louder when I turned the television off. The afternoon I showed a *Project English* video, the kids watched silently as smiling Tom Hutchinson (the author of *Project English*) drove around in his fancy looking red sports car, getting lost in several expensive looking portions of England and all the while yakking away on a car phone. Then Hutchinson proceeded to introduce everyone to his happy family who had a large two-story house and lots of gadgets and extravagant furniture (it appeared smilin' Tom was making a pile of money somewhere). After the bell rang, there was not the usual commotion and clamor for more video. Instead, the students quietly filed out of the class. One girl, Mary, lingered behind.

"Teacher?" she asked with big wide eyes. "Do all people have a phone in their cars?" I assured her that they *certainly* did not. They usually had two.

13

Growing Pains

The new government was having its share of troubles. Although plans for the economic transformation were solidly enacted, there was constant debate and differences surrounding a number of key issues, including the aforementioned Slovak desire for more autonomy and the drafting of a new constitution.

The thorniest debate surged around the question of how to prosecute past crimes against the Czechs and Slovaks by the Communist government. To me, it is perhaps the most fascinating question, legally and morally that has arisen in the country. It is complex and unforgivingly cruel, cutting through families, friendships and the workplace.

From a distance, the untutored observer might find the question elementary: simply find those who did bad things and then put them on trial. But if one considers the civic structure of the country as a cake, the issue quickly becomes alarmingly unclear. On top are all the big fish—the high-ranking officials from the former government: Czechoslovak President Gustáv Husák and the leader of the Communist Party Miloš Jakeš and the chief Prague boss Miroslav Štěpán (a notoriously sinister fellow who ordered police to attack student demonstrators in Prague on numerous occasions).

Probe deeper with your knife and the questions and doubts begin sprouting from within this layered, rotten cake. A few inches below you'd find all of the top level Communists who were spread out across the country in various National Committees and in the vitally important trade unions. Down a little further are the low-level functionaries who kept the party going day in and day out. Some of these people had as much contact with the top of the party as you and I have with our own Senators and Congressmen. They were simply cogs in a machine, grinding gears so they could receive their extra fat paycheck or get their children into a better school.

Near the bottom of the cake lies a thick layer of average people who informed, listened and betrayed their fellow citizens on a daily basis. These people range from your next door neighbor who once gave you a nice present for your birthday to the employee down the hall or your best buddy on the soccer team. This is a murky zone, a rotten conspiracy of lies and hatred built on other people's weakness and deceit.

"What are we going to do, blow up the whole goddamned country?" a Czech friend raged one night when the issue was being fully played in the newspapers and in Parliament.

Havel, as usual, summed up the question most eloquently in his 1990 New Year's Day address:

"We had all become used to the totalitarian system and accepted it as an unchangeable fact, and thus helped to perpetuate it. In other words, we are all—though naturally to differing extents—responsible for the operation of the totalitarian machinery; none of us is just its victim; we are also its co-creators.

"It would be unreasonable to understand the sad legacy of the last forty years as something alien, which some distant relative bequeathed us. On the contrary, we have to accept this legacy as a sin we committed against ourselves."[1]

The Communist Party had hardly folded its tents and stolen quietly away into the night. Although they were reeling from mass defections—membership declined from 1,717,000 in May, 1988, to 750,000 in November, 1990)[2] and internal disputes—Communists still held a fair number of seats in the Federal Assembly. Some even thought there might be a chance to recapture power. Vasil Mohorita, a relatively young and energetic Communist who had been considered something of a reformer, emerged with a blistering and chilling statement on October 3, 1990, saying "the period of national understanding has ended and a period of hard struggle has begun" and encouraged a Communist takeover by aggression if necessary.[3]

The angry protests that followed Mohorita's comments led the government to propose a series of new measures, including the confiscation of the Communist Party property. Taken with a law on judicial rehabilitation that had been passed in April making it legal for citizens to claim redress of wrongs for persecution, it seemed there would be some sort of mass popular action against the Communist Party.

But no action was taken, and the issue continued to bubble rather than overheat. Part of this was due to resistance from Communists in the Parliament, and part was due to the numerous other pressing concerns facing the country. There wasn't even a proper Supreme Court set up to deal with the possibility of hearing appeals or the broad consideration of constitutional law. What's more, a final constitution hadn't even been approved.

Instead, the government set up a special commission charged with investigating not only the various lists and information left behind by the former state police, but also the events leading up to the November 17 attack on the students in Prague that had sparked the revolution. The names on the list were being kept a secret, as opposed to the *Staatssicherheit* (Stasi) files in East Germany, which had been opened for public inspection (although the process of getting to actually look at the material was slow). The Stasi files showed that releasing personal documents could be dangerous for many public individuals, as often the material contained errors and heartbreaking information about the past.

On the purely political level, the leading party, Civic Forum, was undergoing a fissure that eventually caused it to rend in late October when Klaus, the economics minister, was elected Chairman. Although Klaus had won plaudits with the adoption of his economic plan, his victory over a Havel nominee, Martin Palouš, was stunning indeed and marked Klaus' arrival on the political scene. It also marked the end of Civic Forum, as Klaus had extremely clear ideas about which way to go and that direction was firmly to the right.

Since the election in June, various factions had been fighting with each other over whether to pursue a fundamentally left- or right-wing course. Civic Forum had been created essentially as an umbrella organization to fight the hard-line government, so was only natural to expect that eventually various people within would have to go their own ways.

By January, 1991, the split was irreconcilable and two new parties—Klaus' Civic Democratic Party (ODS) and the leftish Civic Movement (headed by the Foreign Minister Jiří Dientsbier) emerged from the division. In Slovakia, the same situation occurred with a number of different groups rising from the ashes of the original party, Public Against Violence.

Some of the children's parents were helping us by giving us little "welcome" gifts when we visited their homes, including a number of nice full-color books about Prague and Czechoslovakia. "We thought you would like to see some nice photos," one couple told me, "but the book is not for reading." When I got home and flipped through the text, I could see why. Like in the English grammar books, the authors had laid on the glory of socialism so thick it nearly dripped from the page, making the book all but unreadable.

"The Czechoslovak economic reforms in which this aspect is strongly underlined draw upon the experience of the former system of planning and management with its endeavor to inject technological advance into the economy almost exclusively from the top," one book proclaimed. "The Fourth Five-Year Plan (1966–70) makes big demands in this respect since its dominant note is the widespread reconstruction and modernization of engineering, textiles, glass, the food industry and transport (especially the railways)."

Huh? Little of what they had written made sense. But they managed to get all of the major points: people in Czechoslovakia had come to their rightful senses in 1948 and decided to continue the "correct" path to socialism; the people only wanted peace with "imperialist" countries; and everyone had enough to eat. The Soviet Union was exemplified in slobbering prose, as having liberated the helpless Czechs and Slovaks from the clutches of the Nazis in 1945. Socialism was only heading forward, the people were happy and peace and friendship was the mainstay of relations between all Comecon nations. After a few pages of this drivel, I felt as though I'd eaten a box of laxatives.

Over the next few months, I began to acquire a weird collection of old pamphlets, posters, books, buttons and other memorabilia from the pre-revolution days. Not surprisingly, Czechs I showed this material to didn't think much of it. Some laughed at the stupidity of it all, but most seemed fatigued and uninterested in the ridiculous potpourri of literature.

"I've seen it all many times," Jarka said, sighing and changing the subject. "I'm not interested in it." Renáta wasn't terribly keen on the material either, so I eventually kept the things to myself. Dan and I happily filled our rooms with posters of Havel and the other odd totems and trinkets we were gathering. There were pictures of Havel eating breakfast, Havel standing on the balcony overlooking the center of town, Havel with the Rolling Stones and Havel meeting Frank Zappa. And, we had a really big poster of Havel lounging on a sofa. The words on the poster came from Havel's favorite saying: "Truth and love will triumph over lies and hate."

Visitors would silently take all of the material in as they wandered around the apartment and then give us odd looks.

"Geeze, you guys really like Havel, don't you?" they'd remark with kind of a bemused look and then shake their heads. We were too blissed-out in our own Personality Cult to notice that we were looking suspiciously like fanatics following a deity or 16-year-old girls who just have discovered a teen idol. "Yeah!" Dan and I would shout, almost in unison. "We really respect Havel! He's great!"

One afternoon at school, I came across a pile of posters, books and magazines that was earmarked for the trash. That is, until I busily dug into the material and found that it was loaded with all sorts of Socialist goodies. I asked Dana, who had come walking down the hallway, whether I could take some of the things home.

"Of course you can. But I don't know why you'd want it. In there is such terrible things." I understood Dana and the others in wanting to forget about the past, but to me, the material would be priceless someday.

159

Looking back, I can't quite grasp what possessed me to keep back issues of the English-language *Czechoslovak Life* ("Solving industrial disputes where they arise: the workplace") and *World Youth 1982,* which included a insightful commentary by Jaroslav Jenerál, Chairman of the Central Committee of the Socialist Union of Youth (SSM) on "Our vital interest—a creative life in peace" and a report on the activities of something called the FDJ ("an active force in the struggle of progressive world youth for peace and disarmament"). Despite my best attempts at wading through the turgid prose, I was never able to figure out what the FDJ was or what it was supposed to do, except that it seemed very opposed to "imperialism." Later, a friend told me the FDJ was the East German counterpart of the Socialist Union of Youth.

I even came to love some of the old Socialist working songs, including this gem, which was lampooned by exiled singer Karyl Kril every morning on *Radio Free Europe*:

A Tractor Song

Merrily, merrily
A worker goes to the factory
Merrily, merrily,
He goes to the factory
Merrily, he smiles
When his lathe is singing to him
Tell me, mother, my mother
What are the engines singing about in the factories?
What are the engines singing about in the factories?
They are singing, singing like the birds
That people are glad
That they have jobs!

160

August 1990: Czechoslovak President Václav Havel (right) with fellow dissident and then Foreign Minister Jiří Dientsbier.

August 1990: Havel with the Rolling Stones at Hradčany.

Summer 1992: As Havel struggled to keep Czechoslovakia unified, the strain was mirrored in his eyes.

The reluctant First Lady: Olga Havelova.

The good old bad days: Czechoslovak President Gustav Husak with Communist Party leader Miloš Jakeš at May Day celebrations in 1988.

November 17, 1989: Students lighting candles shortly before being attacked by police on Národní in Prague.

November-December, 1989: Signatures on a poster saying "Havel to the Castle."

March 1992: Pensioners eating at the opening of the first McDonald's.

July 17, 1992: Slovaks cheering news of the Slovak National Council's sovereignty vote in Bratislava. Prime Minister Vladimir Mečiar is featured on one flag.

Photo courtesy of the Czech News Agency

January, 1990: Statue of Klement Gottwald, "First Worker's President of Czechoslovakia" being prepared for removal. Graffiti on statue reads: "Murderer of the Nation."

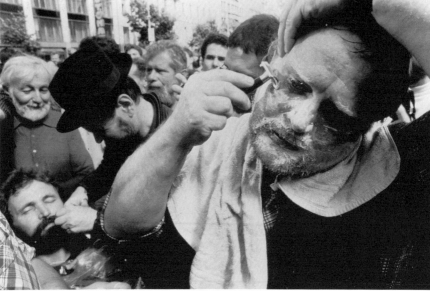

June 25, 1991: As the last Soviet tank leaves Czechoslovakia, Czech men shave beards they began to grow in 1968 to protest the Warsaw Pact invasion.

14

Meeting the Parents

In the afternoons, I sometimes taught a special discussion class with older children who could speak English well enough to talk in full sentences. But despite their linguistic dexterity, prodding them to discuss anything was often a challenge.

"Well, is there something you'd like to talk about?" I asked, not wanting to ram contrived topics down their young throats. A pretty blonde girl raised her hand.

"Could you tell us about America?" she asked sweetly.

"Well, I was more hoping you'd tell me about yourselves."

Silence. I tried a different turn.

"How about I tell you something about America and then you tell me something about Czechoslovakia."

Stares from the gallery. I started out. "America is big," I said. "Jan, what is your country?"

"My country is small," he said. "Teacher, what is Disneyland like?"

Rats! Foiled again! A few of these dreary sessions and I could begin to see the importance of preparation and careful planning. It is one thing to direct a class casually, and another to have it steer off course into La-La Land where the teacher gets frustrated and the kids just get bored.

My complaints about the children's lack of concentration worked their way up through the teachers until they got back to the parents in ways I never expected. In early October, I received an invitation to dinner at the home of one of my brightest students. The 11-year-old boy, whose name was David, lived in a beautiful neighborhood not far from school where the buildings all have elaborate stone facades and the streets are lined with trees. It was sleeting through the trees when I arrived at the appointed hour. David's parents, Milan and Věra, served a delicious dinner of duck and dumplings and cabbage. Both parents were doctors and both spoke very good English, so I didn't have to worry for one evening about making myself understood. Milan, who was tall and lanky with a receding hairline, asked about my health and I told him about my ongoing sinus infection and my trouble getting it treated properly.

"Well, you know, good Western drugs are hard to get here, but I will see if I can find something at the hospital," he said.

Věra asked me if I was enjoying my work.

"Well," I said, "I often don't feel that I know what I'm doing. But I'm trying my best."

"We hope you won't go home too soon," she said with a smile. "They told us at the parents meeting at school that the children were being so bad to you that you might go home!"

I very nearly spluttered on my beer.

"What? I never said that," I cried. "I've had some problems, yes, but I doubt very much that I'd go home. It hasn't been that awful."

"Well, we hoped that," Věra said, "but it was funny that night after they told us you were unhappy. David was in the bathroom crying because he thought that perhaps you would go away."

Milan broke in to the conversation at this point.

"The other day, I had a conversation with a parent of one of David's friends. The parent was most upset that you aren't giving enough homework or tests at school. He feels that his child isn't learning enough. I said I was most happy because David is doing exactly what he should be doing at school and that is speaking English. He has time enough to learn proper writing and grammar rules, but I can see that he is speaking better. And he enjoys it, so what's the problem?"

I thanked Milan sincerely and told him that I would try and keep up the good work. Walking home that night, I realized how much was going on that I didn't know about: Teachers saying I might leave if the children didn't behave. Parents unhappy with the teaching. Grumbling

162

about my personality, my salary and the fact I was an American. It was a lot to try and manage.

Several days later, David brought a package of very expensive antibiotics to school for me. I thanked him effusively and asked him if his parents wanted any money. David waved me off.

"No, no, they are from the hospital," he said. I went back to my office and took immediately took one of the pills. As I let the pill roll over my tongue, I thought about how kind people had been here. It seemed almost too good to be true.

Over the first few months, I gradually came to understand the various quirks of each of my students. I got to know their parents as kids would tell me what their parents did for a living.

"My father drives a tram," one said. Hands shot up all around the classroom.

"My mother works in a shop."

"My father is a doctor."

Sometimes the parents would stop by the school if their child was ill. Absenteeism was incredibly high, as a lot of the children suffered greatly from asthma and other lung diseases. A lot of them ran constant colds. Once, after I complained about having so few students in class one day, Dana said, "Now you can understand why we need the school in nature program. If the children don't leave Prague, so many of them will be just unhealthy."

I myself didn't feel healthy for days on end and would get unexplained headaches in the late afternoon. "It's the coal," Viktor told me. How could one feel well when the air was filled with a faint gray mist from morning until night?

Suddenly, it was time for the first parent-teacher night where all the parents assembled in school to receive an update about how their children were doing.

Jana clucked when she told me about the parent-teachers' meeting.

"You will see, Douglas. Like student, like parent. They're all the same. If student is stupid, the parent will be as well. Ugly, short, fat or beautiful. You'll see it in their face."

163

Dana told me to come to school at about 7 P.M. so I could meet with the parents. What she didn't mention, or make clear, is that I would be talking to them all at once. I have been rarely as terrified as when I pulled into my first class and discovered more than 40 parents listening to a report from an art teacher. Even though Jana was there to help translate, it still was a lot of people to speak to. They sat there, dwarfing the tiny desks, staring at me like I was a suspect politician sent to tell them about the need for tax hikes.

"Ahhm, first," I said, nearly coughing up my dinner, "I'd like to say that I'm very sorry that I don't speak Czech. I am taking lessons and I hope to learn to speak something soon." I tried to smile, but it seemed difficult. However, more than a few of the parents smiled when they heard Jana's translation. I told them that I was happy with the class and I hoped that their children were learning something. I said that all parents should feel free to come to school and see me. I asked them what they had heard from their children. Jana translated it all and then one of the parents put up her hand to ask a question. I looked at Jana while the parent smiled at me.

"She is asking about Maria. How is she doing in the class?"

I groped for a reply. I hadn't expected to be forced to evaluate students in front of everyone.

"She's doing fine," I nearly blurted out. "She is very nice." The parent seemed pleased with the answer and went on smiling at me. Others raised their hands to ask about their kids. One by one, I said the same thing, that all the students were trying hard. Luckily, the several parents I did want to see to discuss problems were wise enough not to raise their hands. I asked to see some of them after the meeting. In one case, I was concerned about the case of a girl who always cried whenever things got difficult. I told her father what was happening and he laughed a bit.

"It think it is her nature," he said in English. "She cries a lot. But don't worry, she seems to like you."

The Czech obsession with slippers went a little too far several times at school, when parents would show up for a meeting with me and would immediately change into their slippers before entering my classroom. While I could deduce the thought behind the practice—

i.e. they are showing respect for my "home" and workplace—it seemed completely impractical, especially since often they were often there for less than five minutes. And besides, the floors were usually a dirty mess.

On the nights of the big parent-teacher meetings at school, the hallways would be lined with pairs of shoes and plastic boots, a strange sight that even drew chuckles from some of the Czech teachers.

I wandered the hallways that evening, moving from classroom to classroom. Jana was right: like student, like parent. If the kid was slow, the parent often was slow. Bright and speedy, ditto.

In the end, I only received a few tough questions, including one from woman who demanded to know why not everyone was using a new textbook called *Project English*.

"Because I don't think the school has the money to purchase enough copies for each student."

"That's not good enough!" the woman stormed in excellent English and then turned to the assembled parents and spoke sharply with them. There was a brief flurry of discussion and then Jana turned to me.

"They are discussing whether or not they should buy *Project English* for their children. They say they will."

But that wasn't all. The woman asked whether it was true that I had a video player in my classroom. I said it was, and she asked me why I wasn't using it.

"I don't have any tapes for it," I said.

"Well, let's get some!" she said, looking at me. Then she switched to Jana and stormed at her in Czech.

Later, after the meeting was finished, Jana hurried out of the classroom and back to the office. She was fuming. After sitting down, she explained that the strident woman at the meeting was also an English teacher.

"She was probably trying to show off in front of the other parents," Jana said. "It's quite common."

Interestingly enough, about two weeks later, the same woman, whose name was Gabriela Klímková, wrote me a note thanking me for teaching her son and inviting me to come see her school, which was a new private language school. After a brief tour of the school, we settled with coffee and she told me a bit about herself. She was a single mother and had learned English slowly over the years to the point that she had mastered it quite well. She only wanted the best for her son, Tomáš, who was quite bright and motivated.

"I was lucky enough to visit some relatives in Pennsylvania several years ago," Klímková said. "And I must tell you, when I returned from seeing them, and seeing the style in which they lived, I was so angry about our government and what they have done to us. I won't wait any longer to try and help myself or Tom." She was a big believer in quickly acquiring everything that a real school should have and, indeed, her language school was already much better off than Prokopová. They had a copy machine, lots of shiny new books and magazines for students to read in German and English.

The next year, Klímková removed Tomáš from the school and sent him to a new private school that had just opened.

One early Saturday morning in early November, I took a night train to Berlin, leaving at shortly after 2 A.M. Clambering into an empty compartment, I fell asleep almost immediately, only to be roused somewhere in Northern Bohemia by a family of gypsies that had purchased reserved seats. The woman was extremely furious at me for occupying her seat, and gave me holy hell as I sleepily moved into another empty seat in the compartment. It took them a long time to get settled, as they seemed to have a ton of luggage. When we reached the German border, sometime after 4 A.M., there was a long wait while the customs authorities searched the train. As I was an American, they didn't bother with me, but instead seized upon the family in my compartment. Within minutes they had them empty nearly everything in their bags, the contents of which appeared only to be composed of cigarettes. The next thing I knew the gypsy family was unceremoniously escorted from the train and herded into one of the customs offices on the border. So much for smuggling, I thought, sinking back into a light slumber.

For the uninitiated, Berlin is perhaps the best way to truly examine the huge canyon that existed between the Western and socialist countries.

On the cold Saturday morning I arrived, I took the S-Bahn ground-level subway across East Berlin, past the gray, forbidding Alexanderplatz, to the Hauptbahnhof Friedrichstrasse, the station closest to Potsdamer Platz. I figured that way I could walk across the main square where Hitler had met his demise and where the wall had once been.

In the early morning light, the huge square was nearly deserted and still terribly in need of renovation, having served as a no-man's land for more than thirty years. The Brandenburg gate was there, imposing as in the pictures, but covered in graffiti and political posters. I tried to picture the final Soviet shells spitting down on the cement and the chaos of Hitler's final hours. I carried on, walking through the lovely wooded Tiergarten and was astonished to think that after the war it had vanished because Berliners needed the wood to heat their homes. Everything seemed so tranquil, so perfectly in order.

After having been in Prague for nearly four months, I was totally unprepared for the cultural and commercial shock I received when I entered the Ku'damm, or Kurfürstendamm, the main shopping avenue that dominates the heart of downtown West Berlin. Although it was still early by the time I wandered up the street, I was amazed by the array of goods crammed into every available shop window and store.

Everything seemed like it was bulging with color. I gawked at the advertisements telling me to do this or buy that or eat something. All the Germans looked so resplendent in their fancy coats and well-pressed shirts. They were smiling and their teeth were straight and there were no restaurants with indifferent waiters slopping coffee on the customers or telling them sourly to go to hell because everything was reserved. My eyes took in this panorama of pleasures: healthy looking couples wolfing down sandwiches and ethnic food and drinking coffee like they were posing for a television commercial. It all seemed so unreal, so completely out of the ordinary. And it became even more so after I changed some money and entered one of the shining cafes, dreaming about breakfast—*ein Früstück mit einem grossen Milchkaffee.*

When it all came, exactly as I had ordered, I wondered whether I should bow my head and give a short prayer. Rarely have I been so thankful for something so small. I ate and drank the coffee that wasn't Turkish-style, but filtered, buttered my bread which was fresh and flaky, and felt extremely peaceful as I read The *International Herald Tribune*. And then I received *den grosse shock* as I was cheerfully handed *ein grosse bill* for more than 6 DMs!

"Six marks!" I loudly said to myself. I looked around and saw several of the happy Germans staring at me. "That's like twenty-five beers in Prague!" I paid and left feeling like I had been slapped in the face. I paused to consider my guidebook which only now told me that West Berlin was fantastically expensive: "As expensive, if not more, than the best areas of New York." Well, I'm no stranger to the streets of New York, and I can tell you coffee doesn't cost that much. And you get as many refills as your pulse rate and bladder can stand.

After absorbing the blow, I spent the entire day walking through the beautiful, tree lined streets, drinking in the stores and the people and keeping my wallet firmly in my pocket. Finally, at the end of the day, my feet sore, I bought a few cassettes in a huge music store called *World Of Music* and then bought a few food items that weren't available in Prague (sage, green apples). I wandered slowly over the line marking the wall and watched the colors slowly fade away until everything around me was again like in Prague: rusting Trabants, cracked buildings and dirty walls, dim lighting. As dark settled over the city, I bought a chunk of the Berlin Wall from a man on the street and took the S-Bahn back to the train station in East Berlin and disappeared back into the clutches of the socialist housing complexes, now completely confused about the amazing division between the Western and Eastern countries.

Not long after our "blind date," Renáta invited me to go see Půlnoc, a Czech rock band that had managed to sign a contract with Arista Records in the United States. They had toured in the United States and had been in San Francisco shortly before I left for Czechoslovakia, but I hadn't had time to see them. I was quite keen to see them live as they were the only Czech band I had read about (interestingly enough I had come across them a year before when Robert Christ-gau, the influential rock critic for the *Village Voice* in New York, had named one of Půlnoc's unreleased live tapes as his album of the year. I recall having thought Christgau was bonkers and wondering where the hell the band was from!).

Půlnoc (pronounced "pool-notes"—it means midnight in Czech) had a long and storied history that stretched back to the late 1960s, when several of the band's musicians were in The Plastic People of the Universe, the band that had sparked Havel and other dissidents into action when the band and its manager were arrested in 1976. In the mid-1980s, the Plastics broke up and formed several different groups, one of them being Půlnoc.

The controversy surrounding the Plastics and the attention bade them by members of the international rock press eventually brought Půlnoc to the attention of major record labels, which were signing up numerous bands from Eastern Europe and the Soviet Union. Record executives assumed there would be a big interest in the United States in hearing "previously forbidden" music from behind the Iron Curtain.

"We don't play to change the political system," their bassist and leader Milan Hlavsa said while on tour in the United States. "We play because we're musicians. The system forced us to be political."[1]

In fact, the entire nature of the Plastic's music had been over dramatized, Hlavsa said. "We suddenly became the representatives of the underground. The public turned us into guerrilla fighters. We never wanted to be political and we didn't enjoy being political. *Other* people made politics out of us."[2]

Several weeks after arriving in Prague, I had bought a copy of Půlnoc's first album, which was simply called *Půlnoc*. Although I couldn't understand the lyrics, I found much of the music absorbing. It was a blend of numerous sounds and influences: the Velvet Under-ground, dissonant art music, and three-chord garage rock. Over the layers of murk and sonic texture, the seven-member band introduced two fairly unique touches that gave the band somewhat of a signature sound: Michaela Němcová's opera-trained voice and Tomáš Schilla's mournful cello (a carry-over from the Plastics). The lyrics are street-wise and serious, moody and ominous. Despite Hlavsa's comments about the music not being political, I found it hard to believe, especially while listening to songs like "Kanárek (Little Canary)" which featured Hlavsa's pounding bass and thudding drums:

> *"The little canary died*
> *Or perhaps he kicked it*
> *Or perhaps someone ripped him off."*

We took a long tram ride out to the club where Půlnoc was playing, a medium-sized hall called Junior Klub. It was already quite full when we arrived, with lots of people sitting on the floor and milling about drinking beer from paper cups or wine from bottles. Not surprisingly, the atmosphere was typical: long hair, faded denim, bandannas, endless smoking and drinking. But many in the audience looked more studious than Americans; many wore John Lennon-like round granny spectacles which gave them a vaguely bookish character.

As opposed to clubs in America where one can wait until the wee hours of the morning before the music begins, Půlnoc came on shortly before 8 and ended at 10 P.M. Part of this was inherently cultural and part is the numerous early morning jobs that get people out of bed before 5 A.M. It was refreshing to see a band when I was fully awake or not nearly unconscious from drink and still be able to go out afterwards.

Půlnoc played, and in sharp contrast to American clubs, the audience sat on the floor and applauded respectfully after each song. There were some whistles and loud cheers, but the reaction to the music was more akin to a jazz club or a classical concert. This too, was refreshing in people's desire to see and hear the music, rather than make loud spectacles out of themselves by cheering like they were at a football match or applauding like trained seals hoping for a fish. When Půlnoc came to take its first break, I happened across Teresa, one of my older students from school. I liked Teresa immensely; she had a good attitude but wasn't an apple polisher. She had big saucy eyes and a flirtatious personality. When she saw me, she gave me a huge sheepish look and tried to slink away.

"Jesus, Teresa," I said. "What are you doing here?"

"I like Půlnoc," she said. "You will not tell ..." she said, a pleading look in her eyes.

"Of course not," I said, a grin spreading across my face. "It's OK." Renáta was suitably impressed with my fine students who were out on the town.

"I wish my students were like that," she said as we got in line for beer. While we were waiting, a tall man with long black hair and beard came up to us with a camera bag and a several cameras slung around his neck. After hugging Renáta, he introduced himself to me in excellent English and said his name was Daniel Vojtíšek.

"I'm taking pictures of the concert for a rock magazine," he said peering at me from behind large aviator-like glasses. After he and Renáta talked for a few minutes, he led me over to another man who was waiting by the door to the club.

"This is Ondřej Konrád," he said, "he is an editor at the magazine." Konrád, who also spoke English, shook my hand.

"I think you have chosen a good concert to come to," Konrád said. "Půlnoc often doesn't play very well live and this happens to be one of their better shows."

I asked Konrád if he liked Půlnoc and he said that he thought they were just all right; he liked the blues better.

"You know, Muddy Waters and Stevie Ray Vaughan and so forth," he said.

Daniel took me backstage to meet to meet Tadeáš Věrčák, the guitarist for Půlnoc. Věrčák was just packing up his Fender Stratocaster when we walked into the small dressing room off the stage. With long straight hair set off by round spectacles, Věrčák looked shy and bookish. But he was very polite and asked me lots of questions about the American music industry. When he heard I was from San Francisco, he tried to enlist my help.

"Do you know Bill Graham?" he said, referring to the legendary concert promoter from San Francisco. When I said I had worked with Graham's office in the past as a reporter, Věrčák asked me if I could get in contact with people there.

"We really need help in learning how to record and produce our own music," he said through Daniel's translation. I was very surprised,

171

because I knew that the band had toured at least once in the United States and had recorded an album there. Didn't they already know a lot of people through their American record label?

"Well, things aren't always as they seem," Věrčák said. Indeed, the band's American record label had saddled the band with a highly restrictive recording and management contract and several members of the group were very unhappy about what had transpired.

We migrated to a nearby pub where we talked into the early morning about music.

"I think life for me now means it's more funny, less money," Daniel said as he started in on what must have been his fifth beer for the evening. "I think while most of us like the freedom, many feel worse off simply because they are no longer guaranteed a stable salary."

Petr, the manager of the Junior Klub, eventually joined us and told me about his experiences working for the Rolling Stones when they had played in Prague.

"I learned so much about promotion in those few days," he said. "I learned that we have much to learn." Petr said the Rolling Stones concert was the first time any of them had been able to see modern sound equipment up close.

Sitting at the table with the many people, drinking the excellent beer and listening to their stories, I suddenly felt tremendously happy and relaxed. I drank a lot, but didn't feel drunk—only open and in tune with the conversation around me. Up to that point, I had been having a good time, but hadn't felt easy like I would have in San Francisco. There was always the fear of wondering where I was and how to act and what to say. The transcendent moments I may have been having weren't warm and comfy and there was always a raw layer to my emotions.

Underneath the table, Renáta grabbed my hand and I didn't try to pull away. I realized I was attracted to her. She was bold and I liked her spirit.

Daniel invited me to come to the magazine's offices and see them. "Perhaps you can write something for us," he said.

"But I don't write in Czech," I said, surprised and embarrassed by his generous offer.

"We can translate it. Besides, you may be one of the few people to have seen many of these musicians." He was right. After visiting their offices, I discovered a group of writers who passionately loved their subject matter, but were having to compose in arcane, abstract ways without having seen the true product. Imagine having to describe cottage cheese without having seen or tasted it.

Owned by *Lidové noviny* (The People's Newspaper), a Prague liberal daily that had been the first independent newspaper to come out of *samizdat* after the revolution, the writers at *Rock & Pop* had grand plans for the future: television shows, concerts, records. Unfortunately, like many small, young businesses, the line between fantasy and reality are sometimes very far apart. Just getting the product onto the street each month was a trial. There were numerous printing headaches, writers would disappear for days on end and sometimes the magazine's staff would be too much into the proverbial sauce by mid-afternoon to accomplish anything. But they were all good-hearted people who were happy to read my articles and encourage me to write more.

What's more, the enthusiasm they had for running their own magazine was inspiring. Even though they didn't know what they were doing half the time, they didn't care; they were free to do as they pleased and they'd find a way to make things work. Do you want to write about the Velvet Underground? Great! Give us the story! Chris Isaak? How about next week!

The kids I first met in Prague were often very interested in so-called "underground" music like Půlnoc and other bands that had played at the very edge of disaster with the government. But four years down the road, Prague's youth is interested in the incessant drone of techno, hip-hop and trendy music like Roxette and Ace of Base. The move away from serious music to youth-oriented culture meant that *Rock & Pop* lost a big readership.

Daniel told me an interesting story one night when we were having dinner.

"I was in a pub and this man was complaining about 'how everything now is so expensive.' And I said, well, that is true, but the most important thing is that I am allowed to do as I please. I can work, or

173

I can choose not to work, and that alone is my decision. I can tell the government to go to hell and I won't go to jail. I can think what I want and tell others openly what I think."

"And what did your friend say to this?" I asked.

"He agreed, but was still pissed off that everything costs so much more!" Daniel said, laughing. "I think he will never understand."

Over the next few weeks, Daniel took Dan and me to see other bands, including Žlutý pes (Yellow Dog), a Southern rock band that played letter-perfect versions of songs by the Allman Brothers and Lynyrd Skynyrd.

We also went one evening to a punk concert at the former Stalin monument high above Prague. In the 1950s, workers had spent several years laboriously erecting a mammoth 100-foot high bronze statue of Stalin, Lenin and other Communist leaders in Letná Hill, a huge green expanse overlooking the city. In 1962, years after Khrushchev's so-called "secret speech" condemning the Stalin cult, Czechoslovak president Antonín Novotný realized that the time had come to removed the eyesore, which Praguers sometimes referred to as "the largest bread line in the city." However, it took more than a few well-placed blasts of dynamite to get the statue down.

As a side note, a statue of Lenin that stood in the middle of another square also was the butt of numerous jokes—literally. Because a beer pub was located squarely behind Lenin's back, most local folk always referred to the pub as *za prdelí*—"behind the ass."

Underneath the statue, the state had constructed a series of interlocking bunkers which were to be used in case of nuclear attack by the Western imperialists. However, the bunker project remained mostly unfinished and, after the revolution, some local students co-opted the space for music and art shows. They called it the "Totalitarian Zone" and staged numerous concerts in the dank and dark unfinished space that featured dirt floors and cement beams. The night we went, there was a punk band of sorts and a group of teen-agers politely and carefully stage diving, like their mothers were watching.

Despite the tentative attempts by the band to play punk, the music was not new to the country as the first real Czech punk band—Zikku-rat—was formed in 1979. Through the 1980s, there were dozens of underground punk bands that came and went.

We stood around in the cold air drinking beer out of paper cups and watching the kids jump about in the dirt. Lights from the edge of the stage cast strange, eerie shadows across the cement walls and somebody had hung some moody, dark blue formless paintings on the walls. The room felt haunted. As I wandered about, I thought of the Russian word *zona*—zone, but with a forbidding presence—and the whole spectacle reminded me of a Andrei Tarkovsky film. Just before we left, I picked up several pieces of cement left over from the foundation for the Stalin monument. There was tons of the stuff lying about. I kept it as a souvenir of sorts next to my chunk of the Berlin Wall in my room at the Dům.

15

Mr. Bush Comes to Town

In early November, 1990, the White House announced that President Bush would be coming to Prague on November 17, the first anniversary of the student demonstration that eventually led to the downfall of the Husák regime. My Czech friends and the Czech newspapers were very divided about whether it was a good thing that Bush was coming to Prague.

Jarka and Viktor both said they didn't mind that Bush came, but why did he have to come on the anniversary? They felt that Bush was coming only to exploit his own policies and programs and pay lip service to the Czechs and Slovaks.

Others said they were glad that Bush was coming. It was a symbol, they said, that Bush stood behind Czechoslovakia in a difficult time. It would validate the revolution and give it new life.

"Well, I just hope somebody can write a decent speech for him," Dan drily remarked while pouring over press releases that we had picked up at Havel's offices.

Dan was in heaven, as he finally had some reporting to do. Since arriving in Prague the month before, he had difficulty getting organized. With the exception of several radio pieces for Pacifica Radio, he had been hoping for a good news story to report.

"The teaching is OK, but I really wish I hadn't signed up for quite so much," he said during a coffee break. "I feel like I'm not getting anything else done." I felt the same way. By the end of the afternoon,

I really didn't have the energy to go try and dig up stories that might be interesting to a newspaper in the United States.

Receiving credentials to sit in the press gallery was ridiculously easy. I merely showed my expired press card from the California Highway Patrol and was issued a press pass.

Several days before the big event, workers began to assemble a huge platform near the top of Wenceslas Square. On top of the platform, they built a huge box with blue-tinted bulletproof windows. Because Bush had received many threats from terrorists opposed to his Gulf War policy, and Havel had received several threats from Slovak extremists, it was deemed a good idea that both of them deliver their speeches from inside the Big Blue Box. Later reporters dubbed it the "fishtank," and the name stuck. It wasn't planned as much of a visit; Bush was in Prague less than 24 hours as he was in Europe to sell allies on preparations for the coming Gulf War and eat Thanksgiving dinner with the troops in Saudi Arabia.

On a cold, cloudy Saturday morning, Dan and I arrived near Wenceslas Square about three hours before Bush and Havel were due to speak. There were already thousands of people in the square, carrying banners and Czechoslovak and American flags. The streets and buildings along the square were lined with flags.

From the beginning, it was clear that Bush intended to use his visit to promote United States participation in the Gulf War and help his chances at being re-elected in 1992.

Not surprisingly, the American Embassy had reserved the front of the square for Americans, who were all conveniently provided with little American flags to wave. A lot of the people from the Dům were down there waiting in the chill. In addition, someone, probably the American Embassy, distributed thousands of little buttons to Czechs featuring Bush's face and the inscription, "Thank You!" on them.

Without any effort, we literally wandered just feet from the fish tank and then took our places in the press gallery. With visions of Lee Harvey Oswald dancing in my mind, no one even bothered check our tags or search us.

A loudspeaker near the small "fishtank" blared out American patriotic music for the chilly hours before Bush and Havel arrived to speak.

A stiff wind blew up the square and it looked like it might rain or even snow.

About a half-an-hour late, Bush and Havel appeared and climbed onto a nearby platform to wave at the crowd before entering the safety of the fishtank.

Havel spoke first, thanking Czechs and Slovaks for their loyalty during the long year, but also warning people of the upcoming hard times. Havel dubbed the manic, somewhat crazy year following the revolution the "Velvet Hangover."

"The time of hard, everyday work has come," Havel said, "a time in which conflicting interests have surfaced, a time for sobering up, a time when all of us—and especially those in politics—must make it very clear what we stand for."[1]

Bush's speech was, in contrast, one of the worst addresses given by any modern leader in recent memory. I have heard tipsy luncheon speakers at the Rotary speak better. Even worse, Bush's turgid sentences were hurt by the need to pause every three sentences so the material could be translated. "In the face of force, you deployed the power of principle. Against a wall of lies, you advanced the truth.

"We will not fail you in this decisive moment. America will stand with you to the end!" Bush dragged on in his shrill voice, before reminding everyone that they should be united in his cause to go lay waste to most of Iraq. "It is no coincidence that Czechs and Slovaks should be among the first to understand that there is right and there is wrong. There is good and there is evil. And there are sacrifices worth making."

He ended the speech by presenting Havel with a small replica of the Liberty Bell. Two years later, Bush traveled to Poland and repeated the speech (sans the Gulf War material) almost word for word.

"I will ring the bell three times," Bush said happily. "Once for the revolution, once for the people and once for the children of the revolution." The first time he rang the bell, someone failed to turn on the little microphone attached to the clapper and so Bush had to ring the bell a fourth time. After the speech, Bush and Havel again climbed out onto a little platform to wave briefly, sing a few bars from "We Shall Overcome" with the crowd and then they departed the square.

179

True to form, the White House, led by the droll Chief of Staff John Sununu, put the most ridiculous spin on Bush's visit, radically inflating the number of people who saw Bush in the square from 100,000 to 800,000. *The Los Angeles Times* reported that one "White House official" berated a reporter for not sticking by the White House numbers and said the reporter had "insulted the Czech people and the president."[2]

A reporter friend of ours from the BBC saw Sununu (could *he* have been the official yelling at the reporter? Surely not ...) beaming not long after at a press conference, exclaiming that Bush's visit had been a complete success. During the day, Barbara Bush read stories about Millie the dog to students at a local elementary school and visited a school for the handicapped with Olga Havel.

In the late evening after the speech, Dan and I walked through the huge square again and watched workmen dismantling the fishtank. Nearby, a group of children tried gamely to keep the literally dozens of candles burning in the memory circle. Their faces glowed in the flickering candlelight as they dashed about with bits of burning twigs and sticks.

Dan and I were interested in the Havel's concept of a "Velvet Hangover." Havel's commentary was not new, as the hangover theory had also surfaced in Karel Vachek's *New Hyperion,* a massive, three-hour documentary about the first and sometimes bitter election campaign in June, 1990. The film makes no judgments about the election; it shows the hundreds of people who were all working for one single goal: the introduction of a free and civil society. But as the election approaches, it is clear that people are agreeing less and less. While it is absurdly easy to see the need to get from point A to point B, there are many arguments on how to get there. Thus: the hangover.

"Whoever hasn't got a hangover from the last twenty years won't live to see the catharsis," Vlasta Chramostová, a noted Czech actress says cryptically in *New Hyperion.* "Actor, citizen, whatever, as a nation, we have to have one to get the other."

I was starting to try my hand at cooking Czech food and Jana gave me a recipe for making cabbage to go with the meat and dumplings:

Cut a head of cabbage into small pieces and take out the core. Boil for a few minutes, then pour out the water. Reboil the cabbage again with fresh water. Pour out the water after the cabbage is soft, but not mushy. In another pot, fry some onion in butter. Mix the cabbage with the onion and add one spoon of very soft flour. Then add salt and vinegar and one spoon of sugar. Keep mixing, tasting and adding vinegar or sugar until you get the desired flavor. Finally add caraway seeds and heat until ready to serve.

While it sounds simple, it isn't so easy to get the desired taste like one gets in a restaurant. When I came back the next day, Jana was quite keen to hear how my cooking had progressed.

"You know, I'm just amazed that you and Dan are doing this cooking!" she said. "At home my husband would never do such things for himself. If I was not at home, he would either eat at the pub or die of starvation! You know, Douglas, we women in Czechoslovakia are slaves." She said this without much humor. Despite being guaranteed equal rights under the Czechoslovak Socialist constitution, and despite the supposition that socialism had done away with inequality, racism, sexism and a whole host of other "isms," women were generally kept too busy to ever consider something like feminism.[3]

In one newspaper article, the Czechoslovak minister of Foreign Affairs, Dana Hunatová, described how she rarely had any food in her household as she simply didn't have time to go to the store. Hunatová had to scrub the floor with her hands, do much of her laundry by hand, stand in the endless lines and cook for her husband.

"When I don't have to spend four hours doing the laundry," one woman told me one afternoon, "I'll have time to consider being a feminist." Other women just seemed suspicious of feminism, sensing it was yet more dogmatic propaganda for them to swallow. Some told me they were afraid feminism was something that would turn them into lesbians or force them to give up their femininity.

Renáta put it most plainly: "There was, under socialism, a special day on March 8 just for women. It was called International Women's Day and everyone was supposed to celebrate the importance women

181

had in building socialism. Men would begin their day by buying flowers for the women and taking them to their sweet wives. Then the men would finish in the pub in the early afternoon and in the late evening the women would have to go around all the pubs and collect their drunk husbands and take them home and put them to bed. That was our feminism."

Not long after, when a friend in the United States wrote us that she was having difficulty with her husband, Jana was sympathetic.

"Once I packed my husband's bag and told him that he would be leaving. I was going to turn him out. But then I realized that he would have no place to live, as Czech women are always given custody of their flat in a divorce. So we are still married."

Depending upon who you talked to or which statistics you read, a large sexual gulf existed between men and women. Perhaps the largest gulf of sorts between men and women in the local culture was sexual. Despite that sexual intercourse is common among teen-agers and sexual infidelities were common, women never were given an opportunity to develop their own sexuality. While a study in 1992 showed that only a tiny fraction of women considered themselves to be orgasmic, and an even higher number didn't know what an orgasm was, a Czech friend of mine violently disagreed.

"Women have not given themselves a chance to develop their sexuality properly because they've been too busy fucking since they were 15!" he told me heatedly. My friend, who spent seven years teaching at an all-girls high school recounted numerous stories of girls having multiple partners during the course of a month or even a week. "What *is* typical," he continued, "is that a husband and wife will have several minutes' sex (if any) with one another, while in their extra-marital activities they'll engage in five-hour marathons with their lovers."[4]

Worse, birth control was usually limited to condoms. True to the socialist habit of fouling up every product possible, the Czech-made condoms were painful to wear, and consequently a lot of men simply rejected them. The Czech-made pill contraceptive, which was available was essentially a shotgun blast to the ovaries and consequently, many women avoided it. Only 15 percent of women of fertile age used IUDs and only 5 percent used the pill.

"You don't force a man to wear a condom?" I once asked a woman.

"The man just knows when it is time," she said, shrugging. Knows when it's time? I think not. Even the best musicians sometimes mess up their parts.

As it was, abortion was extremely common in Czechoslovakia and there were as many as 160,000 in 1988. An abortion could be performed legally twice a year and cost about 500 crowns (today its about 4,000 crowns).[5]

If women hadn't even begun to consider feminism, homosexuality was a taboo that few would admit existed. Viktor once told me straight-faced that he was sure he had never met a homosexual in his life. While there were gay clubs in Prague, they were hard to find. Marc Huestis, a gay filmmaker from San Francisco, told me once that he had had a great time visiting Prague because there was a reclusive, mysterious element to gay life in Prague that simply had vanished in the United States.

"I had all these guys trying to sleep with me so that maybe I'd fall in love with them and then take them to the United States!" Huestis said laughing.

Shortly after Bush's visit, Dan and I began planning a Thanksgiving dinner, which we both agreed was of vital importance to our spirits. Jarka and Viktor volunteered the use of their flat and Pavel, Milena, Renáta and Jarda were invited. The week before Thanksgiving, we fanned out like detectives searching for every available bit of produce. Jana kindly arranged for the school to order a large turkey through the canteen (turkey wasn't very popular, we discovered).

"Really, I can't believe you men are going to cook!" Jana again laughed as I lugged the 4.5-kilo turkey up the stairs to our office. "I don't think my husband can boil water!" Jarka also seemed very skeptical that two men, even if they were from America, could make a large dinner.

By Friday night, we had assembled a number of ingredients, but were missing traditional spices and side dishes like yams or even small onions. But we had plenty of carrots, potatoes and garlic. I made stuffing by leaving bread out for several days to make it stale and then proceeded from scratch. On Saturday morning, we prepared everything we needed at the Dům and then loaded it all into boxes which we attached to a luggage cart. On the metro, people smelled the cooked garlic and butter and poked each other, all the while looking around to find the source of the smell. We had to trundle the cart through the metro, onto two trams and finally, down the hill from the castle, the cart rattling and the boxes shaking so much we thought we would lose everything.

Once at the flat, we worked like bandits to get the turkey into the oven by 3 P.M. and then boil potatoes and slice bread and make a small salad. Gradually, the others appeared dressed in their best clothes. As we hadn't said anything about dress in advance, both Dan and I were very pleased and even humbled by their respect. Shortly after six, Pavel staggered in with a case of beer and I suspected that the evening would be a good one. I was right, because even if our friends didn't grasp the meaning behind Thanksgiving, they seemed to understand the concept of a feast as everyone sat down to one of the largest dinners I had ever seen.

Sometime before midnight I crept off to try and sleep some of it off. When I got up around three o'clock, much of the gang, Dan included, was still hard at it, now diligently working their way through a bottle of a bitter liquor called Fernet while playing more Phil Collins and Ozzy Osborne.

Several days after our feat, Jarka appeared during one of our breaks at school and informed Dan and myself that Viktor wanted to make dinner for us the following week.

"He saw that two American men can cook and now he said he wants to try," Jarka said, barely containing her spluttering laughter. "It will be perfect!"

On the appointed night, Dan and I presented ourselves at their flat with a fresh bottle of wine. From the minute Jarka opened the door it was clear that things had not gone so well.

"Viktor has been fighting with the food. I think the potatoes are winning," she said in a near whisper. Wisely, Viktor had chosen to make potatoes *au gratin,* which was fairly easy to prepare. Somewhere along the line, things had taken a turn for the worse and Jarka had to help. Then the two of them had ended up arguing. Dan and I found Viktor sitting at the dining room table with a long face.

"I'll do something I know how to do," he said irritably and reached for his wallet. "I'll get beer."

"So what if you needed Jarka's help," Dan said later, digging into the supper. "It's great." We all praised Viktor's cooking and his spirits seemed to lift a bit. But he never bothered trying to fix a meal again.

16

Winter Blues

The national song of winter in Prague is the sound of someone blowing his nose. From the gentlest, daintiest sniffle to the most generous honking bellow, noses and sinuses can be heard being cleared everywhere: from the worker on the tram who whisks out an extremely sodden and soiled handkerchief and lets fly, to the child who has a perpetually running nose like a leaky faucet. If the cold air doesn't make your nose run, the coal smoke and general poor health endured by people will. Normal American-styled tissues seem to be unable to withstand the fury of a Czech-sized snort in winter. In my house, tissues are kept everywhere within handy reach.

Our bodies were buried under layers of sweaters, overcoats, thick socks and clumpy, ungainly boots. Entering shops, businesses or restaurants was a burden: there was the ceremonial searching for a coat rack, which was usually full, forcing you to drape your overcoat over the back of your chair where it got stepped on or tripped over by a waiter. Then there was the removing of the gloves and the wet scarf and the blowing of the nose and the adjusting of the tangled sweater. While this was transpiring, I was stuck at the door, blinded temporarily by fogged over glasses. It's a pity they don't market glasses with defrosters like in the rear windshields of cars.

Old-timers like to remember winters in Prague when it regularly snowed up to a foot. I have seen photos from after the turn of the century of crowds gaily skating on the Vltava river in a sort of winter carnival. But with the tremendous amount of heavy industry and pollution in Prague, the air in the city rarely creates snow in great amounts.

When the snow is fresh, or just beginning to fall on the frozen streets, Prague is a wondrous sight. Streetlights tinkle and glow, reflecting the drifting flakes. Gradually, the snow piles up in crevices, along sidewalks, on railings and across the red tiled roofs in a perfect way that cannot be recreated by any artist. Whether you view it as the work of God or Mother Nature, it is breathtaking to behold in its still, crystalline beauty.

The first time it snowed enough to remember, we were out celebrating Dan's *svátek* or "name day." One of the sweeter events in Czech culture is the celebration of a person's official "name day," an event unique to European calendars. Each day has a special name, drawn from Christian designations: Monday is David, and the next Eva and the following day Markéta and so on. Usually the event calls for the giving of small gifts like flowers or candy and a special dinner. And—yes, you guessed it—yet another reason to drink.

When Dan's appointed day came round in mid-December, the two of us and our circle of Czech friends trooped off to a good restaurant where we drank schooners of beer and ate the house specialty, a huge potato pancake cooked around a pork chop. Entering the restaurant in the early evening, the weather had been threatening. Leaving the restaurant shortly before midnight, the world was transformed: huge snowflakes were falling out of the sky, landing on cars that were already drifting in snow. There was already an inch or more of snow on the cobblestones.

Ten seconds later someone threw the first snowball and suddenly the street erupted into a huge snow fight. I dove for cover behind a car and hurriedly assembled a pile of fresh snowballs.

It was all very jolly, with each of us whooping and laughing madly. That is, until the police drove up in their small yellow and white car. They stopped the car, rolled down the window and spoke sharply to us.

"Get out of the street! Immediately!"

I generally have problems with big, leering authority figures, so I told the police to go to hell. It was not a good idea.

"What'd he say?" the policeman asked one of my friends in Czech.

Pavel, who is tall as a center on a basketball team, stepped in front of me and quickly explained that I was a foreigner who didn't understand the rules and that we would all very happily get out of the street. The police drove off and we continued quietly towards the metro stop.

"I know what you're thinking," Pavel said as we walked along, the snow dancing onto our foreheads. "But the same rules don't apply here. The police can do what they want and although they are stupid, they will do with you what they want."

As we walked off into the night, enjoying the new snow, throwing an occasional snowball, I silently reproached myself for acting so angrily in a country that wasn't even my own. Not only what I had said wasn't a smart idea, it was unfair.

Within two days, the snow was reduced to a muddy, slushy mush that stuck to boots and became a nuisance, filling potholes, dripping off eaves and splattering across the roads whenever a truck or car rumbled past.

The gray winter had begun. Days rolled by without a glimpse of the sun. Just a unending series of cold mornings, afternoons and even colder evenings.

Both Dan and I were sick of cabbage nearly every night, but it seemed to be the only vegetable I could find in the stores anymore. My mother sent me a clipping from *Sunset Magazine* that detailed new Czech recipes called, "Ask the Czechs about a serious winter meal," which showed a group of happy people busily digging into plates of fresh green asparagus and spooning up dishes of blackberry cordial and drinking glasses of Alsatian Gewurztraminer. Ask the Czechs about a serious winter meal indeed, I thought sourly as I scanned the article. Several days later I chipped a tooth on a slice of raw cabbage.

One of the more interesting diversions Dan and I found during the winter season was attending a series of balls held in the city from late fall until early spring. As opposed to youth in the United States, nearly every teenager, male and female, still regularly attends dance school where he or she is properly instructed in the finer points of the waltz, polka, tango, foxtrot and cha-cha. The kids then use these skills at their school ball—called a *ples*—held by various groups. It seems there is a ball to fit nearly every social group. The police have a dance, and so do the railway workers. The various political parties chip in with their own events and the various departments from the universities also sponsor balls. One of the most popular each year is the Hunter's Ball, where guests can win freshly killed game. Depending on where the event is being held, and who is staging it, the ball can either feel exceptionally classy and elite, or you can wind up feeling as if you've crashed somebody's wedding by mistake.

The ball season goes well back in Czech history, to the time when Czechs were attempting to revive their national identity in the early and mid-1800s. Although balls were a traditional part of the bourgeois nobility, in Prague, all types of people came out to dance, especially to several particular "Czech Polkas" that became very popular.[1]

In late December we joined Jarka and Viktor at a graduation ball for a local high school. It was a lavish affair, with several live orchestras and maybe a pop band to close things off. We danced to a 1920s-styled jazz orchestra and then finished off in the early hours to the Velvet Underground Revival Band, a well-known Prague group that featured several of the members from Půlnoc. The band's letter-perfect cover versions of songs like "Sweet Jane," "Heroin" and "Rock & Roll" were almost chilling—so good, in fact, the group had backed up Lou Reed in concert when Reed had visited Prague earlier that year. In one of those strange quirks of music, the Velvet Underground became very popular in Czechoslovakia in the 1970s as the band's dark, brooding observations about life meshed perfectly with the difficult first years under "normalization." It was a very strange experience to find myself dancing around an ornate ballroom to Lou Reed's "Head Held High" with a group of students who were not even alive when the Velvets recorded.

At one point during the night, the students paraded about on one of the lower floors with a huge sheet stretched out while guests hung over the balconies and threw money down onto the sheet and the students "for luck." The money went to pay for projects like the ball and other student activities. There were some speeches and each graduate was introduced. Then everyone got back to dancing again. I staggered around the floor like an elephant who had just been crammed into shoes for the first time. After several turns around the dance floor, I decided to respectfully watch from the safety of a table where we had assembled an array of wine and champagne. The dances in Prague tend to go on into the wee hours of the morning, and there seems to be a bit of a contest to see who can stay out longest. I lost, early on.

17

Klaus: Privatization Architect

K laus was quickly emerging as perhaps the second most important figure in the government behind Havel. Although Klaus' quiet, unassuming physical presence makes him appear rather bookish, he is one of the few politicians to emerge from the former Warsaw Pact countries who truly can hold his own against Western politicians.

The first time I saw Klaus in person, I was surprised, as he didn't necessarily mesh well with Havel's slightly swinging crew of dissidents and neophyte government reformers. A moderately sized man, with a carefully trimmed mustache and owlish face, Klaus seems to peer daintily at the world from behind his silver-rimmed glasses. As opposed to jocular, personable Ministers like Dienstbier, Klaus was more guarded and reserved. He wasn't a dissident, and despite having been placed in several obscure clerk jobs because of his outspoken economic views within the Czechoslovak State Bank, he never signed Charter 77 or worked with any of the traditional groups opposed to the government.

Fastidious, wonkish and seemingly with a perpetual chip on his shoulder, Klaus is the yang to Havel's ying. It is hard to imagine two men who are so uncommonly dissimilar, yet it is also hard to image the development of Czechoslovakia after communism without Klaus's presence in the government. Klaus' economic theories were sharply focused, drawn from the playbook of traditional free market economists like Milton Freedman. As much as Havel has represented the people's right to an open and free society, Klaus has represented the other face of the revolution: the right to work in an unregulated economy, to direct and master one's own future based upon your own work and ideas; ultimately, the right to make money and hold title. Klaus seems to be eternally looking towards the future, rather than towards some murky past. He rarely speaks of the struggle to overthrow communism and surrounds himself with people who were but shadow figures in the dissident movement.

"He was different than the other economists after the revolution," a factory worker told a reporter for *The Prague Post* in 1992. "He looked like a professional manager who could put the whole economic mess that the Communists had left behind in order."[1]

He likes jazz (I once saw him sit through a ferocious Ornette Coleman concert without squirming) tennis and skiing. This is not a man who prefers whiling away hours in a pub over endless glasses of beer. He is highly articulate and speaks wonderful English, a byproduct from a short stint spent at Cornell University in 1969.

Yet, for all his accomplishments, Klaus remains somewhat in Havel's shadow, the person everyone wants to meet second. He can be suffocatingly arrogant in both Czech and English and does not suffer fools gladly, as I have seen him practically garrote reporters in press conferences like they were errant children sent to annoy him during an important lecture.

Klaus has had to steer the country through some extremely difficult periods, especially just before the first wave of price liberalization and privatization in January, 1991. And it was a potentially difficult period. Many reporters who arrived to cover Bush's speech in November had written stories about how the "Velvet Revolution was not going so smoothly in Czechoslovakia." The reporters pointed to the arrival of a peep show in downtown Prague near where students had first clashed with police before the revolution, as a sure sign that things had changed—and not for the better. As it was the only peep show in town—and it closed less than several months later—God help them if they ever blunder into Times Square in New York.

While there was some hoarding going on in anticipation of price hikes, it was hardly the panic buying being described in these doom and gloom articles.

"Back last November when people went into the streets, they thought communism would fall and they would have cars," Rudolf Blažek, one of the key student leaders from the 1989 revolution was quoted in *The Boston Globe.* "But now, people don't know what is coming. People are uncertain."[2]

In municipal elections held at the end of November, the Communist Party gained an impressive 17 percent of the vote, which led to concern that perhaps enthusiasm for the economic reform was fading.[3] But most people, including Renáta, were unmoved.

"These people voting for the Communists are in the small towns and villages where they have this stupid loyalty to such people," she said. "They know many of the candidates personally, too." I was amazed, however, that so many people could continue to support a system that had ruined their country.

The day after the elections, we arrived at school to find Jana smiling broadly.

"You see," she said, "there are people here who are concerned about the future and don't think it will be so easy!" If Dan and myself were having trouble understanding why some people had voted the way they had, many Czechs we were meeting had terribly misguided notions about life in the United States. One evening, we had dinner with Hanna and Tomáš, a fine newlywed couple whose greatest dream was to travel to America and pick oranges just like Jack Kerouac in *On The Road.*

"Do you think this is possible?" Tomáš asked us. Dan, who had an uncle who was a farmer, said he would look into the matter. I tried to think how to tell him about migrant workers' camps.

Then Tomáš showed us pictures of "flower children" in San Francisco's Golden Gate Park and asked us "where do these people live today?" I hadn't the heart to tell him that a lot of them had become computer programmers, gas station attendants or school teachers.

Over and over, Dan and I were quizzed about life in America: Yes, we had our own cars. Yes, we all had telephones. Yes, these things were generally normal—provided of course one had a job and was lucky to have money. But my words about the need to have money went unheard. It was assumed all Americans had money, were tan, had good looking wives, girlfriends, husbands and lovers. Life was easy like the oranges on the trees.

Others wanted to know if I was scared walking the streets with so many dangerous people (read: minorities). What a vision people had of our country! Of people being shot as soon as they step off the plane or being handed a million dollars just because they are Americans! It would be funny if the violent side of America wasn't so pronounced, threatening and real.

Often, after meeting people for the first time, they would inevitably question me, after an appropriate interval of time, on how I felt about "America's *meeenority* problems." While I would try and explain as gently as I could, that I couldn't care less what the color of somebody else's skin was, my words always seemed to fall on deaf ears.

While the racism I usually encountered in Prague on the surface seemed less virulent and more naive than American racism, I gradually came to see that racism is essentially the same all over the world. Much of the inherent racism in Prague seemed to spring from a general uninformed perspective as there weren't many minorities in the country over the years. In short: Africans were still living in huts and dancing, American Blacks rioted and were still barely out of slavery and blacks (or any other minority group for that matter) in Czechoslovakia circa 1989 were oddities to be observed, from a distance.

Not long after, one of my students brought in a set of flash cards with English words and helpful pictures. I had visions of using the cards in class. That is, until I got to the "negro" card which featured a Little Black Sambo rendering of an African holding a spear.

There was, and still is, a number of food and domestic products that incorporate racist drawings into their packaging, including strange bags of "Chinaman" rice from Cambodia that had a sketch of a bucktoothed Chinese person wearing an oversized coolie hat. One day, while hiking in the Beskydy mountains near the Polish border with some older kids from school, we happened across a small snack bar along the trail. There are dozens of these snack bars located everywhere in tourist walks; Czechs like to joke that there will be a snack bar outside St. Peter's Gates.

After persuading my kids to order Cokes instead of shots of vodka, I purchased a bag of chocolate-covered chunks of banana that were delicious. The bag contained a lovely illustration of yet another bug-eyed black woman, this time with huge white lips and a huge bone through her nose.

If Czechs and Slovaks were curious about blacks, they displayed an open and undisguised hatred for the thousands of Gypsies who lived in the region. I can't for the life of me imagine two cultures that are as diametrically opposed, as the loud, generally uneducated Gypsy culture (a byproduct of not being allowed into Czech schools) is in direct conflict with the quiet, more reserved Czech and Slovak culture. While there is a Gypsy political party, little has been done to integrate the Gypsies (more properly called Romanies) into society. Czechs say you can't trust a Gypsy; the Gypsy says the Czech won't give them a chance to be equal. Very few people understand who or what the Gypsy culture is all about, and even fewer can speak their exotic tongues, which are often a mish-mash of languages — from Romanian to Farsi. In a public opinion poll published in 1994, more than 62 percent of the people said they would like to see tougher discrimination laws passed against certain parts of society, including the Gypsies. Vietnamese and Arabs were farther down the list.[4]

One evening we went to a local club to see Jasná Páka (Sure Thing or Safe Brake), a popular band that had long been part of the Czech rock scene. While we were waiting for the concert to begin, a huge middle-aged man with thick square glasses near us picked up a small girl and started spinning her around by her hands. The girl laughed and yelped with pleasure as she spun round and round and the man, who obviously had already consumed a lot of drink, obliged the girl by spinning her faster and faster.

At first, people were laughing and smiling at the scene, that is, until the girl's feet started to hit some of the people in the head. Curiously, no one said a word, and when the girl's feet swirled clipped my head, I was less than pleased. The man, who had a receding hairline and was sweating heavily underneath the big glasses, didn't seemed to notice anyone. He was just intent on swinging that girl around. When the girl's feet clipped me again, I got angry.

"Goddamnit!" I shouted in Czech. "Watch out!" Renáta grabbed my arm and hissed at me.

"Don't say anything, please. You don't know who he is," she said.

"I know who he is," I said. "He's an asshole."

"Not really. I will explain to you later about him." So I rubbed my head and watched as the man, who had set the girl down and now was was still swaying and dancing to the music coming from the PA speakers. Suddenly, he began undressing. First he took off his shirt, revealing a sagging beer belly and then he began playing with his belt. The belt came off, as did his shoes and finally, his trousers. People were smiling and watching and pointing. Down now to only his jockey-styled underwear, he danced and jiggled to the music with a big happy grin on his face. This dance went on for about ten minutes and then he stopped and put his clothes back on and sat down.

I got up to go to the bar, all the while thinking what a crazy person this guy seemed to be. I was patiently waiting in line at the bar when the man came tearing out of the auditorium and marched up to the bar. He physically shoved me aside and gestured loudly at the bartender for a bottle of wine. When I get angry, I lose my ability to say anything rude in Czech, let alone anything coherent. So my next sentence came out in English:

"Listen you asshole, why are you so rude?" The man turned and looked at me.

"Fuck off," he said in English through a heavily accented, slurry voice. "Fuck you again." Then he turned away and mumbled to the bartender. I decided I didn't need a drink that badly and wandered away. Several days later at the *Rock & Pop* offices, Daniel explained to me who the loudmouth was.

"His nickname is Magor, which means 'crazy person' in Czech. His real name is Ivan Jirous and probably everyone here knows of him or has seen him before. He's very well known."

An art history professor at Charles University in the late 1960's and writer, Jirous had become the manager and "spiritual leader" of the Plastic People of the Universe. Wild, unpredictable, clever and often brilliant, Magor served as a sort of Czech Ken Kesey to the Plastic People, helping them arrange concerts, lecturing to them about Czech history and in the process becoming a guru to the legions of young Czech fans who followed the Plastics throughout the 1970s. When the Czech authorities tried to keep the band from performing live, it was Magor who found ways around the legal blockades and managed to obtain permits for live performances in rural towns in the Bohemian and Moravian hinterlands.[5]

Eventually the government put an end to all of the shenanigans and threw several members of the band into jail for various amounts of time. Magor himself received an eighteen month stint. Through the 1980s Magor and the Plastics had continued their elusive tango with the government, going through occasional stretches where clearances to play live seemed within sight, only to be snubbed out in the end. Magor himself moved away from the group, but had shed none of his characteristic lunacy.

"And now," Daniel continued, "he likes very much to dance naked, or almost naked. He recently got arrested for fighting the police and dancing naked, even though the bartender said it was all right. It seems he went to this pub outside of Prague in the afternoon and told the bartender when he arrived that if he got drunk, he might want to dance naked. Jirous asked him, 'Do you have a problem with this?' and the bartender said, 'No, we're all adults here.' So Jirous went and got drunk and took his clothes off and danced about. The police came and arrested him for dancing naked in a public place and Jirous got terribly angry and as they were carrying him out he was screaming that he had asked permission."

Later Jirous was fined 4,000 Czechoslovak crowns by a court for disturbing the peace and attacking a public official. At the trial, Jirous' defense said that he had only been inspired by the Frank Zappa song which goes: "You can even take your clothes off when you dance."[6]

Daniel laughed very much and then recounted other times when he had nearly gotten into fights with Jirous.

"When he's sober, he is brilliant," Daniel said, "but when he is drunk, which is often, he can be a real fucker."

And so it seemed. Since then, I have seen Jirous numerous times (although not doing the naked dance again), always with a drink in his hand and always with a small group of followers parading behind him, hanging onto his every utterance.

A spin through the Plastics' music is challenging, even for people who may appreciate the modal squall of extreme free jazz or Frank Zappa-Captain Beefheart compositions. It is a heady stew of sonic disturbance: viola, free saxophone, throbbing bass and hypnotic lyrics. Although the group foundered into several different musical projects after the revolution, including the aforementioned Půlnoc, the Plastics have regrouped several times to play live and in 1993, they released an extensive, elaborate multi-CD box set that for the first time brought together many of the recordings which beforehand had only been available on *samizdat* cassette.

Havel described the Plastics' music as "a profoundly authentic expression of the sense of life among these people, battered as they were by the misery of the world. There was disturbing magic in the music, and a kind of inner warning. Here was something serious and genuine, an internally free articulation of an existential experience that everyone who had not become completely obtuse must understand."[7]

Interestingly enough, Magor appears, dancing naked, on the cover of Půlnoc's second album *City of Hysteria*.

Dan and I spent a lot of evenings trying to see as many Czech musicians and bands as possible. In early December, we attended the Prague Jazz Festival, which has had a long tradition in Prague and was one of the few officially sponsored major musical events of the year (the other being the Classical music oriented "Prague Spring"). While we sitting at a table backstage with Daniel and several other photographers waiting for B. B. King to take the stage, Daniel introduced us to Lubomír Dorůžka, a slightly stooped, elderly man who had been one of the main festival organizers for years and one of the country's premiere authorities on jazz.

"I have always had trouble arranging things for the festival," he told us in halting English. "Every year it was difficult, but of course now, we have no problems, but we also will have no money for these Western artists."

He told us, how in the mid-1960s, he was able to arrange for many well-known jazz musicians to come to Prague because the government was slowly liberalizing its restrictions on culture.

"I brought Louis Armstrong here in 1961," he said proudly, raising a finger in the air for emphasis. "But then after 1970 and the invasion, we couldn't have such nice festivals." He went on to tick off the list of important musicians and bands that had come to the festival over the years: Duke Ellington, the Modern Jazz Quartet, John Hammond, Jr. and Sarah Vaughan. More often than not, Dorůžka said, the government knew next to nothing about jazz.

"Once," Dorůžka said, "I got a call from the authorities who said, 'we have an offer here from a musician named Count Basie to come to the festival next year. Do you know of him?'"

Consequently, promoters were able to sneak through some of the more adventurous jazz musicians including: Sonny Rollins, Dexter Gordon, Cecil Taylor and John Scofield.

Jazz has an important place in Czech culture and has undergone several flourishing periods, followed by repressive years. The Nazis forbid any jazz performances, having branded it "Judeo-Negroid." Still, as Czech writer Josef Škovorecký recalls in an essay about the history of jazz music in Czechoslovakia, people used to play the music and dance in small country shacks and mountain villages where the *Schutzpolizei*—Nazi police—couldn't hear them. There was even a jazz band at the ghastly Terezin Ghetto in northern Bohemia called the Ghetto Swingers.

"The hours we spent racking our brains over song titles we couldn't understand," Škovorecký wrote. "'Strutting with Some Barbecue'— the definition of the word "barbecue" in our pocket Webster didn't help us at all. What on earth could it mean: 'walking pompously with a piece of animal carcass roasted whole?' We knew nothing—but we knew the music."[8]

In the early 1950s, traditional jazz became very popular as a number of groups, including the Czechoslovak Washboard Beaters, the Prague City Stompers and Memphis Dixie, took the music around the country. Predictably, the Stalinist government took a dim view of jazz and restricted it whenever it could. However, after the rise of rock n'roll in the late 1950s, jazz took a backseat to rock as the most despised music.

18

Christmas and Fried Carp

Christmas came in a ever quickening rush, kicking off the first week of December with Mikuláš, a traditional Catholic holiday celebrating Pope Nicholas 1, who died in 687 A.D. Mikuláš was a fun, light affair for children who go to parties where they are visited by angels and devils whose jobs it is to determine whether the children have been good all year; a few harsh questions from the devil (usually a local neighbor dressed up in red clothes and clutching a hastily made pitchfork) and the children are rewarded with candy to tide them over until December 24.

I'm not sure when or where I was when I learned that the traditional Christmas meal in Bohemia begins with a fish soup and follows with fried carp with tartar sauce, potato salad and beer, but I'm sure I must have looked fairly confused. I wasn't sure if people were kidding me until I looked into one of my guidebooks about Prague and found several references to the aforementioned Christmas Carp. While I certainly didn't expect the Czechs to have precisely the same Christmas traditions as Westerners—ham or roast beef, say—the notion of eating a rather bland fish that was deep fried and slathered in a mayonnaise-based sauce was rather startling.

But owing to Bohemian and Moravian tradition, carp had been the Christmas meal for hundreds of years. Supposedly, carp was the only meat poor people could afford at Christmas and eventually, a whole carp industry sprang up in Bohemia to feed the hungry peasants. At one point between the 14th and 16th centuries, there were more than

78,000 fish ponds in Bohemia alone.[1]

About a week before Christmas, special stands selling carp appeared all over the city. As opposed to the normally limited number of options available to consumers, one actually had many choices to make when buying a carp. First, you could choose your carp from the huge tank or barrel that was set up at each stand. Then, after the wriggling, gray fish was unceremoniously removed from the tank with a net, it was weighed and the customer could decide whether they wanted to take it home alive or have it killed and gutted on the spot.

Some families liked to keep their carps in the bathtub for several days so the fish could be fresher on Christmas Eve. Others liked to have the fish handler at the stand deal with the carp so it didn't stink up the whole house. One afternoon, I stood watching for at least twenty minutes while the fish handler dispatched one poor carp after another with a series of blows to the head with a rubber mallet. One of them was particularly stubborn and refused to quit twitching even after being whacked at least five times. The butcher and the customer giggled and the butcher gave the fish another whack on the head just for good measure. Fish innards, blood and scales trickled off the wooden stand and onto the frozen ground. It was disgusting.

Jana and Dana laughed as Dan and I told them about watching the carp.

"Once I bought the carp alive and took it home and our son played with it in the bathtub for a week," Jana said. "When it came time for Christmas, he started crying when I took it to the kitchen and so finally my husband had to take it to the Vltava and let it go. We ate pork that year!"

A hot Christmas gift that season was a Monopoly-like board game called *Marxeso,* in which the object of play was to avoid being taken to jail for anti-state activities. The game was on sale all over Prague, as were various leftover uniforms, hats, buttons and medals from the departing Soviet army. Most of the people selling these collectors items knew they had something unique and charged fairly steep prices for the little tin badges of Lenin and Marx.

Dan was tired of Prague and interested in doing something different than assemble at Viktor's house for more beer and madness every night during our vacation. He went off with a group of Czechs and Americans to ski and teach conversational English in the mountains. As I was planning to travel on my own right after Christmas, I remained in Prague. Viktor invited me to his mother's home for the traditional meal. His mother was a polite woman whose home was beautifully decorated with oriental rugs and rooms lined with tall bookcases. It was a very festive, warm affair as we ate the carp, which I thought was extremely bony, with tartar sauce and drank several bottles of beer. There was also *kompot*—a mixed canned fruit salad— and plates of good ham and cheese. They had gone out of their way to include me in the gifts and gave me a beautiful crystal pitcher for ice tea or beer. Czech glass is among the best in the world, and it's usually on the top of most shopping lists when people visit Prague.

Later, we went to the Saint Mikuláš (Saint Nicholas') Church in Malá Strana for Midnight Mass. The church, which dominates the Malá Strana area, was built in the early 1700s and is a simply stunning representation of Baroque architecture, with a huge dome that rises high above the other buildings.

As Jarda was working with Czechoslovak Television on a live broadcast of the service, he escorted us high into the normally closed rafters of the building, up towards the front of the altar. From so high up, the choir and organ was nearly deafening.

The church was overflowing with people who were experiencing only their second free Christmas in more than forty years. Although it was so cold inside you could see your breath, there was a feeling of unity throughout the ceremony that I found almost loving.[2] I couldn't understand much of the liturgy being read in Czech and Latin, but I did find the service interesting. In the early morning hours, we walked back up the hill to Viktor and Jarka's flat under the Castle.

Early the next morning, I scrambled quickly to organize my things at the Dům because I was headed for Cologne and Amsterdam. By mid afternoon, I was deep in Germany riding a zippy EC train, marveling at how fast and clean and efficient train travel could be. Amsterdam was a wonderful city, and I would have been happy to walk through its many canals for hours if there hadn't been a steady rain that soaked through my clothes and shoes within minutes. Even worse, the rain never showed any sign of abating during the two days I was there. I spent most of my time running quickly from one doorway to another, keeping warm in various coffee houses and museums. The final blow came when I realized I either had lost, miscounted or been robbed of a significant amount of the colorful Dutch money.

Dan and I spent New Year's Weekend in the Beskedy Mountains, only a few kilometers away from the Polish border, with seemingly every Czech person we had met, including Viktor and Jarka and four-teen others. Even though I was feeling worse and worse from a flu I had picked up from my soggy trip to Amsterdam, I arrived at the bus station in Prague shortly after 7 A.M. to find Jarda opening a huge bot-tle of wine for the trip up to the mountains. He was in a loud, expan-sive mood, and spent much of the three-hour ride loudly singing while he and the others passed the bottle. I held my head in my hands and thought I would be ill.

Despite my dodgy health, I went skiing and took long walks through the snow covered trees (great idea when you're sick!). One evening everyone went out to a local pub and I lingered behind, as I really didn't feel well. I was given sharp instructions before everyone left that I should make sure all the coal heaters in each room were well stoked with coal.

"If they go out," Jarka said severely, leading me through the cabin's seven rooms, "it will be very hard to start them again and the house will be extremely cold."

Later, as I wandered from room to room with a little bucket of coal, I thought about how I had spent the previous New Year's Eve in Pismo Beach in California. Three hundred and sixty five days from a beach to pouring lumps of coal into little pot-bellied stoves near the Polish border. So much could happen in so little time.

New Year's Day brought more than just a few hangovers and quiet despair. The weekend had not gone well for a number of the people in the cabin and there had been fights and bickering between the var-ious couples. Dan and I had avoided the heavy drinkers back at the house and spent the afternoon skiing. By early evening, many of the men were so drunk they could barely rise from their seats.

"I told you it would be like this," Dan said sadly as he helped me assemble a New Year's Eve dinner. "I was having a fine time teaching English and skiing just two days ago and now I'm here with these lunatics." Although people seemed to be hungry, no one seemed sober enough to make any supper. They had spent a generous portion of the day consuming several bottles of peach- and lemon-flavored vodka. After those were gone, they started in on straight vodka. The house was a wreck of beer bottles, overflowing ashtrays, ski boots and sleeping bags.

"Why aren't you drinking, you fuckers?" Jarda said, stumbling up to us. In the background, someone put on a Phil Collins tape for the twenty-fifth time that day. Dan banged a cutting knife on the board in frustration and looked at me angrily. Earlier in the day he had packed his things and tried to leave quietly for Prague before the others had woken up, but Jarka had cornered him at the door and persuaded him to stay.

As the evening grew later, their energy seemed to increase sevenfold until people were outside in the bitter cold, diving from the roof into the deep snow drifts and wrestling each other on the hill. While we shot off handfuls of fireworks and lit sparklers in the dark, several of the men passed out in front of the fire like fallen horses in battle.

"Happy 1991," Dan said, raising a toast at me. "We survived."

The new year saw the introduction of the first major economic restructuring since the revolution. The Czechoslovak crown was revalued and, for the first time, prices were greatly liberalized as subsidies to industries were removed. Overnight, the cost of all consumer goods, including beer, wine, soda, cheese, milk and bread, shot up dramatically. The cost of riding public transport increased from 1 to 4 crowns. It was strange to walk into stores and see the higher prices everywhere. Up to that time, almost every product in the country had the price directly printed on the label, as the cost of food and beverages rarely changed over the course of a year.

Not surprisingly, the new reality caused many to panic and shout that the economic transformation was happening too rapidly and too cruelly.

"Do you know what this is?" Jana said to me one afternoon as she handed me a bottle cap. "It's a frying pan for a family of four!" She must have chuckled over the joke for several minutes. It was a strange thing to watch people facing inflation for the first time in their lives. Up to that point, the economy had all been a game where the government would dole out a small amount for every family to live on (unless one was in the Communist Party, that is) and keep prices relatively in line with the salaries. A family would be able to put food on the table, have a second home perhaps—even a car if they managed to save money for several years. Despite the fact that the stores were generally full, there was no variety to anything, no quality to the goods or services, no chance that one could stumble over more than two varieties of bread or four different kinds of yogurt.

Concurrently, to keep foreign visitors and rich Czechs happy while they were visiting Prague and other bigger towns, the Communist government set up special stores called "Tuzex" that stocked foreign goods, including cigarettes, liquor and clothes. The stores accepted foreign currency and special coupons issued by the government. Tuzex stores carried things the average Czech could never afford, or find, in a normal shop, like foreign-made denim jeans, imported chocolate and foreign liquor and cars.

Trading on the black market for the Tuzex coupons was fierce, and so occasionally, a Czech might be able to afford the coupons and then go to Tuzex.

One afternoon, while heading home from school, I passed a clump of Czechs crowded around something in the subway station. After a few minutes I could see what they were staring at: an automated teller machine. Workmen were still wiping away dust and debris from where they had installed the machine, and the crowd was staring at the machine like a Martian had landed in the station.

"Imagine having enough money to actually store something in there!" a teacher told me the next day over lunch. The ATM had made the front pages of most of the local newspapers. It was actually fairly useless as none of the machines were linked together so one never knew how much had been removed over the course of a month (of course, banking statements were only available monthly).

To prevent companies from merely raising salaries to compensate workers against the inflated prices, the government passed a series of wage caps. In addition, interest rates were jacked up significantly to prevent inflation from taking more of a bite than necessary.

Daniel and other Czechs we spoke with had difficulty understanding how milk could cost five crowns at one store and only four at another. No one had any conception of supply and demand, price competition and most of the normal economic rules that American business lives and dies by. For the first time since the nationalization of the country in 1948, the Czech word *sleva*—sale—took on new meaning for shoppers.

A large fall in industrial productivity throughout the country was due in part to the ending of arms production, particularly tanks, throughout the country. When Havel had first become president, he had solemnly announced Czechoslovakia would no longer make tanks or other heavy weaponry. Before the government's collapse in 1989, Czechoslovakia had produced equipment for many nations, including Syria and Iraq. Havel's policy was gradually reversed and was one of the sticking points between Slovaks and Czechs since Slovakia relied on its majority share of tank factories. There was just too much money to be made making weapons of war.

The privatization of businesses allowed people to stock a larger variety of goods in their stores, so some businesses, like tobacco stands, became more useful as they began offering newspapers, drinks, liquor, gum and other conveniences.

The economic downturn was boosted by the fact that the Soviet Union and other Warsaw Pact countries were no longer buying goods from Czechoslovakia in great numbers—in some case as much as by two-thirds. The Soviet Union was just entering its final death throes and the shock waves from the initial nationalist uprisings in the Baltic States could be felt in Prague.

One morning in January, the teachers called a meeting during a break to raise money for several groups in Latvia, where Gorbachev had recently sent troops to squash an uprising by the local govern-

209

ment. A number of people had been killed at the television station in Vilnius.

"As you can expect," Dana said, as I joined the teachers in their lounge, "this violence is something we can understand." We all chipped in money for relief supplies and one of the teachers cried. After the meeting ended, Pavel, one of the few male teachers at the school, poured himself a large shot of Becherova, a sweetly bitter Czech liqueur (he took any excuse to do this) and said dramatically before downing it, "To the death of Bolshevism!"

19

The Winter Grows Colder

As soon I heard a discussion on the BBC about the "bombing rolling on," I knew the Gulf War had begun. Rolling out of bed, I went in to see Dan, who was already listening to his radio.

"It's started," I said, sitting down on his bed. After listening to the radio together, he got up to take a shower and I went to watch—what else?—CNN. Czechoslovak TV was broadcasting CNN on all of its channels and had brought in translators to cover the English audio.

By the time we got to school, the trams and streets were buzzing with people talking about the *válka* (war). My kids chattered endlessly about how America and the other allies would "be best" and filled in the conversation with the appropriate sound effects of dive-bombing jets and explosions.

With the littlest students, I taught my normal series of classes, but with the older children, I turned on CNN in my classroom and tried to discuss, in reasonably simple terms, the meaning of the war. After hearing of my concern for my several friends who were serving in the Gulf, some of them grasped the fact that the war was a serious business and not a laughing matter.

In the evening, all of us in the dormitory gathered in the television room and watched CNN until our eyeballs nearly fell out. The scene repeated itself for several days until we finally realized that the world wasn't going to blow up. Then we learned to live with the war.

One evening, Dan and I sat in a pub and listened to the Czech edition of *Voice of America* describe the day's activities in Iraq. The pub was noted for having regular live music provided by locals who would come down each night with their instruments and sing Czech folk songs until the pub closed. Somehow, the pub owner had managed to acquire a whole range of interesting beer glasses, including some marked for the U.S. Thirty-Second Airborne Division, whose motto, "Death From Above," was cheerfully printed with a skull and crossbones on the side of each glass. Despite being terribly smoky, the pub had a friendly atmosphere. The musicians played well and one could stay as long as they wanted.

It was good to have lively places to hole up in each night as there was no doubt about it: the winter was becoming terribly cold. The cost of coal had gone from 180 to 400 crowns in one day, a jump of 234 percent.[1] More than fuel oil and gas, coal is a key lifeline for keeping things running as it is used in more than half of the buildings and homes. Even worse, the country couldn't afford to import supplies so there was a growing shortage of coal.

Jana's face was tense as she told us school might be shut down temporarily.

"It's very cold, you know, and there simply may not be enough coal for the school. It's easier to keep children at home. Besides, if we can't heat the school, we can't have classes. We'll know next week."

In early February, it was announced the school would shut down for more than a week to save coal. It took more than thirty seconds to restore order in my class after the message was read on the loudspeaker by the vice principal. I asked Dana what it all meant.

"It means you are free, Douglas, to do whatever it is you'd like. We are very lucky," she said. "In a strange sort of way, I suppose. Relax, enjoy yourself."

Dan and I kept ourselves busy by skating and playing hockey on a frozen lake near the Dům and working on various articles for newspapers in the United States. I also spent several days traveling east with Jarka and one of her friends to see the large town of Olomouc and then on to her grandmother's home in Moravia. The grandmother served me so much food I thought I would be ill. There is a Czech expression, said while drinking, that you must always have a second drink, because "you have a second leg." That weekend, I must have had fifty legs.

Olomouc, which has a large university, was an extremely lively and pretty town, especially as it was covered in snow. We walked past a huge botanical gardens and along the lovely Morava river which makes a slow s-bend through the city. Once, we came across a series of billboards that had been used in the past to display pictures of the party leaders. Now, the frames were full of pictures of Havel and the other government leaders.

"Look at that," Jarka said, pointing at the display. "Two years ago, I remember the signs saying something like, 'Peace and prosperity for all' or something. Now it is all Havel. But it just seems like so many words."

On the trip back to Prague, the train roared through empty, snow covered fields and past aging train stations that were deserted except for a lone station operator standing in front with a little indicator light, watching as the cars rumbled along. In the severe cold, everything seemed to shine and shimmer. It was so cold the Vltava had frozen clean across for more than 200 years.

One bleary evening it was too cold to do anything useful and Prague was suffering one of its occasional "inversions," where foul air gets trapped down at ground level for days on end. It hurt to breathe outside. I was bored at home, there was nothing on television worth watching and I didn't want to go out to a pub. I couldn't even open the window because the air was unhealthy and smelled.

"You remember this," Renáta said. "This was socialism. You couldn't do anything new or different and instead were stuck in the same place doing the same thing every night. There wasn't anywhere to go and you couldn't leave the country. Everything was broken and still you couldn't fix it. And now you can't open the window."

Her statement reminded me of something Pavel had told me some months before.

"The worst thing that the government may have done is that it just plain bored people to death," he said. "There was nothing to do and everything was generally mainstream because it couldn't be controversial."

The so-called theory of "normalization" after the Soviet invasion in 1968 was aimed at pacifying the people into submission. Writers who had published openly during the Prague Spring were forced from their jobs, film directors were demoted and all open protest stifled. Normalization was presided over by Gustáv Husák, who, despite having been persecuted and jailed during the 1950s show trials, attempted to make Czechs and Slovaks "forget" the Prague Spring had ever happened.

The longer the winter continued, the more I wondered if it would ever be warm again. "Like everything, Douglas," Jana said one morning at school, "we have a saying for this: Březen za kamna vlezem, duben, ještě tam budem. *In March, we go behind the heater. In April, we're still there.*

"I'll save you a place," I said.

The winter was dominated by a series of trips, including two one-day excursions with the kids from school to Munich and Furth I. Wald, a small German border town. In Munich, Dan and I watched an anti-Gulf War parade and a pro-war protest file by the window less than four minutes apart. We nearly froze to death on one of the coldest days of the winter as we walked about the town. One of my students told me he was going to go look at the McDonald's.

"It's too expensive to eat there," he said sadly and walking away in the direction of the Golden Arches.

On my birthday in March, Dan and I rented a car and spent the weekend driving all over southern Bohemia. We slowly covered several beautiful towns, including České Budějovice and Český Krumlov, where the cities are built up almost like they were in the middle ages, with main squares featuring medieval architecture and small, narrow streets. Around the towns—once one gets away from the ever present identical housing complexes—the land rises and falls in great, sweeping undulations through green fields and dense forests. From moment to moment, little villages appear, resplendent with one local pub, one small meat store, a bread or ice cream establishment and perhaps several houses. Off in the distance, there are ruins of castles. Cows, goats and sheep meander though the fields. As in northern Bohemia, this area was once rife with German speaking citizens, but they were all removed from the country after 1946. Today, Southern Bohemia is a playground for rich Austrians who drive the few hours north to walk in the Šumava mountains that line the border between the two countries.

I felt close to a breakthrough of sorts. Despite a light snow on the day of my birthday, the terrible winter chill had eased. I could also see the end of the school year within sight, and I was feeling more settled in what I was doing at work. Although I had some bad days, the kids and I generally understood each other. What's more, I was also able to test them properly on the material from the year and I could tell that many of them actually had learned something.

"How funny it is," I said to Dan one afternoon, "I thought someone like Nikola would be the person who would show me this country, but it hasn't been the case. She gave me the courage to run into this adventure, but now isn't around to see what I have learned. It's a pity."

20

The Pink Tank

In April a 23-year-old local artist named David Černý clambered aboard a Soviet World War II memorial near the center of town and painted an aging T-34 tank with shocking pink paint. Local residents had been petitioning the city to remove the tank, which many citizens believed represented a flagrant distortion of historical facts. Myth had it that the tank in question—no. 23—was the first one to enter Prague when the Red Army liberated the city in May, 1945. In actuality, the first tank to enter Prague was destroyed in battle.

The Communist Party predictably reacted with anger: "I propose that the names of those who sign this petition be made public," wrote one commentator in *Naše Pravda* (Our Truth), the Communist Party newspaper. "This is an insult to our people, a shameless decision by the leaders of Civic Forum (the leading political party) to remove everything that recalls the liberation by the Soviet Army."[1]

The prank, which Černý managed to pull off with the aid of ten friends and a falsified permit from the Mayor's office, generated crowds, conversation and lots of laughter until the memorial was dutifully repainted olive drab several days later by city workers. Apologies were dispatched to the proper Soviet authorities, who obviously were not pleased. Černý said he was just trying to turn "just a weapon on show into something more human. "I don't understand art which is about nothing," he told *Prognosis,* an English-language newspaper in Prague. Earlier in 1990, Černý had added human-like legs to the frame of an East German Trabant, painted it gold and placed it in the center of Prague's Old Town Square.

But the question of whether to prosecute Černý persisted and became a point of debate between reformers and older members of the government who wanted to try Černý under the terms of the "paragraph no. 202," a flexible law created by the Communists in order to arrest and charge people for *Vytrznictvi*: disturbing the peace.

About a month later, on May 16, a handful of Czechoslovak Parliament members came and repainted the tank pink. Apologies were once again dispatched to Moscow, and Havel was forced to discipline his errant colleagues—some of whom were his personal friends from their days as dissidents—like some kind of college fraternity house president.

"I've got to confess that the act of those deputies doesn't garner my admiration," Havel said in telegraphing yet more apologies to Moscow. Havel criticized the deputies for taking justice into their own hands, wondering aloud whether others would join into the act and paint other important sites all over Prague. Soviet Foreign Minister Vitaly Churkin responded several days later, calling the incident a "vile act of political hooliganism" and expressing his desire to see the Parliament members prosecuted.[2]

The Parliament members were immune to prosecution, thanks to a new law giving them immunity over their actions, and the issue of the Pink Tank became a *cause celebre*. A local promoter quickly organized a "Pink Tank" concert, t-shirts and postcards were cranked out showing the tank in all of its pinkness and the parliament members made their point: the country was under new management and the future of paragraph no. 202 was moot.

Czechs with whom I discussed the issue of the Pink Tank told me they believed it fit perfectly with the crazy year.

"Before, Communists used to say, 'What's not allowed is forbidden,' said Aleš Horáček, a friend who was studying to become a doctor at Prague's Charles University. "Now we say, 'What's not forbidden is allowed.'"

Dan had become friends with a young Czech woman named Martina whose family had emigrated in 1968 to Australia. Martina and her brother, David, were living with their uncle who was the drummer and leader of a very popular rock group called Lucie, which played pop-metal appealing to many teenagers.

One afternoon the drummer showed us some of his band's videos and the grandmother had a good time mimicking the ridiculousness of the music, which was a cross between Bon Jovi and Poison. Although he admitted that Lucie was sometimes silly, the uncle was doing very well by Czech standards. He was a nice guy and totally unpretentious, despite having one of the most popular bands in the country.

One of the things I loved most about holidays was discovering various traditions that were totally unknown in the United States (the carp, say). Easter brought an especially good one. I had been noticing long canes made from braided, soft wood in many stores around Prague. Some of these sticks were elaborately adorned with colorful paper and ribbons, while others simply looked like a high school art project that had come to a sad end. I asked Jarka about these objects one afternoon and immediately Viktor began to laugh from behind a magazine he was reading at the table.

"Oh, you mean the *pomlázky,*" he said. "It's an old Bohemian and Moravian tradition. On Easter Monday, men are supposed to hit the girls with the sticks. Then the girls are supposed to serve the men a great breakfast or give them a gift."

"What? Easter Sunday brings a license to beat up the women?" I replied. "And then they feed you?"

"Well, it's supposed to be a bit gentler than that. Anyway, that's what the sticks are for," he said.

"I hate this tradition," Jarka said sharply. This quirky Easter habit varies from place to place, as in parts of Slovakia, women are supposed to be covered in cold water or dragged into a river or lake. Swatting your woman with a stick or pouring cold water on them is supposed to give them new freshness and strength after the long cold winter.[3]

As I had finally begun to feel comfortable in Prague, life seemed easier than it had in the first frantic months. Without thinking much about it, I decided to continue teaching in the fall. I wasn't ready to return home to find another job. I also felt I owed it to the school and the parents to try and correct some of the mistakes I had made teaching during the first year. I was sure that, with more Czech, I would be able to get through to the students with a little more ease. I also wasn't sure about what I would do if I didn't teach English. I still was determined to try and make more money off writing, however.

At about the same time, Viktor discovered that he had been accepted to do a year's physics research at the University of North Carolina at Chapel Hill. He agonized for days trying to decide whether or not he and Jarka should go.

"I don't want to be so far away from here, my friends," he must have said 100 times, despite knowing that there were dozens of Czechs who would give anything to spend a year in the United States.

"I think this is perhaps the best possible thing for Viktor," Jarka told me one afternoon. "If he does not take this, I don't think he will have yet another chance in Prague." There were few jobs open in physics at the university and Viktor also hadn't been working very hard to try and find one, either. He had spent much of the winter bouncing from job to job, and at one point, been working on the street, selling magazines in front of a subway stop. Dan and I had met him one day trundling his magazines in a little cart up the long, cobblestoned street that led up to their apartment.

In the end, Viktor decided that he should go. He and Jarka would be leaving in early May.

Viktor organized a final weekend party at a cottage southwest of Prague in a small town called Rokycany. All of Jarka and Viktor's friend turned out. They had now come to feel like family. Rokycany was filled with small, A-frame houses and cottages and a main street lined with stores. The party was four kilometers from the town.

Before setting out to the cottage Dan and I stopped in for some lunch at a pub in Rokycany, While we were sitting there, a stooped elderly man approached our table. He didn't speak English, but he sure seemed to know a lot about America and the West. He sat down with us and told us about himself.

His name was Václav Sach and he had lived for years in Rokycany.

"I know everyone in town," he said with a twinkle in his eye. "I was twenty-eight in 1945 and was arrested by the Nazis just before the end of the war. But then they had to leave because the American army was coming. I was lucky," he said. He waited for our friend to finish translating and then continued.

"I was the first to see the Americans coming into town," he said, touching his chest. "They came down this street." He stood up and led us outside the door of the pub so we could see the street. Then he tugged at Dan's arm and led us outside. He took us next door to the pub and showed us a new memorial sign that read in Czech:

"To our liberators of the 9ths Inf. Reg, 2nd Division. US Army. In everlasting memory. 7.5.1945–8.5.1946."

Sach pointed at the sign.

"The day in 1946 was the day the Americans left."

We went back inside the pub, Sach talking up a storm.

"I taught everyone here how to play softball after the Americans left. The soldiers taught me how to play the game." Suddenly, he looked up and excused himself.

"I'll be right back," he said and left the pub. We continued to chat and drank another beer. After about 20 minutes, Sach came back into the pub, a softball in his hand.

"This is the softball I had then," he said. "I still have it." I took the ball into my hands. It was almost too soft to use, but it was a softball. It had seen a lot of use. The leather was very worn. We went outside and took some pictures of him in front of the sign with the softball. It was a nice warm moment. Before leaving, Sach gave Dan and myself a five-crown coin each "just for luck."

We left, completely amazed at the man's stories, and carried on to the cottage. The fields all around were green and growing tall with grass. We played soccer and volleyball in the center of a high school soccer field and walked through the small village. While we were walking, Dan and I stumbled on a *zabíjačka*—pig killing. This procedure is deeply rooted in tradition, and each part of the killing is carried out quickly and simply. First, the pig is caught by the village men and either shot or its throat slit with one fast flash from a long butcher knife. Then the carcass is hung from a doorway and the dripping blood collected in a bucket. The belly of the pig is opened from head to toe and the various entrails and organs are removed and rushed into the kitchen where the women work to store or prepare the different parts. The nose and tongue come off, then the legs and other portions of meat. Everything is saved. Even the blood is turned into a thick and bitter soup. Usually, the killing ends in the early evening with a huge feast, featuring some of the fresh meat.

When we returned to Prague, Dan and I organized a softball game for our friends, some of whom had played the game before. Although I had brought my own personal glove from the United States, it was difficult to assemble all the equipment one needs to properly play softball. I finally turned to Robert Shipley, the pleasant official from the embassy, who loaned us baseball equipment owned by the Marines.

On an amazingly warm and sunny Saturday, we assembled in the large Letná Park that overlooks Prague and played a good game for more than three hours. Most of the Czechs not only understood the game, they played extremely well, except for one fellow on my team who couldn't understand why he couldn't smoke when he was batting.

One pleasant spring evening Renáta and I headed out to a suburban theater to see *Music Box,* the highly acclaimed Costa-Gavras film. Upon arriving at the box office, we discovered the theater locked and dark. But since we were more than 45 minutes early for the first screening, nothing seemed terribly amiss, and so we went next door to a restaurant to have a cup of coffee.

When we came back about ten minutes before the scheduled start, the theater was open, but still mostly dark. An elderly woman, presumably the ticket seller, was reading a book while sitting on the couch in the lobby. About six patrons lurked near the theater entrance.

"Can we buy some tickets?" Renáta asked the woman sitting on the couch.

"Not yet," the woman responded and returned to her book.

"Why not?" Renáta asked.

"Because there aren't enough people here yet," the woman said curtly, barely lifting her head from the book. "You need ten people tonight and there are only eight here now." Clearly the ticket matron was trying to play one of my favorite games from the socialist economy, the "I don't see you game."

After a few minutes of shuffling silence, during which time the woman read her book like she was trying to memorize holy scripture and I considered the ramifications of commandeering the projector and showing the film myself, a couple walked in the door and looked around at the group of us in the lobby. A man who had been dejectedly sitting in a chair by the door jumped up excitedly and waggled his finger at the box office matron.

"See! See!" he spluttered. "That makes ten! Show the film!"

The woman sighed, closed her book and went to sell tickets, all the while wearing a tired and hurt expression on her face. Even Jesus probably didn't look so spent as he staggered towards the Cross.

By the time the small group of us had made our way to the seats, the projectionist had already started the film. In the dark, Renáta whispered to me, "Be happy we didn't have to purchase two more tickets."

The auctions to sell off small businesses and stores were continuing apace, with several being held every week in various cities and small towns. Curious, I went to see one of the auctions, which was being held in a large auditorium at the main city hall in Prague. There were more than 100,000 stores, restaurants, hotels up for grab throughout the country. These were the properties that hadn't been claimed in the restitution process. That is, by either the original owners from before nationalization in the late 1940s or by the owner's descendants.

To qualify for the bidding, a party had to deposit at least 10,000 crowns (about $420 then) into a bank and then attend the auction where they had 30 days to pay the remainder of the balance if they were the winner. Most of the businesses went for far more than $420— usually they ranged from $20,000 to as much as $500,000.[4]

Money to buy the businesses came from everywhere: workers who decided to pool their money, investors and Communists who had large savings and were now taking advantage of their previous wealth to play the new game in town. And although foreigners were excluded from the bidding until after the first wave of auctions had been completed, it was clear a lot of money was simply being fronted to Czechs and Slovaks who were in turn buying the businesses for outsiders. Banks were only able to finance a fraction of the loans that people wanted to help them buy a business.

The day I attended, it was loud and stuffy and the properties moved quickly. Like me, a lot of the people had come there just to watch. There was a bread store going out and a small laundry, among others. None fetched a considerable amount of money.

The question of money sources was a thorny one, and more than a handful of people were very angry that the government supposedly wasn't doing more to check on people's backgrounds and stem the flow of so-called "dirty money."

Alex Angell, an employee at Živnostenská Bank in Prague, told a reporter for *The San Francisco Examiner* that he shared the fear of dirty money scams.

"The legitimate fear is that only the people who have the financial resources to buy these businesses, and the people who know the mechanics of running a business, were the very people who the Velvet Revolution was trying to disenfranchise," Angell said. "But the fact is, the privatization process must be pushed through quickly or the momentum of political and economic change will be lost. To do this, people must close their eyes and hope that in five to 10 years, property will be redistributed."[5]

An additional problem was posed by extortionists who forced bidders to raise their bids.

"Some traders search for someone interested in buying something in an auction," said Ivan Cuker, secretary of the Prague privatization committee. "During the auction, these traders drive the selling price incredibly high while their accomplices pressure their 'mark.' They say for instance, 'Give us a few hundred thousand crowns and we'll stop it."[6] The police said they didn't have time to watch over all the auctions and eventually, penalties for false bidding were introduced later in the year. There were also reports that some managers tried win control of their companies and stores and then refused to pay with their whole goal being just to slow down the liquidation process of their businesses.

21

Remembering a Liberation

Not long after our encounter with the Czech softball teacher in the small village, Dan and I traveled to Pilzen for the second annual World War II liberation day ceremonies the first weekend in May. For the second year, Pilzen was honoring World War II veterans because it had previously been illegal to do so. As ridiculous as it sounds, Czechs were taught that the Soviet Union actually liberated Pilzen and the other towns, wearing American uniforms and using American equipment. While this fantastic ruse may have been accepted by some in other parts of the country, in Pilzen, where people had actually met the soldiers, people never forgot.

The government had even torn down a memorial to the American soldiers, but every year, a few brave souls would dare the local authorities by coming to put flowers on the empty block of granite where the statue had rested. Despite the fact that Pilzen was a huge industrial town with huge trade unions (these things supposedly helped guarantee stability in the socialist world), the mere presence of American soldiers for nearly two years meant that its citizens were harder to indoctrinate into the Soviet way of thinking after 1948.[1]

Interestingly enough, the Škoda factory had been one of the few sites of worker unrest in forty years of socialism, when, in June of 1953, local workers attempted to take over the city hall in an angry and violent display over harsh currency reforms. The mayor, Josef Mainzer, tried to calm the workers with socialist platitudes:

"Comrade workers, Mainzer said, "you have a workingman for

227

President ... everything we do is in the interest of the workers."[2]

But the workers would have none of the jingoistic prattle. They smashed up some of the city offices and tried to destroy several statues in the town. Despite hopes that workers in other cities would find out about what was happening in Pilzen and then rally to their side, information never traveled very far and the revolt was quickly and utterly crushed with help from the army. Many workers subsequently lost their jobs or went to jail.

The early 1950s were the worst of times to attempt any kind of public disturbance, as the Prague government was in the final stages of systematically carrying out a series of brutal purges and Show Trials in which hundreds of people (many of them Jewish) were either executed or jailed for "crimes against the state," "Titoism," "Western imperialist espionage." Those who were spared execution were sentenced to life in prison and sent off to the Jáchimov and Příbram uranium mines near Karlovy Vary where they often died from exhaustion or cancer.

An older friend once recalled for me what it was like to listen to the "trials" on the radio: "It was all just so amazing," she said. "People would get up and confess to all these sorts of crimes which they hadn't committed. They sounded like robots."

One man, Otto Fischl, who eventually was executed, said at his trial: "Nothing can justify my grave crimes. I am fully aware of the significance of the criminal activity of the Anti-State and Subversive center. I request a sentence that will fit my heavy guilt."

At the same time, the chief prosecutor, rose to new socialist platitudes during the opening of the trial: "The hearts of all working people struggling to build a bright future for our nation were filled with the deepest contempt and just anger at those who sold themselves to the enemies of mankind—the American imperialists—in order to carry out their inhumane, bellicose plans."[3]

Months later, after the sentences had been carried out, the state had a real problem deciding how to dispose of the ashes of the executed, which had been sitting on a shelf somewhere for several months. Finally, they agreed top drive out of town and dump the ashes in the forest. According to official documents that weren't released until the

Prague Spring in 1968, several men from the interior ministry climbed into a black Tatra and headed out of Prague on a snowy evening. As they drove along, the chauffeur laughed and said it was the first time he had driven ten people in his Tatra: three alive and eleven in a sack. Later when the car got stuck on an icy road, the men were forced to abandon their original plan and instead used the ashes to give their car traction and returned to Prague.[4]

The government's heavy hand in dealing with the blue-collar workers didn't always work, especially in 1989 when the government teetered on the verge of collapse. Miroslav Štěpán, the mean and unforgiving neo-Stalinist boss of Prague, helped to hasten his own demise when he went to address striking workers at a locomotive plant in Prague:

"Comrads," he said from a balcony. "No country can afford to to let 15-year-old children decide when the president should resign and who should be president." Within seconds, Štěpán was whistled and booed off the balcony where he was speaking by the workers who angrily shouted back: "We are not children! We are not children!" The government knew they had truly lost the will of the country when they lost the support of the workers. Štěpán later served more than two years in jail for various abuses of power while in office—the only major figure from the top levels of the government to serve any time. He also wrote a book, *I Was a Prisoner of the Velvet Revolution.*.[5]

On this day in 1991, Pilzen had laid out the welcome mat for the American army. Even before our train pulled into the main station, we could see the Stars and Strips and the Czechoslovak flag fluttering off buildings everywhere in town. Even before we had left the parking lot, a large group of men, women and children dressed in army fatigues and other army memorabilia walked by carrying a huge American flag.

We wandered through Pilzen's large, but somehow uninspiring main square dominated by the huge Gothic St. Bartoloměj church and surrounded by sheets of concrete. The day was cool, and everywhere townsfolk paraded about in American Army uniforms. People stood about eating barbecued sausages and hamburgers while listening to Czech bluegrass and country and western bands.

There were some speeches at a huge rostrum under a sign that read "Liberty For All" placed in front of the church, but a man from the American Embassy told me that the crowds and the speakers weren't as impressive as the year before when both Shirley Temple Black and Havel had spoken to a huge throng. Black had sung "Be an Optimist" and Havel had given one of his more eloquent speeches (that's saying something), stating for the first time that he would order the army to fight if the country was ever invaded.

The veterans came out of the city hall where they had received an official welcome from the Mayor. Wearing little white baseball caps to mark them as veterans, they were seized upon by the waiting crowd, which broke into respectful applause. I was surprised at how well many of the veterans looked. One of them headed towards us and Dan and I stopped him for a chat. He thrust his business card at me. He was from Beverly Hills and sold imported rugs for a living.

"Listen," he said, throwing a comment over his shoulder as he signed an autograph for a man in his forties and his teen-aged son, "When you get back to the United States, go on a low-fat diet. Jesus, the food here'll kill you!"

As other people approached him for autographs or pose for photographs, we talked for with him about the war. There was a low moment when a teenager wanted my autograph too, but I reassured him that it really wasn't necessary.

"He's the important one," I said to the boy in Czech, who nodded, smiled and went off in search of other veterans. The atmosphere was the most genuine display of love for the United States of America that I had ever seen. Everywhere people had buttons saying "Thank You, 1945" or "Never Forget" and there were posters of the soldiers and their equipment for sale everywhere. People paraded the American flag around like it was some kind of sacred object. I'd never seen anything like it in my life, not even at political mixers that I had covered as a reporter. In the United States, those political affairs had been a poisoned hybrid of ultra-nationalist screed flavored by people's none-too-subtle personal interests. This seemed to be a love-in of sorts, a taking stock of the past only to remember.

Even more amazing were the large number of perfectly restored

1944–45 Willys Jeeps that had been left behind by the departing American army. In some cases, locals had stored the jeeps in garages, caves and even underground for years. Obviously, no one had been allowed to drive the things around while the socialists ran the country, and so these jeeps had only been out of wraps for little more than a year. There was quite a bit of a cult surrounding all things from World War II and it seemed as if everyone was trying to outdo the next fellow by having even more correct and authentic arrangements of gas tanks, side lights and horns.

I grew up with a 1946 Willys Jeep and have spent some hours waiting in obscure parts stores while my father hunted for the right engine part to keep the jeep running. The one thing I remember was the number of clubs devoted to preserving World War II vintage jeeps in the United States. From what I could see on the streets of Pilzen, these drivers could beat any of the American clubs hands down in both accuracy and love for their hobby.

Out of the milling crowds appeared Michel and his wife, a young couple we had met during our recent weekend in Rokycany. They took us back to their apartment in a *panelák* on the outskirts of the city and we spent the evening in a pub near a small lake, drinking beer and attempting to speak as best we could with the two of them.

There were more than a handful of the faux-U.S. Army men in the bar and they seemed pleased to have a group of real Americans drinking with them. Later in the evening I was invited to play guitar and sing with a local country band, but I was so tired and woozy from the beers I couldn't remember the words to "Folsom Prison Blues." Needing a breath of fresh air, I walked outside and looked up at the stars. I felt overwhelmed by all of the kindness shown us, especially by Michel and his family.

■

I took the bus to Vienna in late May for a weekend in one of the world's most expensive cities. I honestly cannot fathom how people can afford to live in a city where a soda is nearly two dollars and a ride on the subway more than $1.50. Still, the town was jammed with wealthy-looking Austrians who seemed to be having a great time as they walked

along the ridiculously overblown and pompous government buildings along the tree-lined Burg Ring. As it was the anniversary of
Mozart's birthday, the stores were full of shops selling Mozart para-
phernalia—everything from t-shirts to chocolate candies and glass-
ware. I drew the line at a ceremonial toilet seat (no kiddin') emblazoned
with the composer's smilin' face that played the theme from *Eine
kleine Nachtmusik* (A Little Night Music) when lifted. It seemed
Mozart was in danger of becoming the Elvis of Central Europe.

Prague and Vienna seem to have a small war going on trying to
convince the world that Mozart liked their city more than the other.
To be fair to both cities, Mozart had more work in Vienna, but the
people of Prague appreciated him more. Mozart made several visits
to Prague during his life and *Don Giovanni* (dedicated, in Mozart's
words, "to my people of Prague who understand me") had its debut
at Prague's Nostitz Theater.

Now, I like Mozart as much as the next fellow, but an entire year
of Mozart's symphonies, operas, concertos, trios and other assorted
blather got to be a bit much. As I wandered the stalls in Vienna, casually examining everything from earrings to cardboard cutouts of Vienna
showing all of Mozart's travels through the city, I wondered how
Mozart would have viewed this celebration in excess. From what we
know about Mozart and his short life, the composer probably would
have enjoyed the adulation, even if it was coming a bit too late. I was
also discovering that I didn't like Vienna very much. It wasn't the
high prices that bothered me; I couldn't warm to the grandiose buildings, the serious Austrian personality and the lack of warmth or charm
in the faded *konditorei* cafes that line the elaborate Kartnerstrasse in
the center of town. After several other visits, I eventually grew to
enjoy the city a bit more, especially after I found several restaurants
near the university populated by a younger, hipper crowd.

While the small businesses were slowly being auctioned, many people spent their time trying to get rich as quickly as they could. One of
the people who tried, and succeeded, was Michal Horáček, a former
lyricist for the noted Czech rock band Pražký výběr and a leading

232

member of the Civic Forum group that negotiated with the Communist government in 1989. Horáček, a long-time gambler, had transformed his personal passion for gaming into a small chain of betting parlors called Fortuna. There were several Fortuna offices in Prague, and they looked to me just like the *Off Track Betting* shops in New York's Penn Station: groups of men standing around scribbling on pads, furtively smoking cigarettes and talking to each other like they were bond traders.

On huge chalkboards, the Fortuna staff wrote down the odds of sporting events all over the world, including Soccer matches, horse racing and even American NHL and baseball games. I couldn't see the sense of a Czech betting on an American baseball game, but some still did. At the time, Fortuna was taking in $350,000 a day.[6]

Horáček was philosophical, if not contradictory, about whether or not what he was doing was right for the country at the moment. Betting is a way to learn accountability, he told Dan during an interview. "You may have an idea, but if you are not willing to support this idea with ten dollars from your pocket ... then it is better to shut up.

"What really haunted us for all those decades, going as far back as my cradle, was the collective irresponsibility we witnessed. You could never pin down the person responsible for anything. And it was probably the main reason why nothing really worked in the end."[7]

At the same time, Horáček sought to separate his business from many of the other questionable operations that were flourishing.

"I think we are going through an era of a very wolfish kind of capitalism," he said. "We are going to see some ugly scenes. But we have to go through this partly as a punishment for keeping silent for so long."

22

The Soviets Go Home

I was shocked the first time I saw Soviet soldiers in Prague. I was walking along the street one day when a truckload of them drove up. It was quite something to see them in their olive drab uniforms with matching caps pulled low down around their skulls. Square jawed, with angular, hard-set faces, they looked exactly like pictures I had seen in magazines and on television. I wanted to grab somebody's hand and say, hey, look at this! Real Soviets! But then I realized that people here weren't impressed by their presence in the way that I was. To Czechs, the Soviets were the enemy they had become used to. The soldiers had been in Prague for a long, long time—since 1945 literally, and moreover, had invaded to country in 1968.

I only saw Soviet troops a few times while they were still based in Czechoslovakia. Mostly, they were confined to their bases and didn't travel around much. One weekend, when Renáta and I were staying at her father's summer cottage in Nymburk, about an hour from Prague, I saw a whole group of them walking through the center of town. I had trouble believe these were the same soldiers who were supposed to shoot my little pink body in time of war. They seemed so small, so lost, amidst the changing Czech towns. It was barely a month before they were scheduled to leave the country for good, and already there were reports of soldiers offering Czech women thousands of crowns just get married so the soldier could stay behind and not have to face such an uncertain future in the crumbling Soviet Union.

"Everyone here used to be so afraid of these men," Renáta said, as the soldiers passed. "I once came home to our cottage and found a soldier upstairs, hiding in the bedroom. He had his gun with him. He told me he was running away. And he was hungry."

"What did you do?"

"I called the police, of course," she said. "The Soviet police came and took him away."

On the final day of the Soviet presence in Czechoslovakia, Michael Kocáb, a member of parliament who had been heavily involved in negotiations to remove the troops, organized a huge concert at a hockey rink. Of the many outsiders who had found their way into parliament after the change in governments, Kocáb was perhaps one of the most striking. He had been a well-known rock star whose aforementioned band, Pražský výběr (Prague's Choice or Selection) had been in and out of favor with the government over the years. Pražský výběr had recorded a number of hard-edged records that show influences of metal, pop and Pink Floyd-like atmospheric droning all set to quirky rhythms and lyrics. It might be best described as New Wave. Tall, with receding hair and an angular striking face, Kocáb shares with Havel a keen sense of humor and an ability to bring people together.

Earlier in the day, I had been walking through Wenceslas Square and had stumbled on the truly amazing sight of twenty or thirty men shaving their beards in the square. After asking someone in the crowd, I determined that the men had grown their beards starting in 1968 to protest the invasion and had vowed they wouldn't shave them off until the last Soviet had left. There was shaving cream dropped all over the cement; photographers and news people were pushing and shoving each other trying to get the best possible picture of the men shaving off their whiskers, many now streaked with gray. It was a moment of pure happiness that I hadn't seen in the country. One man's eyes literally shone as he sliced through the hair under his chin and then held up the remains proudly for all to see. There were whoops of delight as still more hair fell onto the ground.

The "Adieu CA" concert (Goodbye Soviet Army) later that evening was a huge affair, with several well-known Czech and Slovak bands assembling for the occasion. More than 12,000 people packed into the hall to listen to an evening's worth of ear-splitting music, including sets by Kocáb and his band. At the end, Kocáb's close friend Frank Zappa came on stage for a short, if erratic, performance that was one of Zappa's last appearances.

"This is the first time I've had a reason to play my guitar in three years," Zappa said, strapping on a Fender Telecaster. "Please try and keep your country unique," he told the crowd. "Don't let them change it into something else."

Like the Velvet Underground, Zappa's music was seemingly much more popular in Czechoslovakia than in the United States. Not long after the revolution when Zappa visited Prague, Havel offered the musician the opportunity to be the Czechoslovakian representative for trade relations with the United States. When the the Bush Administration supposedly balked at the idea, Zappa quietly withdrew his name for consideration.

Havel arrived to watch the final few minutes of the show, various ministers clambered on stage to take part in the concert and address the crowd about the impending removal of the troops. Then, shortly after eleven o'clock, Kocáb called for everyone to make their way out of the hall and down to a large open area outside.

Originally, Kocáb had hoped the final Soviet general would be willing to shake hands with him and others from the Czechoslovak government and then climb into a helicopter and fly away. The general in charge of removing the Soviet troops did initially agree, but later word came back from somewhere on high (probably Moscow) that this would not be a funny joke and that the general was simply to leave without any fuss. So Kocáb had arranged for someone to ceremoniously board a helicopter in a Soviet uniform. As thousands of people watched in the dark, the "general" posed with Kocáb for some photos and then flew away in a helicopter, with people waving and shouting their approval. There were fireworks and they played a recording of Smetana's *Ma Vlast,* which was as moving a moment as I could imagine. The helicopter slowly rose into the air, running lights blinking red in the dark, as the first swelling bars of Smetana's composi-

237

tion for his homeland sounded. The helicopter hovered in the air, seemingly considering the assembled people below, and then turned and flew out over the direction of the Castle. Then it turned and made one final pass over the crowd, which roared its approval.

My friend David Koller, who had joined me at the concert, said quietly, "I wish my parents were here to see this. They wouldn't believe it." As the helicopter slowly flew off into the distance, the concert organizers deflated a giant balloon that was shaped to resemble a Soviet soldier.

The days came and went quickly, with strong breezes through Prague slowly, finally, sucking the winter away. It was now truly possible to go outside without a sweater, an amazing concept after months of being trapped inside layers of clothing. The warm weather also meant that it was time to pack my things and head off again to School in Nature, except that it wouldn't be the short trip like last time, but a full two-week haul in a small town called Trojanovice located south of Ostrava in an extremely hilly portion of northeastern Moravia.

Instead of little children, we had most of the older 13- and 14-year-olds from the upper classes with most of my 11 year olds thrown in for good measure. The relaxing pace of the days (teaching in the morning, long walks in the afternoon, nights free) meant that I was able to relax after months of hurrying around Prague trying to keep up with a series of moving targets. In the evening some of the teachers played cards or bought drinks from the owners of the hotel. Shortly before ten o'clock, we'd head down the hallway, checking each room to make sure the kids were at least attempting to sleep.

The flip side of the quiet meant that for the first several nights I was able to actually sit and concentrate on my life up to that point. The resulting self-scrutiny uncorked a series of sleepless nights in which I pondered whether coming to Prague had been a good idea or not. I was surprised that after all these months I was still harboring doubts; but then again, there it was.

While I had been learning a tremendous amount about the Czechs and their culture, I didn't feel all that successful; teaching hadn't been a complete success, my Czech still wasn't totally usable, I hadn't been able to write as much as I had planned and I wondered whether I would be able to get a job when I went home. But where was home?

Despite my best attempts to put the thoughts out of my head, I felt troubled for several days, especially during one longer excursion through a nearby town. While the children ran about buying ice cream and poking in stores, I wandered through the unkempt, cracked main square and glumly considered the faded writing on a nearby building: "Socialist Workers Are Building Peace and Prosperity."

It was a gloomy day—urinal gray skies and a chilly wind cutting through a poorly planned cultural center made standing exposed that much more unpleasant. Hoping to beat the inevitable rain, townspeople in their faded denim and ill-fitting polyester clothes rushed about like chicken heading for the slaughterhouse.

"What if I die here?" my mind yelped, with the next series of questions flooding down almost immediately. "What if I can't leave here? I don't want to grown old here stung down by bad coffee that sticks in my teeth. What if I can't leave Czechoslovakia? I gotta get out of here. Soon. I'm tired. Can I quit next week? I can quit anytime. I just have to go to the border. These people are everywhere. I'm tired. They're all pathetic. *You're* pathetic. What do I do now?"

Just as I was turning all these ridiculous and pitiful thoughts over in my head, the skies opened with a leaden crack and the rain came down hard. It was a late spring storm headed out of the nearby mountains and the tank was overflowing with rain and hail. I barely had time to dodge into a little supermarket before I got soaked. The rain was useful in that it allowed me to break the train of thought that had nearly incapacitated me.

I rode the school bus back to the pension with the kids in a soggy and foul mood, unsure of anything. Luckily, Dan and Renáta arrived early the next day to spend the weekend with me. I told Dan about my concerns and he simply told me to relax: things would work out. Dana let me out of teaching for the day and the three of us spent the day hiking in the forest.

We spent the rest of the next week taking long hikes in the beautiful mountains along the Polish border. In the afternoons, Dana and

239

I would take long walks through the rolling countryside, past dozens of small cottages.

"Look at this one," she said, pointing to a newly built house. "I wonder whether the people had to pay for all their materials or whether they stole it from the local construction company." She went on to explain how in the past no one had ever paid for much of their cement or wood; they had merely "borrowed" it from the local contractor.

"But didn't the contractors get angry?" I asked.

"Why should they have? They could just order more materials and their jobs could last that much longer." Her story reminded me of an afternoon I had spent with one of my private English students. When I visited his tiny, one-room flat for the first time, he took several minutes to show me the various parts of the room he had built with supplies from other construction sites.

"The shelves came from near your neighborhood," he said deep in thought. "And the walls, well, I got those down the street. Or did I?" He ran a hand over his chin thoughtfully while he considered the source of his pilferage. I shook my head in amazement.

By the time we returned to the school, it was time for an early dinner and then some kind of group program. The kids were generally always good and on one day, we had a special series of silly athletic competitions for them to mark "International Children's Day," a holdover from the past. In the evening, we had a disco for the kids and I stood by the lone cassette player inserting a succession of teen-dream music, including New Kids on the Block, Roxette and some drippy Czech singers. It was funny to watch the older kids who were 11 and 12 years old attempting to decide whether they should dance slow or fast, touch their partner or merely just stay away. Kids are kids all over the world. I saw my past mirrored in their doubts.

When we went back to Prague, I was happy to get back to the city. The school year was quickly winding down and the days were warm. The kids' attention spans were even shorter and Dana told me not to worry about trying to complete much more work.

"You should just review with them and try and make sure they remember what has been given so far," she said. "They'll just forget anything else."

Not long before the end of the school year, the teachers gave a lunch for Dan who had said he definitely wouldn't be returning to teach the following year. Jana, too, had announced she would be teaching English the following year at a new private school one of her friends had opened.

"I think it will be better for me there, there won't be so many changes and I will be among friends," she said sadly. If Jana was miffed by the excessive amount of attention bade the Americans, she didn't say anything, except to make an offhand comment about how much "everyone likes the Americans." Despite the various stories we had been told, I did feel somehow sad for her as she had served with the school for many years and was not even being recognized in any way.

Near the end of the afternoon, the school's vice principal gave Dan and myself cards (perhaps they thought that I would change my mind over the summer) with the following inscription:

"On behalf of our school, we thank you very much for your successful work and charming attitude to all of us."

The Vice Principal rose to speak. "I don't speak English very well," he said in Czech to us. "But if I could say something, it would be what they have said in Pilzen . . ." he hesitated and then repeated slowly in English, "Thank you boys. We will never forget."

23

Anniversary One

We knew there were a lot of Americans in Prague, but no one knew just how many had arrived since 1990. Certainly there were more than 500, and most people figured the number was probably over 1,000, but beyond that it was tough to figure. Many of the arrivals had failed to properly register with either the American embassy or even the Czech government. If anything, it felt like a small community, in that you could always be guaranteed of running into someone you knew at a movie with English-language subtitles or at a western jazz or rock concert. If something hip was going on in town, like the times when Wynton Marsalis and Suzanne Vega performed in Prague, chances were good that the Western contingent would be out in force.

In the spring of 1991, a handful of recent graduates from the University of California at Santa Barbara had started the first English language newspaper in Prague. Called *Prognosis,* it was published once a month. It looked suspiciously like a college newspaper, and was making an attempt to be hip and modern-looking without really having the resources to do so. Intrigued, I did a story for *The New York Times News Service* about the staff and its work.

The first several issues of *Prognosis* were a jumble of some impressively written stories, bits and pieces of useful information and some not so great articles that wandered dangerously into the "arrogant American points a finger at the Czechs and laughs at them" territory. There were articles about how to get a job teaching English, buying glass and cooking and shopping in Prague ("Cooking in Prague is first and foremost about lowering one's expectations.").

Both Dan and I agreed that the newspaper had great potential but seemed to be wasting its time on too much fluff and "save my weak American ass in this hellhole" kind of stories. Dan did some work for the newspaper; I chose to concentrate on selling stories abroad and teaching.

Prognosis was the first of many business and cultural ventures led by Westerners—generally Americans—in Prague. Beyond the large number of economic and private sector advisors, there were a lot of people coming to Prague simply to pursue other projects: play guitar for money on the Charles Bridge, paint, write poetry or simply drink beer. Back in the dark early days when we lived in the Dům, we often fantasized about starting businesses or companies in Prague; these were business-types who were actually doing it. Several restaurants opened, offering everything from New York-styled pizza to vegetarian food and Mexican burritos and tortilla chips. Since the Czechs didn't have these things, the Americans decided that they would jolly well provide it for them. Trouble was, most of the prices in these places were so high that the average Czech person couldn't afford to frequent them.

"That's disturbing," the Croatian writer and essayist Slavenka Drakulic told me once in Vienna. "A separatist culture like that is almost colonial." Whether or not the Americans were consciously being separatist is doubtful, but many Czechs were angered by places where barely anyone spoke Czech and the menus were written in English. Worse, there was sometimes a know-it-all, show-off attitude to some of the businesses, as in the pizza restaurant that dressed its employees in red, white and blue uniforms with inscriptions that said: "Work hard, play hard."

"I'm tired of the arrogance of some Americans who seem to think that we need these things in our life, that we have been deprived of something," one of Jarka's friends said one afternoon while we were walking through downtown Prague.

"Aren't you curious about other cultures?" I asked.

"Yes, but I would prefer to take these things on my own terms, and not be made to feel as if I have been missing something all my life and I will realize that American food and culture is simply so much better than our own." It wasn't so much that she was rejecting the new array of foods: she was unhappy with how it was presented to her. After being a closed society for so long, to have new cuisines like falafel and gyros was bewildering. Suddenly being told that one should exercise more and not smoke or eat fattening food was irritating to many people.

"You can't imagine how much the Party always told us what to do and lectured to us," Dana had said one day at school. "President Husák always began his speeches with the words, 'Dear friends' like we were some kind of children."

The paternalism shown by some Americans towards Czechs was often simply wrong-headed. Once, after *The Prague Post* printed an article about how Czechs weren't warming to the introduction of the *Yellow Pages* in Prague, a Czech teacher friend of mine was incensed.

"The article implied that Czechs are stupid because they can't use the *Yellow Pages*," he told me. "What the reporter didn't bother to find out is that our old information books were arranged differently and that we grew up learning to look for things in a different way."

While the general assignment reporter usually has more than his fair share of naivete lurking in every story, American reporters covering a foreign country are often capable of huge cultural faux-pas and blunders via their writing. The reporter can make tremendous mistakes from a lack of information.

I spent several weeks during the summer in San Francisco. I reveled in the purity of moments, the closeness of friends, the ability to speak to strangers and have them understand. But the things I had always hated still made me angry—the slack-jawed, zombie-eyed jadedness of America's youth parading through the malls, the traffic, exorbitant car insurance, unemployed friends and endless arguments about racism and political correctness, glass ceilings and Madonna.

For those who have money, America or any country offers up a variety of chosen moments. Prague still lacked many of the small details that ease the stress of everyday life. However, America simply cannot offer the pleasure of certain chosen moments found in parts of Europe, including the gentle tolling of a church bell through a centuries-old square on a Sunday morning.

Moreover, I found my friends in the United States stuck on a treadmill that, for them, hadn't run very far. My new world in Prague was changing so quickly I couldn't go a day without seeing a new store open or a building being rebuilt. The government was passing laws and there were people making real changes in their society. Something was always happening.

But, try as I might, I couldn't always submerge the feeling that I wasn't truly at home. I admired some of the Westerners who seemed so settled in Prague, so relieved of their past lives. There were days when I would want so much to be back in the West I could just burst. My lungs ached to breath cleaner air and my eyes longed to revel in a range of different ethnic cultures and foods. These moments came usually when I had had a rotten day and the trams were overloaded and everyone smelled sweaty and pushed and shoved and shops were closed by the whim of their owners and I had waited in what seemed to be my 55th line of the day and then didn't get what I wanted.

I had arrived back in Prague on a hot Saturday afternoon in late August, nearly a year after I had first blundered into the train station. I was determined to have a better year teaching English and write more articles for newspapers in the United States. I didn't have to worry much about writing again, as Dan told me on the ride in from the airport that there were plans for another weekly English-language newspaper in Prague. I was thrilled.

Moreover, the newspaper was going to be helmed by Alan Levy, a former reporter for *The New York Times* and *The International Herald-Tribune* who had been one of the few American journalists to personally witness the Warsaw Pact invasion in 1968 and had written one of the few English-language eyewitness accounts of the period.[1] After he was expelled from the country in 1971, Levy moved to Vienna. But he returned after the revolution and now had been approached by

246

two former staffers from *Prognosis* who were interested in starting their own newspaper, *The Prague Post.*

We made an appointment to see Levy at the Post's small office located off Old Town Square. When I had been introduced to Levy several days before, I had been impressed by the fact that he didn't take my credentials at face value and asked instead to see a resume and some clips. Upon arriving for my interview, I was encouraged by the air of professionalism that prevailed. After looking through my materials, Levy pronounced himself satisfied and asked me where I'd like to contribute. I told him I would be happy writing about anything, especially about entertainment. But as the newspaper still didn't have a lot of reporters, the Managing Editor, Martha Jane Pinder, asked me if I could write a news story for them about an upcoming summit meeting of leaders from the so-called Vyšegrad Three of Central European nations: Poland, Czechoslovakia and Hungary.

I also met two of the newspaper's owners, Lisa Frankenberg and Kent Hawryluk, who had been intricately involved in starting *Prognosis,* but had decided there was a wider market to be tapped than *Prognosis* was willing to consider. A third investor for *The Prague Post* was back in Texas.

In addition to writing several stories for the paper, I helped in the office proofreading materials, running errands and gathering other bits of material to run in the first edition, which now was only three weeks away. Pinder and the Deputy Managing Editor, Revan Schendler were tearing their hair out trying to stay ahead of the looming deadlines: the staff had to produce a "dry run" issue and the Post's huge entertainment listings section had to be assembled, checked and rechecked. On the other side, the business staff was busily trying to place ads for the first issue, arrange for distribution of the newspaper and plan a huge launch party and press conference.

This was all being done in an office the size of a small kitchen, with one huge table, a few desks and chairs, two computers and one printer. Even though the newspaper was working on a shoestring staff, it got ridiculously crowded and noisy, with people squabbling over one telephone, bumping into each other as they searched for paper and pencils or tried to make coffee. There was no privacy: people had

arguments in the middle of the room, if you went to the bathroom outside the office everyone heard your business and phone calls were
frequently interrupted by loud conversations. In the early evening,
various members of the staff would stumble down the stairs enroute
to the closest pub for mass quantities of beer.

Although I didn't have nearly the responsibility that others had in
preparing the first issue, I was happy to just be a part of the energy
swirling around me. It was a manic environment, with grown adults
and young reporters all hustling to produce a product they all could
be proud of. There were tantrums and laughing fits, dancing in the
hallway when something went right, and endless amounts of anxiety
over each facet of the newspaper. I hadn't seen this kind of devotion
since I was Editor-in-Chief of the *USC Daily Trojan* in Los Angeles.

I also returned to Prokopová, this time with an extended list of
projects and plans. There was a new principal, as Holíková had been
rather unceremoniously relieved of her job shortly before the end of
the previous school year. In plain terms, Holíková had been demoted
to serve as merely just another teacher. The new principal, Milan
Hausner, was an extraordinarily portly, unkempt man who seemed to
have a limitless amount of energy. Whenever I saw him, he was huff-
ing his way through the hallways with his oversized trousers limping
on the floor and his straight, thinning hair all askew. He had called
me at the Dům in early July to introduce himself. He spoke fairly
good English and told me that he was looking forward to working
with me.

The last time I had been in the school the final week of June, it had
been chaos: flowers, crying students who were graduating and celebrations. We had met briefly to go over the schedule for the following year, and I asked for the maximum possible number of small
children.

"Please, no more 12 year-olds," I asked Dana. "And please, don't
give me 5B again."

But although they had tried to accommodate my request for small
children, they had been forced to give me several older classes, includ-

248

ing one group of 14 year-olds that didn't speak any English.

From the first day, I felt I had my act together. I had class lists of names, I knew where the chalk was located and how to call on each student. I began the first day of school by explaining in bad, but under-standable Czech, that there were limits to each class, that I expected a certain amount from them and hoped they would all enjoy the work, but that they also had to behave.

My littlest kids didn't need such severe lectures and so I concen-trated on making sure they all started properly this time out. We started with the pictures and learned only two to three words a day. I con-stantly reviewed with them, sang songs, played little games and took breaks. Mostly, I was able to keep their attention or redirect events in Czech, a crucial aspect that I hadn't had the year before. If they showed signs of being bored, I didn't get angry. Instead, I merely changed the lesson plan and tried to focus their energy elsewhere. It was a lot of work, but it was also enjoyable.

The older group of kids that didn't speak English, however, was a disaster, nearly from day one. Regardless of what I did, they could-n't have cared less about learning English. Most of them weren't mov-ing on to the next level of schooling, but instead would be going to technical and vocational high schools. It wasn't so much that they were boisterous, they were just plain uninspired. It didn't matter whether I told dirty jokes in Czech or burned a $100 bill just to see their reaction. There *was* no reaction. I could have immolated myself and leapt out the window and the most response I might have elicited was a casual, "Wow."

After nearly five months of this torture, I did something I never thought I would do: I asked to have another teacher replace me. Luck-ily, there was a new English teacher arriving in the school and it was agreed that she would take over for me.

One afternoon during a teacher's meeting, several of the former headmistress' friends attempted to collect money to buy a gift for her.

"We thought we should buy her something because she served this school for so many years," one of them said, waving some money. My colleague, Eva, who shared office space with me, suddenly looked up from where she had been quietly correcting papers.

249

"No!" she said loudly, her normally peaceful face contorting into a scowl. Eva was perhaps the nicest person I had met. "I won't give that Communist cow any money!" In Czech, calling a woman a 'cow' or a 'pig' is extremely serious. Immediately the room erupted into arguments about whether to purchase a gift for Holíková. I stayed clear of the yelling, somehow sorry I had learned to speak Czech well enough to understand the shouting.

24

Building a Newspaper

L ife at *The Prague Post* closely mirrored the swirling world of Prague. We didn't know what we were doing half the time, so we fudged it in spots, worked in groups or merely prayed that the printer wouldn't screw up the photographs or text.

The launch party and press conference for *The Prague Post* the first week of October, 1991, was held in an elaborate baroque room in a building located underneath the Castle. Each of the owners explained who they were and why they were starting the paper. They had managed to get the newspaper out on time.

The goal was to provide a complete newspaper for the reader, with hard news, opinion, business, complete cultural listings and features. In the first issue, there were stories about a failing exhibition of Czech culture and industry, the problems between the Czechs and Slovaks and updates on the privatization process.

Alan Levy read a column called, "Us," in which he charted a course for every American to follow when coming to Prague:

"We are living in the Left Bank of the 90s," he began, reading from a prepared text. "For some of us, Prague is Second Chance City; for others a new frontier where anything goes, everything goes, and often enough, nothing works. Yesterday is long gone, today is nebulous, and who knows about tomorrow, but somewhere within each of us, we all know that we are living in a historic place at a historic time. Future Hemingways and Fitzgeralds, Audens and Isherwoods, Boswells and Shirers will chronicle our course, but even they will need to know the nuts and bolts of what it was like and how it felt to live and be in liberated Prague in the last decade of the 20th century."

Standing in the back of the room, I could almost hear the sound of airplane tickets being purchased and passports being stamped by hundreds of yearning writers wanting to be Hemingway and Stein.

"Congratulations," I told Martha when I arrived at the office the day after the launch party. "What now?"

"Now, darling," she said with a cackle, "we start all over again." Most of the staff was exhausted by the first effort, but there were only several days until the next issue was due at the printer.

Despite all the effort, the debut was still riddled with typographical errors and design problems. Production of the first issue had not gone smoothly, as it had taken hours to print paste-up copy on the newspaper's one small Hewlett-Packard laser printer. The listings were riddled with errors, mostly because the various groups that were supposed to provide the information had gotten most of it wrong. There simply was no attention to accuracy on the part of some cultural groups—who cared if the performance started a 7 P.M. instead of the printed 7:30 P.M.?

If I had thought myself busy after I first arrived in Prague the year before, I was just as frantic, running from school to the newspaper in the afternoons. As Viktor and Jarka were gone, Dan and I saw less and less of their other friends, who it seemed were becoming very involved in their own lives. I tutored Milena for several months in English, but eventually had to give that up because I just didn't have the time.

I took a big step when Renáta and I moved out of the Dům in October to a two-room flat in the center of town. Dan had moved out some months earlier to an apartment downtown.

"It's easier to move out," he said. "It'll make you much happier. No long subway rides. You'll have a some privacy again. You can have a private kitchen."

When Renáta and I left the Dům, the building was being privatized into a hotel. Gradually, over the rest of the year, there were fewer and fewer teachers living in its rooms. The apartment where we now lived was on the fourth floor of a six story walk-up and featured dark wood walls and a tiny kitchen and living room area with a space for tour bed. Both rooms were exceedingly gloomy as there wasn't one strong light in the entire apartment. We called the kitchen the "Andrei Sacharov" because it reminded us of pictures we had seen of Sacharov in exile, always sitting at his small kitchen table. Despite the shadowy light, the apartment was homey and comfortable. Sadly, we were only going to be able to stay for about six to eight months.

In the second half of 1991, privatization moved from the legal, theoretical stage. Changes appeared on the street, as the small business auctions slowly turned over stores to new owners.

One morning in early September, I happened to notice the meat store across from school was being fixed up slightly with the addition of a new sign: Jiří Egbert: Meat. And sure enough, there was Jiří standing on the front step, looking at the sign and welcoming people into the store. His store.

I stood and watched for a few minutes as he said hello to each person who came through the door. No one had done anything like this in more than forty years. There was no need to promote ownership or take pride in anything. But this was changing. Although many owners of stores, restaurants and bars in Prague have had their share of difficulty over the past several years, Egbert's store has continued to prosper by offering a wide variety of meats and fish. The store is always crowded, but people are still served quickly and effectively. Jiří seems to know what he is doing.

Small privatization meant that many people were now able to begin reconstruction work on their apartment buildings and office buildings and seemingly overnight, Prague was filled with skip loaders, huge trucks, new construction sites and the endless sound of jackhammers and other clatter. It became impossible to walk down the sidewalk without having to avoid a construction site and an immeasurable amount of dust and garbage.

Very few buildings needed only a fresh coat of paint. Most needed to be torn apart, literally from the ground up. Walls were ripped out and replaced, floors were dug up and relaid. Windows and frames were removed and resealed. Electricity had to be brought up to standards and conduit installed for eventual phone lines. In some cases, the only thing remaining from the original structure was the facade.

While it was amazing to walk down a street and see several buildings that had been repaired, it was also sobering to look around and see that six or seven others on the same block needed the same treatment.

Commercial advertising was on the verge of obscuring everything in town, it seemed. Trams were leased whole to various companies who then repainted them to advertise their products. Overnight, the city was full of red and gold trams exulting the benefits of smoking Marlboros or blue and white cars praising Minolta, Xerox or Cannon.

Everything, including the film industry seemed to be in flux. While film companies were now able to make the kinds of movies they had always dreamed about, there was no money to finance them because the state had cut off its subsidies. For a film industry that previously pumped out 50 to 60 films a year, the slowdown was quite sad, with numerous actors and directors sitting idly on the sidelines. Concurrently, American and British films were incredibly popular at the box office, and film distributors had to jostle each other to get into the theaters with each big Hollywood film: *Dances With Wolves, Highlander II, Awakenings* and *Postcards From The Edge.*

An extra layer of confusion surrounded the actual privatization of the industry, which was bogged down in endless disputes over who would own the rights to older films: the director, producer or studio. Czech and Slovak film had experienced several golden ages, including a lively pre-war period and the so-called "New Wave" of the 1960s when such films as *The Shop On Main Street* and *Closely Watched Trains* won Oscars for Best Foreign Film. Czech and Slovak films are often brilliant, punctuated by incredibly vivid screenplays and a comic, ironic bitterness that is simply not present in American film. Actors are not chosen for their beauty or bankability; they exist on screen as real people.[2]

I myself was lucky enough to get invited by Jan Jíra, the head of the Czech distribution agency called Lucernafilm, to attend the debut of *Dances With Wolves,* which had won a clutch of Oscars in the spring. The first showing of the film was something of a gala affair with a wine reception before the screening and speeches by the various film people. As I wandered around the theater before the start of the movie with a glass of wine in my hand, I encountered Shirley Temple Black, who was seemed not to be in the best of health, or in the best of moods. After introducing myself, I mentioned that an official at the Commonwealth Club of California in San Francisco, where Black was very involved, had suggested that I call Black's office in Prague and ask for an interview because I was a fellow member of the Commonwealth Club.

"Oh, God," Black said with more than a trace of irritation and lighting a cigarette, "I'll have to make sure they quit telling people to phone me up. I simply don't have the time to meet everyone who comes to town." While she spoke with me, we must have been interrupted twenty times by adoring Czechs who wanted to meet the famous film star or kiss her hand. Black was extremely cordial to each of the well-wishers, but seemed happy and relieved when Alexander Dubček appeared several minutes later. I had never seen Dubček up close, and although he had aged over the years, he still had a kind, expressive face that exuded charm. Despite having a major role in the government, Dubček was often derided by the right-wing as being too naive and unrealistic about the past years under Communism. Moreover, he had never warmed completely to the concept of a market economy.

While Dubček stood alone with only his interpreter and a bodyguard, I moved towards him to introduce myself.

"Good evening," I said in Czech. He greeted me with a handshake and a smile and I was just about to say something when an American man and woman nearly cut in front of me to lay tributes at his feet. I'm not sure what they did for a living, but I hope to God it wasn't diplomacy. They proceeded to make asses of themselves by firing a lot of rapid questions at Dubček, who continued to smile and answer as best he could.

"Could you ask him if he still believes in socialism?" the man asked the interpreter, pushing his white wine glass forward into the empty air between them. I didn't catch Dubček's answer as the American woman was already screaming something about Dubček being the "first Gorbachev."

"You were the first, sir, you were the first," the woman said sympathetically and then patted Dubček on the shoulder. By this point, I had quietly left before witnessing anything even more embarrassing.

Sadly, I never got another chance to meet Dubček. He died in November, 1992, from injuries sustained in a serious automobile accident two months earlier. Upon hearing of his death, Gorbachev said: "I feel respect for this man and I bow before him."[3] His funeral, sadly, was controversial, because many in the government, including Klaus, did not attend. The country was less than two months away from the split and was not elevated to a state funeral because they did not want to draw attention to the issue of federalism. Dubček, who bitterly opposed the split of the nation, did not live to see it happen.

Even with the money crunch in 1991, a number of good films did get made, including *Obecná Škola* (The Elementary School), which ended up being nominated for an Oscar. Jiří Ježek, a noted film producer in Prague, told me in an interview that the most important thing was to make movies that people wanted to see.

"If the film is good," he said, "it will find its audience." Shortly after the revolution Jezek, along with a new company called Bonton, had produced *Tankový Prapor* (Tank Battalion), the first independent film since the industry was nationalized in 1946.

"It was very complicated to finish *Prapor*," Ježek said, leaning forward in his chair as though he was passing me a secret. "In fact, it was illegal." As the film industry hadn't been privatized, making a movie without state permission was technically forbidden. From the first day of shooting in November, 1990, Ježek and Vít Olmer, the film's director, didn't know whether or not they would get shut down by the police. So Olmer worked quickly, shooting literally around the clock. Thankfully, common sense prevailed—they were told by a

256

minister that "there would be a silent agreement"—and Ježek was allowed to finish the film. It was released to great success; more than 2.5 million people flocked to the comedy about life in a tank battalion during the difficult 1950s.[4]

Ježek and Bonton handled everything related to the movie, including marketing and distribution.

"We had no help or advice," he said. "We had to figure out how to do everything, from booking the film to finding the transport boxes for the movie. I think it's not an excellent film, but it was made at a time when Czechs and Slovaks wanted to see a funny movie."

On November 18, 1991, Gustáv Husák, the former Czechoslovak President who had done so much to hurt the nation through "normalization," died at a hospital in Bratislava where he had been undergoing treatment for cancer and heart disease. Unconfirmed reports surfaced in the press that shortly before his death, he had accepted the last rites from a Roman Catholic priest who had been called to his bedside. In Prague, the news seemed to hardly raise a fuss, while in Slovakia, the Slovak Prime Minister, Jan Čarnogurský, attended the small private funeral. Asked whether Slovaks would accept such a gesture, he said: "I think they will accept it. For many years he was president of Czechoslovakia. Yes, he was also a representative of the policy of "normalization," which had devastating effects on the society. But, as usually happens in politics, a politician has not only positive or negative traits; usually, they are combined. In this case, positions held by Husák during his life were sufficient reason for me to honor him as a man, as a politician and a representative of the state."[5]

I wondered how many funerals Husák had attended for all the hundreds—and probably thousands—of people who had been ruined under his command. It had been almost two years since Husák left office, and the country was still trying to find its way. The various major news stories kept the staff of *The Prague Post* constantly on the move during the fall and winter months. And, without us knowing it, the newspaper itself and the Americans in Prague had become something of a story elsewhere in the world.

The first article that appeared about the Americans in Prague, save for Alan Levy's "Left Bank of the 90s" piece, was a short discussion of the two English-language newspapers in town by *The Los Angeles Times'* Charles T. Powers. From this one article, I can perhaps trace the genesis of nearly every Left Bank of the 90s article in print, radio and TV.

"Ten thousand Americans in Czechoslovakia—many of them twentysomethings—is the hip-pocket estimate, although no one, not even the Czechoslovak immigration department, knows for sure. It seems to have happened overnight—and in fact may be just beginning. There was Paris in the '20s; will it be Prague in the '90s?"[6]

For those not connected with the article, Powers' words were pleasant, a somewhat nice affirmation of the strange turn our lives were taking in Prague. Few, if anyone, probably could have hinted at the ridiculous tidalwave of coverage Prague's American community would receive over the next two years.

In the worst conceit of modern journalism, most of the features consisted of strictly follow the leader reporting. Rarely, if ever, did the reporters try and get out and cover a new angle or find a fresh face. It was "round up the usual suspects" and ask the same questions ("Why are you here?"), and hear the same responses ("I could never get a job like this in the United States" or "I can live like a king here and drink and party 'cause it's all so cheap.").

There was CBS with Ray Brady and NBC with Tom Brokaw and ABC's *Prime Time Live. The New York Times* did a piece. So did *The Washington Post.* And *The San Francisco Examiner* and *The Seattle Times.* Then one day, MTV trotted out two jokesters worthy of enshrinement on *Wayne's World.* As I was resident rock guru at *The Prague Post,* it was suggested that I be interviewed. The Wayne and Garth clones knew so little about what they were supposed to cover that they just stuck the microphone in my face and said something like: "We don't know much, so maybe you could tell us why this place is cool." In retrospect, I think even MTV's Beevis and Butthead would have made better interviewers. At the end of the taping, one of the cameramen lay down on the floor.

"Are you OK?" I asked, gazing down at his prone figure.

"Yeah, sure," he said, struggling to keep the camera upright and pointed at me. "I'm just getting those great MTV angles."

In the midst of all this, we were busily working away, helping to fan the flames of the Left Bank myth by producing reams of our own Americans in Prague stories, sometimes on a weekly basis. The paper was a success from the first issue, with advertising being stronger than most people could have hoped for and steady sales.

By the time I became Managing Editor of the paper in mid-1992, we were receiving a torrent of resumes on a daily basis, all saying approximately the same thing: "I'm a recent graduate from a small college in Spotted Liver, Kansas, with a useless degree in journalism and saw this great story about Prague in the newspaper and would be really whacked out of my gourd if I could write for your newspaper. And I'd really like to get tanked all the time on the beer." Actually, none of the cover letters were even that inspired.

While we did get a fair number of really decent journalists to come work for the paper, we also got a whole ton of people who had only the most tenuous connection with reporting ("Say, can I write a story on Václav Havel?" or "I really like to read newspapers. Can I write a story for you?"). At first, we could use just about every person who walked in the door, even if they couldn't report their way out of a school board meeting. But after awhile, the "bottom feeders," as they came to be known, got so out of hand that we nearly had to hire a cleanup crew to haul them all out of the office.

Building a newspaper, as some of us discovered, is a long and tedious project. There were endless problems we kept running up against, most having to do with the fact that we never had enough money to buy enough equipment and computers. The staff was unpredictable and volatile. Often we would come into the office in the morning only to discover that some freelancer had decided to go to Poland on a whim and another "just couldn't take it anymore" and had packed up for America. There were language barriers; people fought like children over the phone, argued about who would be next in line for the translators.

Worse, some of the reporters sometimes treated the Czechs on staff like they were little more than hired mouthpieces who were only there to interpret. Other times, the interpreters didn't understand why they had to be diligent about finding a public official or some document.

"They'll be there tomorrow," some of the translators would say. "We can call then."

If some Czechs were angry about their city being turned upside down by Westerners, they were also amazed at the American spirit to carry on in the face of ignorance.

"I think Americans are very different from Czechs," our translator Misha told me one day while we were walking to an interview. "You can just come into a big city and start a big business like a newspaper and pretend to know what you're doing and believe that it will work. I don't think a Czech could ever do that."

While there were some very good Czech and Slovak reporters, too often the reporting was slipshod or biased towards their newspaper's particular political point of view. Reporters just hadn't gotten used to challenging and asking the difficult questions that needed to be asked. Going to press conferences was sometimes embarrassing as reporters would tiptoe towards the microphone and ask softball questions of major politicians who deserved much harder treatment.

But this timidity, too, like so much around the region, was simply the product of forty years in which no one had been allowed to openly think or speak for themselves without asking permission first. Trying to find who was the appropriate contact in a ministry or a private business was often frustrating and maddening, as one secretary after another would tell us that "they didn't know anything." There would be the usual shrug of the shoulders and then a nervous glance away as their eyes pleaded: "Look, I really don't want to take responsibility, here."

But when you found the right person and did conduct an interview, often the results were amazingly good. I have had interviews with various officials in Prague that have been more revealing than any I have conducted in the United States. Whether it was the changing world around them or just a lack of knowledge about how the press operates, people generally were more open and forthcoming about their own work and their failings. This is not to say that I relished people's failures; rather, I found it refreshing to hear people speaking honestly after so much jargon and double talk in the United States.

"You must see, Douglas, that we often don't know what we're doing," one of Havel's low-level advisors told me one afternoon while I was interviewing him. "We're all just learning." I didn't use these comments in my story, but was happy to see a public official be so candid. And I knew, it wouldn't last.

25

Lustrace: Cleaning Out Communists

In the fall of 1991, the government began discussing a major law called the "Screening Act" that would restrict any person who had ties with the StB—state security—from holding public office. The law was broad: it would prevent high-ranking members of the former government and militia members from holding office for five years. The bill exempted people who had joined or ascended through the Communist Party in the 1968–69 reform period.[1]

The entire question of what to do with informers and collaborators generally came to be known as *lustrace,* the Czech word (borrowed from the Latin) for "cleansing" or "purification." On my visit home to the United States that summer, I had told a Czech professor at Stanford University about the *lustrace* issue and he was shocked to hear how the Czechs had labeled the law.

"That's such a nasty, evil word!" he said. "I can't believe they are really calling it that!" Others, including those who were caught in the government's lists as informers would have agreed, as the law ran quickly into a firestorm. Despite passing 148–31 in the Federal Parliament, the bill enraged deputies from the extreme left and pleased most moderate and right-wing parties, which had accused left-wing deputies of being "soft" on Communism.

"It's the so-called Civic Movement (left-wing party) which is endlessly friendly to the Communists," said Pavel Bratinka, a fierce member of a rightist party. "These people represent a mortal threat to democracy. I hope they are wiped out in the next elections."[2] Some commentators worried that the law was so fierce it would shut out many former Communists who either had been forced out of the party, become dissidents or had turned out to be credible people who were currently working in the present government, including Alexander Dubček and the Prime Minister, Marian Čalfa.

People seeking a role in government or in large state enterprises needed to get a certificate of "cleanliness" that showed their files had been examined by the parliamentary commission charged with examining *lustrace* cases.

The cases were based on the files containing more than 60,000 names of supposed agents and collaborators. People who were trying to prove their innocence often had a difficult time of it, as the lists were maddeningly vague. In fact, the vagueness of the lists later helped many probable agents to sue the government and win on technicalities. The state lost a lot of money and no justice was done. Many dissidents were on the list, along with code names for each person and sometimes specific contact dates. However, as the StB had managed to destroy many of the main files containing the specific contacts and jobs assigned each person, it was hard to tell whether a person might have been targeted for recruitment or was a full-fledged collaborator.

Suppose you are a quiet person who one day is contacted by your local StB agent, who invites you to have beer with him. You accept, as you don't want to give him a reason to try and build a case against you and because this man is more powerful than the law or constitution. Over the beer, the agent tries to get you to inform against your friends. You resist and you and the agent go your separate ways. The StB agent puts your name on a list saying that he contacted you. Now it is after the revolution, and you're trying to clear your name. Is it possible? The files were marked with various codes indicating your status—confidants, contacts and enemy—and depending on who was handling your file, the material could often been vague or just plain wrong.[3]

In the early part of the year, government officials had already been moving against a number of existing Parliament members, informing them that their names had been found in various files and that they had the choice of resigning quietly or having their names read out in Parliament. A number of those accused resigned; ten did not.

While there had been an initial screening of candidates for the Parliament in May of 1990, the screenings had been very quiet and few people raised questions about the propriety of the searches.

However, as the first anniversary of the revolution approached in 1990, many people were questioning whether some of the agents had actually ended their work, or had merely shifted into a different gear and were working to slow the rate of economic change and hurt the government from within.

Petr Uhl, who spent nine years in jail as a dissident, and after the revolution worked as both a member in Parliament and later as the head of the state news agency. He became involved in the search for StB agents from the day that Parliament passed Resolution 94 in January, 1991. The bill authorized a commission to examine the StB question in a serious and more rigorous fashion. In an interview with a reporter from *The Los Angeles Times,* Uhl compared the StB searches in 1991 to the opening of Pandora's Box.

"The first mistake we made was that the resolution didn't address the consequences of the screening," Uhl said. "Second, we thought the registers would carry the appropriate information. We didn't know that the registers had the names of people who never knew they were in contact (with an agent)."[4]

One of the men who refused to resign from Parliament was Jan Kavan, who had been accused of being a "conscious collaborator" from the time he was a student in London in the late 1960s and early 1970s. Kavan steadfastly denied being a collaborator and took the government to court, quickly establishing himself as a symbol for those who were caught in the government's tangled web of incomplete lists and partial files from the past. Kavan, (whose father had been a ranking member of the Communist Party in the early 1950s until being caught up in the purges and sentenced to five years in prison) was a noted dissident-in-exile who spent countless hours working to help his friends who were still in Czechoslovakia. Kavan traveled in and out of the country using fake passports and disguises and brought various documents and *samizdat* material in and out during the 1970s and 80s. He was a tireless crusader for those who were working against the government.

While recounting Kavan's complete story would fill an entire separate book, suffice it to say that the government's suspicions were fueled by evidence in the files that Kavan may have given information to an agent in the Czechoslovak embassy in London. Or did he? From the way the papers were structured, it was impossible to prove one way or the other. Even the agent who dealt with Kavan said he didn't think Kavan was guilty.

"The Kavan file is not clear on either side," said Jan Sokol, a member of Parliament. "But in the Kavan file, there is plenty of documentation. It's not the sort of information a normal diplomatic officer would need. The suspicion is difficult to dispel."[5]

Ironically, *The Prague Post* had hired Kavan to write a weekly column for the paper on what was happening inside Parliament. A tall, imperious but still slightly nervous person, Kavan did not strike me as anything more than a difficult writer the several times I met him. He was continually unhappy with the way his columns were being edited at the newspaper and, consequently, most of the editors did not like dealing with him. Regardless of what one thought of Kavan, he had clearly been denied due process, since many of the proceedings had been done in secret and Kavan himself was unable to examine much of the evidence against him.

Lawrence Weschler, who wrote an excellent account of the Kavan case for *The New Yorker,* told me once that he doubted Kavan was guilty of anything, except being exceptionally paranoid and fanatical about his work. "To live that kind of life, going in and out of the country and taking huge risks, one must be a bit of a fanatic," Weschler said. Although Kavan eventually was given a "cleanliness" certificate by the ministry of the interior on February 25, 1992, the document was suddenly revoked a week later by Ján Langoš, Federal Minister of the Interior, who believed the process had been rushed.

"The people who have been entrusted with this task didn't abide by the law," Langoš said. "I have recalled the head of this department and have given orders to verify all the negative certificates that this office has issued."[6]

The case was returned to an independent commission, which

returned its judgment on October 16, 1992: Kavan was guilty of "willful collaboration" during his school years in England.

"There was no concrete evidence against me, and all the testimonies were for me" Kavan said, citing the large number of people who had testified on his behalf. "All the facts were in my favor, so I suspect they were motivated by (political considerations)." He vowed he would appeal into a Prague district court, and that is where the case remains today.[7]

Despite the difficulties surrounding the various StB cases, Parliament was still pushing forward on other anti-Communist legislation. It had passed yet another law in late December, 1991, equating fascism with Communism and setting terms allowing for punishment of any person who "declares national, racial, class or religious hatred." Predictably, the Communists in the parliament reacted strongly and Jiří Svoboda, Communist Party chairman, spent several days wandering around Parliament with a red star in the shape of the Star of David pinned to his chest. The star read: "I am a Communist."

The see-saw battle between the need to prosecute the past and vindicate those who were truly not guilty of crimes against the state would always be a murky issue. Despite the original contention that "everyone was guilty," even Havel's generous position towards ex-Communists seemed to harden over time. In his New Year's Day speech in 1992, he expressed disappointment at the many former agents and Communists who were still abusing others in the country.

"We all underestimated the extreme cunning of our former opponents and their extraordinary capacity to adapt to the new situation," he said. "Once I announced in Václavské náměstí (Wenceslas Square) that 'We are not like them.' If we do not want to be like 'them,' we must not allow ourselves to be blindfolded by fanaticism, longing for revenge and hatred. But it does not mean that we will tolerate everything done by 'them' and that we should not prosecute those who committed crimes."[8]

In the early fall, signs appeared all over Prague advertising the arrival of *burčák,* the first pressing from the wine harvest. Thick and sweet with the color and appearance of apple juice, the young wine is powerful stuff and capable of inducing mind-splitting hangovers. One must drink the juice quickly as it spoils in just several days. Bottles of burčák have been known to burst in the refrigerator, as the rapidly fermenting wine puts off a lot of gas. Thank goodness the season only lasts for about a month.

On a pleasant fall weekend, Renáta and I headed southeast with her father and step-mother through the rolling Moravian hills to help the family with the wine harvest. The original idea was to finish the picking and prune back some of plants for the following season. But as the day was clear and warm, we didn't accomplish a lot and instead sat in the vineyard, swatting away wasps and drinking the remains of the previous year's vintage.

The family had a small vineyard that crawled up a sloping hill looking out towards Austria. Czech wine ranges from badly bottled commercial table wine to some surprisingly good local varieties grown in Moravia. Often, the only way to get this wine is to go scour the various small wineries that range across the land near the Czech-Austrian border southeast of Brno. The atmosphere in wine bars across Moravia is as lively as in a beer pub, except that the vintner walks between tables refilling glasses from a huge glass beaker of wine that balances on the shoulder.

As the early evening approached, we went down the street to the family's wine cellar and crushing room, which was located in a small garage dug into the side of a hill. There was a large wooden crusher and various small wooden and plastic tanks for holding the wine. The men, clad in faded denim overalls and dirty jumpsuits, were already hard at work, unloading the last of the grapes for the season into the vat and taking turns turning a huge crank that rotated the crusher. They laughed as I was given a long pole and told to stir the grapes as they cranked and cranked.

"Look, the American is doing some real work!" one of them joked as I slogged the pole about in the bubbling, purple muck. Periodically, the foreman took a huge sugar thermometer and checked the grapes for the sugar content; the juice must be poured off at just the right moment or the desired kind of wine will not be possible. One of the men filled several glasses with fresh juice from the vat and they were passed hand to hand among the sweating workers. Clear as liquid sunshine, the juice was as sweet and refreshing as I had ever tasted. That weekend, there no beer served at any of the meals. Instead we had tall jugs of wine the family had made over the last several years.

We hitch-hiked back to Prague early the next morning in a large interstate truck making the run from Bratislava in Slovakia to Prague. It is still relatively safe to hitch-hike. Before the war in Yugoslavia, Czechs often worked their way around the region in the summers with only the aid of their thumbs. Viktor was very sad when the war came, as he had had grand plans for Dan and myself to travel with them up and down the coast of Yugoslavia—from Split to Dubrovnik—after he and Jarka returned from America.

Not long after we came back from the wine harvest, I attended my first soccer match in Prague. Until now, I hadn't had time to get over to any of the large, hulking stadiums in Prague to see either an international or a local match. With the help of several friends, I gradually gained an understanding of how the complex soccer leagues in Europe work and how both clubs and national teams play throughout the season, which generally runs from the early fall until May or June. Although I played in a soccer league when I was younger, I—like so many Americans—never warmed to the game. But after my first game on a cold, frosty night in November, I began to enjoy the sport. Although there's not enough scoring for me, the hooligans and rabid fans who show up at the matches makes it all worth watching.

I had heard about European and Latin American soccer fans, but had never seen them up close. Long before we even arrived at the game, which was featuring a "friendly" between a team from Scotland and the major city team, Praha Sparta, I could hear and see the die-hard fans. They were everywhere: packed in the trams, walking along the road waving banners and huge flags and singing and shouting. Moreover, you could smell the fans around you as most were already drunk beyond belief. There seemed to be enough police on hand to stamp out a military coup. The police were ready for anything, armed with snarling German Shepherds and truncheons. They carried white helmets with huge visors. A helicopter patrolled overhead.

In the United States one goes with an air of expectation to a game— in hopes that one will see a great play, grab a suntan, eat great food that's bad for you, relax. Attending a big soccer match is a little different, as one goes with an air of expectation that one might easily become caught up in a riot, get hit on the head with a bottle, have one's ears ruptured by menacing fireworks or be crushed to death by unruly fans. Not a lot of women go to soccer games.

While I came to see that Czech soccer matches didn't have nearly the amount of ferocious fans that England or Holland did, they still provided plenty of amazing moments. When Sparta Praha scored its first goal against the Scottish side, the stadium came unglued, especially down below where the really fanatical supporters were standing, walled in by high, cage-like fences. While they had been prevented from coming up to the fence by the police and the dogs, when the goal came there was a roar like a jet engine and hundreds of them surged forward in a mighty wave, climbing the fence and shaking it so much I thought it would collapse. The police responded by setting some of the dogs loose and wading into the crowd with their black truncheons flying. A lot of the security on hand was specially hired by the club for the evening and were known as the "Black Sheriffs." They were dressed in black uniforms and wore stocking masks so they couldn't be identified on video later on. They took their jobs seriously and beat the holy hell out of some of the fans.

Once, during the game when one of the security units was hit by a flying Roman Candle, the security agents waded into the crowd until they found the supposed offender, who was desperately trying to get away. They caught him; two men held him against the wall while one of the agents kicked the man in the groin and punched him repeatedly in the ribs, stomach and face. When the man fell limp, they dragged him out of cage area and threw him out of the stadium. The security goons also assaulted a photographer for *The Prague Post* after he took photographs of an incident outside the stadium.

Several months later, during a "friendly" match between Germany and Czechoslovakia, German fans began a rampage at one of Prague's train stations that continued through the center of town during the day and finished with a violent clash outside the stadium after the two teams finished in a 1–1 draw.

Not all the games were this intense. Many were simply run of the mill Saturday afternoon matches between the league teams. But at the really big matches, I made sure I got to the stadium early to watch the arrival of the opposing team's fans, who usually had to travel a long way. When the team from Barcelona arrived to play an away game for the Cup Winner's Cup, the Spanish fans marched from far down the street in unison behind a huge team flag. Even though the procession was surrounded by police, passing Czech fans hurled bottles and verbal abuse at the Spaniards. The Barcelona game ended in a draw, and after the game, more than 100 people were arrested outside the stadium. It was a quiet night.

26

A Country Breaking Apart

While privatization may have been steaming ahead, the Slovak separatist issue was still circling around like a shark that refused to go away. While there were many levels of debate, the key issues surrounded the amount of autonomy the Slovaks would have in the new federal constitution, which was slowly working its way through the Parliament despite having been presented in late 1990. Slovaks wanted to have "a loose form of co-existence" and the power to conclude separate treaties with other nations and control customs and other economic issues. The majority of Czech deputies disagreed, saying what the Slovaks wanted amounted to outright independence. Even with these various conflicts, in the fall of 1991 I still doubted heavily that the country was headed for division.

The bitterness between Czechs and Slovaks dated from the early days of the Czechoslovak state. Even then, there was a disagreement about whether Czechs were dominating the white-collar job sector, inside and outside of Slovakia. Czechs complained they had to control the post office and other civil services in Slovakia because there weren't enough qualified Slovaks.[1] In addition, Czechs contended that their half of the country was forced to pour large amounts of money into building up Slovak schools and Slovak infrastructure, which previously had been largely non-existent. Slovaks, on the other hand, complained that the Czechs have always demeaned them and reneged on promises to share profits equally.

While Klaus' party was the most popular in Bohemia and Moravia, in Slovakia, the Movement For a Democratic Slovakia (HZDS) had climbed to the top of the polls. Led by a former Communist named Vladimir Mečiar, HZDS was actively proposing that Slovakia be given outright sovereignty and be allowed to make more decisions for itself.

To many Westerners, reform in the Warsaw Pact countries is confusing, especially when entire countries willingly vote to return former Communists to power—as in the case of Bulgaria or the Ukraine. Ronald Reagan preached the Soviet satellites would all happily choose Democratic governments for themselves. However, this just isn't so, as recent developments have shown. Democracy is something best appreciated by those who have lived under it, and most of the Warsaw Pact hasn't. Thus, to understand Mečiar and the nature of Slovak nationalism is to appreciate the extraordinarily precarious situation all across Central and Eastern Europe.

Mečiar is generally stereotyped as a big and tough. If he had been an actor, he would have made a perfect extra as a butcher or teamster. I once saw him at a press conference dressed in a shiny, pin-stripe suit and I wondered whether he had taken up moonlighting as a pit boss in a Las Vegas casino. His face is wide and somewhat flat, dominated by a prominent jaw and heavy set eyes that seem to swish about like radar seeking the enemy. It is not surprising to discover that when he was young, he tried his hand at amateur boxing. His voice, deep and coarse, is instantly recognizable, as is his speech, which comes in staccato-like bursts. If he is angry or trying to sound impassioned, he can bellow, and chop his arms through the air. Despite his tough exterior and these thuggish characteristics, it is easy to misread Mečiar, and more than a handful of journalists have done so, labeling him as everything from a tinhorn dictator, neo-fascist, neo-Communist or hard-liner. All of these things Mečiar is not—just as Mečiar is not simple.

The son of poor, working-class parents from a tiny village in central Slovakia, he exudes a rough kind of streetwise charm. He is a good public speaker and has succeeded politically because he knows his people. He rose to power on a strange mixture of populism, left-of-center politics and benign nationalism that played extremely well with disaffected Slovaks who were suffering high unemployment and

274

a bleak economic future. While Klaus promised abstract concepts like European integration, free-markets and strict monetary controls, Mečiar went for the basics, promising a pie-in-the-sky Slovakia that was independent, financially secure and strong.

While other politicians in Bratislava were debating the various issues of what it meant to be Slovak over coffee and cigarettes, Mečiar was out on the stump. He didn't need to debate what it meant to be a Slovak: he knew. "I've spoken to ordinary Slovaks," he said. "I understand their problems perfectly." He sometimes invoked a concept one could call "two pigs and a cow," appealing to agrarian hearts and minds with promises of largess for all under a Mečiar government. If you were a steelworker, there would be more steel to produce. Farmers would be cared for and respected. And most of all, Slovaks would speak Slovak and Hungarians could either speak Slovak or leave the country.

While it is true that Mečiar had been a Communist, he had been tossed out of the Party in the "normalization" period following the invasion in 1968. He earned a law degree during the 1970s and impressed many with his keen mind and ability to command a room.

He had originally become Prime Minister of Slovakia in 1990 when he was still a member of Public Against Violence, which had been the majority party in Slovakia after the revolution. In 1991, he was removed as Prime Minister after being accused of blackmailing politicians with their StB files. The charges included tampering with his own secret police files from the early 1970s and ordering a break-in of government files relating to the StB issue. Although many believed Mečiar's career was finished, it was really only just beginning. He left Public Against Violence and formed the Movement for a Democratic Slovakia (HZDS). And he vowed he would return to the political arena.

"What they did was dishonest, immoral," he said, describing his political enemies, including the media. "They were trying to make me look like someone who rapes small children."[1]

If people weren't charmed by his promises, they were taken in by Mečiar's strength and character. It has been said many times that the people across Central and Eastern Europe desire strong leaders.

Whether this is always true is debatable, but in the Slovak case, people were seeking someone who could command more respect in Prague.

Snapping at the heels of the HZDS was an even more nationalist party—the Slovak National Party, which advocated a complete divorce with the Czechs. Together, the two parties had gathered a considerable amount of clout.

Roman Zelenay, a Slovak Parliament member, reached back to the earliest days of the Czechoslovak state in defending his peoples' right to self-determination: "The Czechs have failed to keep their promises," he said. "We've had this before and we don't want it again. That's why we want an international treaty which would have international validity."[2]

Not everyone in Slovakia, however, was a rabid nationalist.

"The nationalists have nothing better to do than to exploit the poor Slovak people," said František Sebej, a member of the moderate Civic Democratic Union, which had been created when Public Against Violence fell apart in 1991. "This is what you have, when a large group of people feel threatened this way. For the last 40 years they were led to believe in the horrors of capitalism—so it's a sort of collective fear and insecurity. It's the best time for demagogues to appear with simple solutions for our problems—a fear of conspiracies, a fear of outside forces."[3]

There were now calls, led by Havel, for a referendum to decide the future of the nation. Havel played this card in the early fall of 1991, hoping that a referendum would settle the issue once and for all, as opinion polls showed that only 10 percent of Slovaks strongly favored splitting off from the Czechs.

"Barely two years ago, people were chanting, 'There is power in unity!' in the streets," Havel told the Federal Parliament on Sept. 24. "An echo of this chant reaches our ears from various sides today. We are obliged to listen carefully to this strengthening civic voice. Let us try to find again within ourselves a generous mind, a spirit of mutual understanding and good will."[4]

Sadly, there were few generous minds, little mutual understanding and almost no good will as the question of a referendum quickly became bogged down in semantics. While the wrangling went on, people gathered at the statue of St. Wenceslas to sign a petition calling for a referendum.

In mid November, Havel organized a mass rally in Wenceslas Square where he could appeal to the people that the unity of the country was at stake. Already, tensions were rising to the boiling point, as Havel had been nearly attacked several weeks before in Bratislava when he tried to address a rally. When he tried to ask for two minutes of silence to honor those who had died attempting to being freedom to the Czechoslovak nation, many in the crowd threw eggs at him.

With the egging firmly in mind, Havel hoped to appeal to a broader group of people than the Slovak nationalists who had met him earlier. The night he spoke, more than 40,000 people gathered in the dark evening to listen to a parade of speakers.

As I shivered in the cold air along with the thousands of others, I was pleased to get a chance to see what it must have been like during those demonstrations nearly two years before which had brought down the government. Havel and the others were speaking from the same balcony on Wenceslas Square where he had emerged with Dubček in the revolution.

"Do you want to hear him?" a man said through the loudspeakers. The crowd roared its approval. "Do you want to hear him?" Then Havel appeared at the balcony and the square erupted in cheers. In a short, impassioned speech, Havel urged Parliament members not to waste more time and heed polls showing that people wanted a referendum and, ultimately, a unified state.

"The fully-elected Parliaments are not our enemy," he said, looking down at his speech card. "You elected them. You have a right to ask them to clear the uncertainty."

Czech singer Marta Kubišová ended the evening by singing the Czechoslovak national anthem and all around me, hundreds of people took off their hats in the freezing wind and sang along with her, steam from their breaths rising into the inky night.

The next morning at school, Martin Opel, who was a teacher and also a member of the local town council, called a meeting of all the teachers. We signed a petition urging the government to take action.

I wasn't sure whether I should sign, but Martin said the government probably wouldn't care.

"It'll be helpful," he said, passing the petition on to the next teacher.

Instead of quickly settling down to work, however, many of the deputies in Parliament were angry and criticized Havel.

"If we say 'No,' then it will be 'No,'" said a Slovak parliament member, explaining why he and other Slovaks would vote against Havel's various proposals, including increased presidential powers and the referendum.[5] In particular, Mečiar's party, HZDS, opposed the referendum, saying a referendum would not determine whether or not the country could have a constitutional future. In reality, the Slovak nationalists knew that they would probably lose the referendum. Ultimately, Havel's various proposals were stalled, withdrawn or rejected.

In December, *The Prague Post* had moved to larger offices, as we had outgrown the original small one-room office near Old Town Square. We ended up, surprisingly, in the building owned and operated by the Communist Party of Czechoslovakia, which made for strange bedfellows as we had handfuls of squeaky-clean Americans, Brits and Canadians wandering the halls next to some of the most horrid, old Communists left in the country. The building was filled with leftover busts of Lenin and pictures and posters from before the revolution. Czechs visiting our offices were either bemused by our location or extremely wary about entering the building.

The Communist Party was going through various divisions and reductions, as it struggled to reconcile itself with the past and chart a path for the future. After long and sometimes bitter debate, a number of the extremely hard-line Communists were not allowed back into the party and the goal was to create a party along the lines of the French or Italian Communists.

January, 1992, brought more price hikes. In his New Year's address, Havel warned people not to expect much good news in the coming year: "Production and the standard of living continue to drop, but unfortunately, the worst is yet to come," he said. "We should be prepared for our economy to be recovering for a long and difficult time from the unrestricted calamity of forty-one years of Communist mismanagement."

I packed up my things and headed out to yet another extended stay at a school in nature. I was lucky to go, as the school in nature program was rapidly being phased out. There simply wasn't enough money to send all of the kids off for two weeks anymore, and the parents, except in rare cases, didn't have the money to be able to carry on the tradition. On a gray Friday afternoon, we herded thirty kids onto a bus and roared off to a hotel located in the northern mountain range near the German and Polish borders. It was a fairly uneventful two weeks of classes and long walks in the snow covered forests, except for a day-long trip to Ještěd, a mountain peak more than 1,000 meters high. When we reached the summit by cable car, the view was spectacular, with clear views stretching into Germany and Poland. To the south, a cloud bank stretched like a blanket into the far southern horizon. I felt like I was flying on top of the world. The wind gusts were chilling.

On one side of the mountain, the trees were fairly healthy. The western side which faced some of northern Bohemia's most devastated areas was a textbook case of devastation. The trees had been burned and scarred by acid rain until they were little more than lumps in the snow. I hiked down the side of the mountain about 50 meters and broke off a tree branch: black as coal, the wood crumbled in my hand like charcoal. From where I stood, I could easily see mile after mile of trees cut low to the ground, all looking like there had been a recent forest fire.

In other spots, many of the trees were stripped bare. Near their tops, there were needle-heavy branches, where the trees were able to get a bit of fresh air. But often, even these branches hung limp, like exhausted arms. Other branches jutted out in strange, abstract arcs. Withering bark peeled away from the trees.

In extreme cases, the trees had weakened so much that they collapsed and toppled over in tangled heaps. Loggers had come to take

279

what they wanted, wantonly, without plan or regard for the future. They harvested the best of the lot, leaving the spindly, sick trees behind to cast strange, eerie shadows through the yawing cavities.

There were many reasons for this devastation: The burning of cheap brown coal without any kind of filtration system created acid rain that literally burned the trees to death. From below, the open dumping of toxic waste and overuse of pesticides poisoned the soil. Farm chemical use, including DDT, rose 360 percent between 1960 and 1980 alone. Then the rainwater carried the chemicals into the rivers and streams, killing wildlife by the thousands. The land acidified, turned rank, unnourishable. In nearby towns, huge factories belched other kinds of filth into the sky.[6]

Years behind the West in establishing environmental protection standards (and given the West's equally fairly shameless record in these areas, that should make you cringe), most industry was never were upgraded to include filtration systems, safe disposal sites or even basic provisions for dealing with waste management.

The level of sulfur dioxide in Bohemia's mountains is the highest in Europe. Lakes are often heavily acidic and the underground waters are polluted by nitrogenous substances due to the unsuitable fertilization and pesticide use.[7]

In their search for nutrients, the trees gasped for air and pulled at the soil. But it wasn't to be found. So they died.

The major towns of northern Bohemia in the Sudeten and Carpathian mountains, Ústí Nad Labem and Most, are giant toxic waste sites, with enough environmental cleanup work to last two or three decades. In the winter, children wear protective masks and scarves on their way to and from school and don't play outside. The elderly and people with respiratory problems are confined to their homes like prisoners in a jail.

More than 70 percent of the country's rivers cannot be used for drinking, fishing or swimming. More than 5 percent are classified as "dead," like the Cuyahoga River in Cleveland was during the early 1970s.[8]

27

Olga

I don't know where else but in Czechoslovakia the President's wife would answer the door to her own apartment holding a lit cigarette. In the hoary milieu of politics, attempts at maintaining a sense of normalcy and an air of casualness are usually abandoned early on.

But the morning we went to interview Olga Havelová about her work as First Lady of Czechoslovakia, it was more like spending time with a friend than interviewing a VIP. But Havelová and her associates have tried to do as much as possible to protect her privacy while still allowing her to pursue a number of fund-raising projects.[1]

Although some reporters have written at length about Havelová being "ornery" and sometimes difficult to deal with, she seemed as relaxed as anyone could be in such a difficult situation. Tall and impassive, with gray, curly hair, she does not speak loudly or gesture dramatically.

Havelová led us into a large space that had been renovated and turned into a conference room for meetings and guests. Chic modern art hung on plain white walls. I was speaking Czech with our interpreter and Havelová seemed surprised. She asked me how I learned. After explaining about my teaching position, she motioned us over to a long table and waited while we arranged the microphone and tape recorder.

Scheduling the interview had been ridiculously easy, as I had met both her and her personal assistant several weeks earlier at the opening of a new center for journalists. Havelová had been there with Shirley Temple Black, but had spent most of the time in a corner, furtively smoking a cigarette and talking to friends.

This, I have been told by others, is simply Havelová's style: present the program or award with a minimum of fuss and then gracefully retire into the background. While she probably never expected to become First Lady, she has chosen to assume a delicate balance between the personal and the private.

After taking several moments to screw up our courage, a friend and I approached Havelová, who looked like she wanted to be anywhere else but in a roomful of journalists and publishers. An interview? It was fine, but please schedule it with the assistant. Several weeks later, we were in her office.

I had prepared for the interview by trying to read everything I could in advance about Havelová (including a gluey article from *People* magazine written in 1990). I quickly decided to dash my prepared questions after I sized up the situation: I was expected to ask questions that pertained only to the Olga Havelová Foundation which was trying to raise money for the health care system. An American named Deidre O'Byrne, who worked for Havelová, sat in on the interview and I pegged her as even more reason not to overstep the boundaries of the interview. Poof! There went a number of good questions I had hoped to ask, including Havelová's views of women's issues and politics. While I was hurriedly organizing my thoughts, Havelová suddenly learned towards me and asked me a most unexpected question.

"Do you go out to eat much?" Surprised, I said through my interpreter that I used to, but now it was almost too expensive.

"What's a good place to go these days?" Havelová asked. After thinking a minute, I suggested a couple places that weren't very pricey but good in atmosphere. Havelová, listened, nodded, seemed to record my answers for future reference and we started the interview.

I asked her if she worked all the time in her office.

"I try to devote as much time as possible, all my time. But of course, there are moments when I have to find time for my household. The most important thing I've discovered is that we are still doing far too little and that we ought to be doing more."

While our photographer moved about the room taking photos from different angles, Havelová discussed the difficulty she was having changing people's negative perceptions of charities.

"It's a question of getting people accustomed to this approach," she said. "So many people reacted to the Communist pressure by withdrawing into their own little world."

After skirting over a number of subjects relating to the foundation, I tried slipping in some questions about travel, including whether or not her vision of Western countries prior to the revolution was the same as what she had found when she was allowed to travel.

"The idea that we were living under some kind of lid is wrong. Basically, even though we did not have much access to information, we naturally could get it. Of course, we did not have the physical possibilities to travel that we have now. But we do know where a particular state in America or Africa is situated, as opposed to Americans, who do not know where Czechoslovakia is. We have some idea of the world." She laughed, and lit another cigarette.

"Have you gotten used to being photographed?" our cameraman asked as he set up another shot.

"I have some experience," she said, fidgeting with the cigarette box in front of her. "The police used to keep a watchful eye on us and constantly had their cameras pointed at us." Her face broke into a sly smile and she rose from the table. Havelová stared outside at the gloomy, rainy day and then announced that she had to go upstairs and prepare lunch.

"I'm going to cook some soup," she said brightly, wishing us well and leaving the room.

28

Cranking Up Capitalism

C apitalism, as anyone who was born in a Western country knows, has many faces, some more ugly than others. The late winter of 1991 and early spring of 1992 revealed the positive and negative aspects of a market economy in the Czech Republic, sometimes all at once. Klaus' program to enlist the average citizen in the market was turning out to be a success, as the coupon privatization program was selling out all across the country. The venture had begun quietly enough the previous fall when every citizen was entitled to purchase one coupon book for 1,000 crowns, worth about $32, but a lot more in emotional weight. The coupon holder could either choose to entrust part or all of their book to a mutual fund or "play" the new market by assigning part or all of the book to the many companies which were being privatized.

Several motivations led to the coupon program. To involve the public, they would need to have some means of becoming mentally involved with the new market economy. Initial sums of money—regardless of how symbolic they may have been—needed to be put into newly privatized companies. Additionally, the program would help determine a company's relative worth based upon the company's assets and the investors' demand.

There would be several rounds of bidding on companies following share prices of popular companies would be moved upwards and potential investors would be given the chance to reconsider their bids—almost like a horse race.

Companies could generally sell their equity to all forms of buyers—foreign investors, local buyers and banks. Any equity left over could go towards stock generated in the voucher program.

The coupon program, which had never been attempted anywhere before, had run into problems over the winter when the government was forced to delay the deadline for approving companies to participate in the program. Many people in the government and the private sector complained that, as in the case of the small business auctions, the architects of privatization had not required investors to disclose the sources of their investment capital.

"In their drive to create a free market, in our view (the government) overlooked an important element—a certain degree of regulatory infrastructure and disclosure rules to enable them to make rational choices," White & Case's Daniel Arbess told a reporter for *The New York Times* in 1991. "What is likely to happen is that there will be a free market, but those with inside information, like company managers, will have a natural advantage."[1]

Arbess, who was heavily involved in structuring privatization deals between foreign companies, also complained that the government's policies on the process itself were vague and often misleading. Worse, he said, the government office charged with approving each privatization program was often slowing down the process by undoing a lot of work done by each company. While the ministry had every right to reject suspicious or unsound transactions, a lot of time and effort could have been saved if the companies had better rules to organize under.

The government countered such claims by trying to force the large companies to set aside relatively large amounts of equity for future stockholders and mutual funds. Parliament also gamely drafted some legislation requiring people who had bought small businesses the year before to reveal the source of their money.

While the public knew about many large companies, especially those that produced popular goods like chocolate, beer and bread, many of the companies were an enigma of strange products. Why should an elderly woman invest in a company that makes bolts for the inside of ovens when she hasn't a clue about how valuable such bolts can be? No, instead, she was more likely to go for the Grand Hotel Pupp, a popular hotel in Karlovy Vary.

In the end, a lot of people simply decided to entrust their coupon books to a mutual fund, which would accomplish the various biddings and future investments for them. But, in building capitalism, nothing comes easily, and in this case, there were more than 300 mutual funds. Everyone, it seemed, could start a mutual fund and either work with a fraction of a customer's points or buy their books outright and thus increase the mutual fund capital holdings.

The coupon process continued through the winter, with a lower than expected percentage of people turning out to buy books. A number of mutual funds began offering high returns to investors either immediately or within a year. The percentage of people turning out to buy coupon books shot up dramatically. One of the mutual funds was Harvard Capital and Consulting, whose chairman, Viktor Kožený, went to Harvard as an undergraduate. The fund had no link to the university, but the founders probably thought it was good advertising.

Harvard, in particular, offered to pay investors up to 10,000 crowns at the end of the first year for their books. Other companies bought the books outright for as much as 8,000 crowns. Suddenly, everyone wanted to get involved in the privatization scheme. In the end, millions invested in coupons.

Eventually, the government was forced to suspend the voucher program for a month while it tightened up some of the rules relating to who could sell and buy the little voucher books.

"We know it's late and it's our fault," said Vladimír Šuman, a member of the Czech Parliament. "Conflict of interest and insider information are big problems but it is difficult to apply Western practices and rules to our situation and conditions. This is not easy."[2]

The government required that funds spread their investment among at least ten enterprises and ruled that funds could not hold up to 20 percent of any one company. In addition, officials of the government were forbidden from sitting on the management boards of the companies.

"What is Communism?" someone asked on a television show that lampooned the week's news. The answer: "The longest and most painful route from Capitalism to Capitalism."

287

With the inflation, Renáta's salary from teaching didn't go very far anymore. Although she loved teaching, she decided she should begin looking for a job that would pay more. On a Friday in late March, Renáta called me late one afternoon from her school.

"I just wanted to let you know that I'm going for a job interview tonight. I saw an advertisement in the newspaper for a company that needs good English speakers."

"What's the company?" I asked.

"They didn't say, except that it's an large American firm. They asked me to come tonight for an interview. At 7 P.M."

I didn't like the sound of this. "At 7 P.M.?" I asked. "Most companies usually have their interviews a little earlier in the day. Even by American workaholic standards, that's a little late."

"Well, actually, they said that its some sort of organizational meeting," she countered. By now, flares were shooting off in my mind. It turned out the "interview" was at a large public hall. I smelled a pyramid scam.

"Well, if it's a meeting, can I go with you and wait until after you're done?" Renáta agreed and met me shortly before the appointed hour at the metro. While we were walking to the hall, I tried to explain the concept of pyramid-styled companies and how they can induce people to buy large amount of products that the purchaser can't unload on his friends. Sure enough, upon stepping into the hall, my expectations were rewarded. It was Herbalife.

Judging by the large turnout, a lot of people obviously considered themselves to be "good English speakers." All of those to be "interviewed" were given a big button saying "I Love Herbalife" in Czech and information about the gradual step program in which a person can purchase a select amount of materials from Herbalife each month. In this way, a person can wind up with, gosh, a lot of Herbalife products stacked in their garage and family room and bedroom.

Up on a stage, an American in a snazzy three-piece suit and wire-rim glasses was giving the pep talk of his life while an interpreter struggled to keep up.

"And, as you can see by these numbers," the man drawled in a flat Midwestern accent. "If you only find just a few people in your network each month, you can make up to ..." His hands chopped at the air. He was selling! He was dealing! God save Herbalife!

By that point, we were already gone, fleeing out across the carpet towards the door. A Herbalife woman trailed after us speaking in Czech.

"Wouldn't you like to sign our register? Let me give you a balloon." I looked back and saw that they were giving away yellow and red balloons to each person. The room looked like a birthday party gone mad.

Back out on the street, I felt ashamed for the river of untapped capitalist excess that, more than not, seemed to emanate from my country.

"Well, look, since that didn't work out, can we go to McDonald's?" Renáta asked.

It was then that I remembered that the first McDonald's had opened that day, just off the main square. All my life I wanted to see Paris or the Pyramids, not a soggy Big Mac. But I gamely held my head up high and we marched up to the front of the restaurant, only to find chaos. People were stopping in front of the store's large plate-glass windows to gawk at the rows of formica tables and the long counter lined with cash registers. An American employee of McDonald's stood with a walkie-talkie helping to arrange security.

"Clear 2–4," he said into the walkie-talkie. "All quiet down front. We still have about 100 out." From the seriousness in his voice, I thought the president would be showing up. Jesus, all I wanted was a hamburger. Would there be strip searches next?

Like the Herbalife show, the opening was a gay old affair with still more balloons and bewildered-looking Czech children being given little flags and other totems from the McDonald's empire. We entered the restaurant and found a nearly empty line. Needless to say, it was a strange experience ordering Big Macs in Czech. It was an even stranger experience having a tremendous amount of Czech money siphoned out of my wallet to pay for two Cokes, large fries and two Big Macs: over 180 crowns. I didn't let Renáta see the cost of the meals, but she was quick to add it all up off the menu.

"That is a lot for this," she said gesturing to the food as we sat down at one of the super-clean tables. I was blinking like some groundhog in February at the all the bright lights and shiny brass and having one of those freakouts that I usually had only when I went to a Western city like Berlin or Munich. Except now I was having it in Prague. Amazing.

Renáta looked at the size of the Big Mac and said, "I don't think I can eat all of this." So she disassembled portions of it and ate it carefully, piece by piece. I was touched, watching my best girl eat her first Big Mac.

An elderly man came and sat down next to us, carefully balancing a tray that had the smallest size hamburger, a cup of water and the smallest possible fries. After arranging himself, he carefully began to eat the tiny meal like it was gold. I watched from the corner of my eye. After a minute he turned to me.

"Excuse me, but I don't think this food should be very good if you are diabetic!" He nibbled at a fry. I laughed and agreed with him completely. He continued, shaking a fry at me: "And it's so expensive! I told my grandson that I would bring him something. May I have your placemats?" We gave him our placemats that had color pictures of Ronald McDonald and all of the foods one can purchase at McDonald's.

Across from the elderly man, a group of young American backpackers of the Nebraska cornhusker variety sat reading *USA Today* with their feet up on the table. One of them got up to order a drink.

"Hey dude, get me another Mac, would'ya?" one of them called, throwing a handful of Czech crowns at his friend. "I'm still hungry." Next to me, the elderly man saved his straw, cup and french-fry box for his grandson.

"He should be pleased," the man said. "I'll try and bring him here sometime."

29

Fateful Election

W ell before the Federal election in June, 1992, Havel had announced he would be willing to stand again for President of Czechoslovakia. As he opened the final session of the Federal Parliament before the elections, he pleaded once again with deputies to consider their responsibility to the people and not engage in a rush to sovereignty. In what was clearly a dig at Mečiar, Havel criticized the politicians who were spewing out "cheap and seductive appeals to national feelings." Such partisan politics only reduced people to a "herd of aggressive soccer fans."[1] Despite Havel's announcement, most of the Slovak deputies said they would not support Havel in a bid for re-election. Moreover, Mečiar's party was pushing for a separate Slovak presidency.

The issue of *lustrace* also continued to boil throughout the run up to the election, with Havel releasing his own StB file that indicated he once was considered to be a potential collaborator. Czech and Slovak journalists were investigated by the Federal Security and Information Service for their alleged links to the StB.[2]

There were so many parties involved in the election—forty in all—that it was hard to follow them all. Aside from the major parties, there were the Communists and the Social Democratic Party and fringe groups like the Green Party and the Republican Party. The Friends of Beer party was back with a platform contending they would "support any reasonable proposal" and the Independent Erotic Initiative slyly informed voters the party would "do nothing at all, but everything for you." Their political campaign poster showed a happy family—mother, father and children—all enjoying the outdoors in their birthday suits. Our home was soon awash in pamphlets and bits of information from many of these groups. Television was a jumble of commercials—some more professional than others—all proclaiming the correctness of various political platforms.

On the Saturday for voting in early June, we took a train to Nymburk near Prague where Renáta was registered to vote. The entire process was very similar to American voting procedures: the elderly ladies running the election hall, the school classrooms that had been appropriated for the vote, the various rituals of checking people's addresses and identification and finally, the vote itself. As the election was based on parliamentary rules, one did not vote for a single person, but the slate of candidates in your local region. Voting consisted of stuffing the appropriate sheet of names in an envelope, sealing it behind a curtain and then stuffing it in a box.

After we returned to Prague several days later, I asked Dana what voting had been like in the past.

"Well, there was the curtain," she said, "and supposedly you could go behind it if you wished but actually that was not allowed! You were supposed to be such a good supporter of Socialism that you were expected to openly declare your support for the Party by merely making your choice in front of everyone else. And anyway, there was only one set of names—the same set of names each time. As for me, I never looked when I voted, I just closed my eyes and just tried to get it over as quickly as possible." Of course, nearly everyone voted, as the various voting committees would go over the lists and then make follow-up checks asking why people hadn't voted.

The 1992 election produced two major winners: Klaus' right-wing ODS in the Czechlands and Mečiar's HZDS in Slovakia. For Mečiar, the strong showing provided him with an opportunity to serve crow to his critics.

"When I last left here, I said I would return," Mečiar told his cheering supporters in Bratislava after HZDS emerged with the largest percentage of the votes in Slovakia. "Now I'm back and this time there are more of us."

But it became clear it would be difficult to form a government between the Czechs and Slovaks. Klaus and Mečiar, whose diametrically opposed parties constituted more than 60 percent of the entire new Federal Parliament, met the week following the elections. At first, Klaus was optimistic a deal could be struck.

"When starting positions are different, which is the position now, you must negotiate. I think the economic reform is going the right way, but if Mr. Mečiar does not, we will have to talk about it" he was reported as saying.[3] They talked about it for several days and quickly came to a dead end. The Slovaks wanted a lot of autonomy: massive decentralization and the possibility of independent foreign policy; separate relations with the International Monetary Fund; embassies. Then there was also the thorny problem of future economic planning. There was no agreement on who would be the new president. Mečiar and the more nationalist parties said they would not accept Havel.

On the early evening of June 17, we were sitting outside a restaurant on a huge veranda overlooking Prague, drinking beer and watching the sun slowly set over the valley. CBS was in town to do one of the "Americans in Prague" stories and an annoying producer and two cameramen were circling around, filming us and asking insipid questions like, "Do you like the beer?" and "Do you like Havel?" Despite their presence, the air was warm and the evening was pleasant.

Shortly after 8 P.M., one of our reporters came walking out of the dark. Word had just come down from where Klaus and Mečiar were negotiating.

"It's all over," he said sitting down. "Klaus is Prime Minister of the Czech Parliament and Mečiar is the Prime Minister of the Slovak Parliament. They're giving each of the Parliaments until September to decide what to do about the country." There was a visible hush at the table while we all considered the ramifications of what he had just said. Two other reporters got up to hurry off and start gathering information. The CBS producer asked the reporter what he was talking about.

"I didn't know the country might split!" she said. "Will there be war?" Happily, most people were ignoring her by now.

"We still want a federation, but the decision must be made quickly," Klaus said after the meeting ended. "A loose union is not a state foun-

293

dation. There are no precedents in the history of mankind." At a late-evening press conference charged with electricity, Klaus explained what had happened. After seeing that there were few areas where both sides could compromise, the parties had decided to instruct the two Parliaments in each republic to begin laying the groundwork and terms for a split.[4] A temporary Federal Parliament would be formed to preside over the final period of the federal nation. And although Klaus had said he thought the federation lost, he still was holding the door open in various statements he made to the press.

"It is definitely my wish that we stay together in a federation," Klaus told *Time* magazine later that week. "But when I consider the forces involved, I am very pessimistic." Klaus said he was surprised by the strength of the Slovak bid for independence, and said it was irrelevant to try and brand the potential breakup of the country a mistake as "the forces (meaning the Slovaks) involved don't listen to rational arguments."[5]

Despite the fact that his party had not favored outright separation, Mečiar moved further and further towards independence: "New markets will be created and dependence on the Czech economy will be eliminated," he said. "Slovakia will become an element of international relationships, enabling it to defend its own interests. The emancipation of Slovakia must be considered not as a new isolation but as a new opportunity."[6]

Havel continued to stress that a referendum was the "only constitutional and moral way" to solve the future of the nation. But his voice was gradually losing its distinction among the thundering calls for division. For a short period, Slovak moderates proposed a rotating federal presidency, similar to that in the former Yugoslavia, but these concessions were immediately rejected by the Czech side.[7]

Despite the fact that 75 percent of the country supported Havel's re-election, his nomination was defeated in the Federal Parliament on July 3 by the Slovak coalition. Havel's rejection only increased the increasingly ugly amount of public comments flowing back and forth between Czech and Slovaks in the press and seemed to propel the two republics towards a split with even more speed. Klaus and Mečiar began talking about dissolving the federation in earnest.

Shortly after noon on July 20, 113 out of 150 members from the Slovak National Council voted to declare the sovereignty of the Slovak nation, putting the final nail in the federation.

"We have waited for this moment for more than 1,000 years," Mečiar told the Parliament before the vote. "For the first time we are deciding alone about ourselves. The declaration shows the degree of maturity of Slovakia and is a signal to the European lands that we exist and that we are willing to deal with them as an equal." After the vote, the deputies sang the Slovak national anthem, "Nad Tatrou za blýská" ("Over the Tatras There is Lightning") and other Slovak folk songs and drank champagne. Outside, thousands waved the new Slovak flag, a red, white and blue banner with three hills and a cross.[8]

Later the same day, Havel announced he would resign as president, effective the following Sunday. In an a televised address to the nation that evening, he said he was resigning because he believed he had lost the confidence of a large section of the Slovak representation. He didn't want to become an obstacle to change. As early evening shadows crept across the walls of our narrow apartment, we listened to Havel's speech on the radio and I truly believed for the first time that the country was going to split.

"I cannot imagine how under the circumstances and in view of the uneasy times ahead of us I could carry out my office well," Havel said. "I cannot take responsibility for developments over which I cease to exert any influence. I do not want to be a mere clerk marking time, waiting for a few weeks until I leave this office for good, and in the meantime, just passively observing further events and only formally complying with my duties."[9]

After the address, Havel went to the presidential summer retreat outside of Prague. On a warm and humid Sunday evening, while he waited for his resignation to become official, he drank a cocktail with the assembled reporters, signed autographs and changed out of his suit into jeans and a t-shirt. Reporters at the scene said he seemed visibly relieved.

The summer was unbearably hot. Every day, there would be a cool few hours in the pre-dawn hours; by noon, it seemed the sidewalks would melt. Even the dust seemed to hang limp in the air. In the late afternoon, we regularly gathered in the shade of a beer garden not far from our offices and watched tour groups of Germans and Austrians dancing in the sticky heat to various brass bands arranged for their pleasure. It was too hot to do much of anything, let alone swirl around to a polka. By five in the afternoon, almost as if on cue, huge thunderheads would drift slowly over the downtown and soon lightning and thunder would descend on the beer garden, scattering the Germans and drenching half-empty beer glasses with water. Safe under a wooden veranda, we would take all this in and watch as waiters tried to save partially eaten lunches and tablecloths from the downpour.

After the rain had passed, the money changers, usually Arabs or Gypsies, would take up their places in the main square and the hookers would begin to parade up and down the streets. There seemed to be more and more of both groups; I honestly couldn't remember seeing any when I arrived in 1990, despite being told that they were there.

The government couldn't decide what to do about the prostitutes, since there was no firm law regulating or prohibiting prostitution. It was the same way with advertising. The Parliament had tried several times to ban cigarette advertising, only to see the law get overturned or amended at the last moment. In the evening, the area around Wenceslas Square was a blur of blinking neon and back-lit signs advertising every possible brand of cigarette; restaurants seemed to try and out do each other in how many free advertising totems they could cram on the premises—from Marlboro banners outside to Camel ashtrays and "Test The West" placemats.

Western companies seemed to be able to generally do as they pleased in attacking the wide open market in Prague. Advertising was still insanely cheap by western standards, so it was quite easy for a company to go out and buy up as much space as it needed. The month the German liquor Jägermeister entered the market, it was like a full-scale assault. It had never been imported before the revolution and suddenly it was everywhere. Ads on television. Billboards. Brigades of kids were hired to pass out bumperstickers and posters of the drink, while the company set up booths all over town to hand out little shots of the green drink that tastes suspiciously like cough syrup.

All during that hot summer, Czechs in Prague were flocking to see *Les Miserables,* the popular musical about the French Revolution. The producer, Adam Novák, a Czech emigré who had recently returned from Canada, assembled some of the more well-known pop singers to star in the production, which was the most expensive and lavish musical ever staged in the country. *Les Miserables* is a franchise, so Novák had to raise a lot of money before the French company that authorizes productions around the world would allow the show to be staged in Prague. Novák turned to Johnnie Walker, among other groups, to help pay the bills. At the press conference to introduce the cast, the whiskey company arranged bottles of its product on every table, with ice and bottles of soda water. When I returned to the newspaper after the press conference, I had to struggle to hear the proceedings on my tape recorder over the hiss and fizz of opening soda bottles and clinking ice. I tried to imagine the same thing happening in the United States and couldn't; the entire press conference had been too surreal.

In comparison to American press conferences where one is lucky to get stale crackers and tea, Czechs were often serving up wine and beer and snacks to the reporters. I recall attending a press conference held to announce the release of all of Antonín Dvořák's works on compact disk and becoming trapped in an orgy of champagne, served to celebrate the great composer's birthday. We all stood while the executives of the record label toasted each other and Dvořák. I finally left after an hour; the entire affair had disintegrated into little more than a cocktail party at one in the afternoon. Sometimes these relaxed affairs were charming, and one had to wonder why one was working so hard. Take it easy! Enjoy yourself! Other times, the press events were little more than a nuisance of poorly trained reporters asking useless questions and wasting time while they fussed with coffee and the ever-present little sandwiches. Ask the questions and be done with it! Besides, I couldn't work, let alone think very clearly after having even one beer at lunch. The alcohol would just make me sleepy.

Avoiding work, or rather, delaying it, seems to have been one of the more important rituals under Communism. "Work is not a rabbit; it won't run away," the expression went and many people spent their days lazily dreaming and drifting the hours away. I once borrowed the use of a computer from a Czech friend for an afternoon to finish a news story. I didn't have my own computer and I worked hard for more than four hours while my friend was out of the office. When he returned, shortly after five in the afternoon, he was shocked that I was still at the keyboard.

"Are you still working?" he said incredulously. "Have you stopped since I was gone?" When I said that I hadn't, he shook his head in amazement.

"I just went swimming and played tennis! I never work so much. I can't. What would I do if I did?" His last comment sounded like some philosophical question, so I shrugged and just said I was a workaholic.

In the hot and sticky rooms at the Federal Parliament and across the country, the Czech and Slovak governments set up a number of committees which were supposed to hammer out a variety of agreements on division of property, currency and state assets. It is bad enough when a man and woman decide to divide up their property. A country is a much larger business. All citizens had to have their passports stamped with their new nationalities. In addition, both Czechs and Slovaks were allowed to apply for a change of nationality.

A brief spat developed over whether or not Czechs would be allowed to retain the old red, white and blue tri-colored Czechoslovak flag. The Slovaks contended that continued use of the flag would indicate to the world that the Czechs were the legitimate successor to the federation. They asked Czechs to find a new symbol.

Czechs reacted angrily. "This is an attempt by one country to limit another," said Jiřína Pavlíková, a member of the Czech committee deciding future use of flags and symbols. "We have always tried to be tolerant with (the Slovaks). Now it feels as if you have offered somebody chocolate and he took one piece and threw the rest in the mud so you couldn't have any."[10]

Even though the Federal Parliament, as one of its last acts, included a directive that both countries should use new flags after the division, the Czech Parliament voted in late December to take all existing flags and symbols for the new Czech Republic. Despite expressing anger, officials in the Slovak government did not challenge the decision.

Cultural Pioneers. New York Pizza, 16.00 hod.

The Globe Cafe, 13.13 hod.

Cartoons courtesy of Ken Nash

30

Czechs vs. Americans

zechs worried about the split and ongoing economic reform. Many were also starting to show more than a bit of unease with the huge number of Westerners that were roaming the city. I had several bad encounters with Czechs who were angry about the number of Americans in town, the changes imposed on them or that the west—especially the United States—wasn't giving them more money. Always, it seemed these encounters came in pubs when people had been drinking too much and had become emotional.

One afternoon, I was sitting in a pub discussing computer programming with an English student I was teaching privately. The level of conversation was fairly sophisticated and I didn't notice that a man had been listening to our conversation for several minutes. Suddenly he rose up from behind his beer and approached our table.

"How much do you pay him for his American wisdom?" he said, looking down at my student, who merely waved him off and told the man it was none of his business. But the man persisted. "Does he tell you how to shit, too?" My student was embarrassed and waved him away.

"It's not as it seems," he said. "It's just talk. You don't understand."

"I understand, my friend," the man said waving his hands in the air. He gave me a menacing look.

"This is not funny," I suddenly said. Surprised that I could respond in Czech, the man straightened and looked at me. "Please go away," I finished. Although nothing had happened, I was embarrassed and not long after, I gave up teaching private conversation lessons. Not only did I already have enough to do every day, but I found that I was uncomfortable about taking money from my students—most of whom were my age—as I didn't really feel like I was doing anything more than correcting their English over endless cups of coffee and tea. For a time, I had some students from Prokopova, and I didn't mind that as much, because I had to prepare much more for those sessions.

One night, a friend and I went after work to a small neighborhood pub in the Old Town. The pub, which before the revolution had been frequented only by locals, had been renovated and turned into a watering hole for tourists. When we arrived, there weren't many people at the long table, except for a lone man at the other end who was nursing his way through several beers.

I could sense his rage beginning to build as more and more Americans sat down at the table and the table become crowded. Gradually, the man shifted his beer glass closer and closer to his vest until it was nearly against his shirt. After someone jarred the table slightly, the man mumbled loudly in Czech, "Fine! Americans everywhere and my pub goes *do prdele*—into the ass."

As nicely as I could, I turned slightly and demurred: "I'm sorry, sir, but I really don't agree. I am sorry about the noise, however."

After the man had finished being surprised at my Czech, he looked me hard in the eyes. "Fine! So you can speak BOTH English and Czech. But my pub has still gone into the ass!" And with that, he gathered up his cigarettes and left the bar. The saddest thing was the restaurant couldn't have cared less about pleasing the old-timers. Once, when we ordered a plate of ham, cheese and pickles, the bill was outrageous and I complained rather loudly, assuming that we were being ripped off.

"I haven't overcharged you," the waiter replied, showing me on the menu where all the various prices were listed. Although he was correct, it would have taken an anthropologist to figure out how the bill was constructed. "This restaurant is in the center of Prague," the waiter said. "Don't come here if you do want to pay these prices."

That episode was tame, as opposed to a much more violent incident that had transpired the previous spring. It had been a pleasant warm evening and Renáta and I had gone out to a pub with our friend David Koller who had returned to Prague for a visit. After discovering that our favorite restaurant was closed, we headed to another one that was not quite as reputable.

When we wandered in, the first thing I saw was that the bartender was so drunk he couldn't properly pour shots of liquor into a glass. Renáta pointed this out rather loudly and one of the other bartenders laughed. The drunk bartender was not pleased. I took this to be a bad sign, but said nothing. Presently we managed to get a table not far from the bar. We drank for about an hour with two men who were so bombed they had trouble lighting cigarettes. One of them dropped a cigarette on the floor and it took him the better part of ten minutes to pick it up. Once, when David got up to go order beer, one of the men turned and looked at him from behind a stubbled beard and craggy face that looked like melted wax.

"Hey," he said, "buy me a beer would'ya?" When David asked him why, the man responded: "Because we're drinking with an American, and it's well known that all Americans have money." Rather than get angry, I tried merely agreeing with him.

"Yeah, you know, it's funny," I said. "Whenever I fart—whoops! There goes five dollars!" The man thought this was tremendously funny and laughed so hard he must have expended whatever excess energy he still had. He eventually went to sleep with his head on his hands.

About an hour later, when I got up to order another round, the drunken bartender merely ignored me and turned away. I went back to the table and suggested that we leave, as the bar didn't want to pour any more beer.

"That's crap," Renáta said, getting up to look at the closing time on the door. True, the bar seemed to be closing more than a half an hour early. Renáta went to the bar and ordered a few beers in bottles to take home. The bartender wouldn't sell them

"Why not?" Renáta said.

"Because I don't feel like it," he said with a slurry voice. "Besides, your American here should be willing to pay twice as much."

An argument ensued, with Renáta calling the bartender a lazy bastard. The bartender, who was beginning to get agitated, responded with several rather predictable and unprintable insults. As the quarrel between the bartender and Renáta grew ever louder, I tried picking her up and carrying her out the door. I had almost succeeded when David turned around and said in Czech to the bartender, "I'll meet you in hell." I don't know whether this is any stronger than anything else that had been said already, but it seemed to uncork something in the drunken bartender. He came out from around the bar and hit David so hard that he knocked him out the door of the pub.

David's glasses shattered and blood flowed from a cut on his nose, which thankfully, wasn't broken. The bartender lurched after Renáta and took a swipe at her for good measure.

While the bartender's friend followed him out the door trying to make peace, I quickly realized that as I was in shorts, a silly looking t-shirt and rubber-soled tennis shoes, I wouldn't get very far in a fight against these two drunks.

Shaking with rage, I lost all ability to speak Czech or even English. I looked behind me and saw a police station.

"We're going to the police," I said.

"Great! Go to the police!" the bartender called out. "See what they do!"

Ten minutes later we returned with two officers in tow. They took a look at the bar, which had emptied of most people by now, and spoke quickly to the bartender, who was now laughing with his girlfriend and polishing glasses.

"What happened here?" one of the officers said.

The bartender gestured towards David. "He smashed a glass and threatened me with it when it was time to pay the bill." David looked down and cursed silently .

Next to me, an elderly man who had been drinking beer most of the evening got up suddenly and pushed passed me. I grabbed his arm and asked him to stay and help us.

"Surely you saw what happened," said. "Tell the police. They might listen to you."

The man shrugged off my hand and continued moving. "I've got to get to work," he said and refused to look at me. "I've got to go to work."

We went back to the police station and the police told us they couldn't file a report unless David had his proper identification. No ID, no report. I flew into a rage. "How long is this going to continue?" I shouted at the policeman. "How many years are you going to sit around and do nothing? When are you going to be able to do something in this town for people?"

The policeman didn't say anything. He just shrugged.

"I thought Czechs were supposed to be wimps," I said, as we rode the tram back to our apartment.

"Apparently not all of them when they're drunk," David said, wiping blood off his nose.

Even though Olga Havelová had been guarded, she was easier to deal with than Prime Minister Klaus, who was becoming more and more dogmatic in his relationship with the press, especially with *The Prague Post* and others in the foreign press. He refused to be interviewed by *The Prague Post* for a profile and complained that we were too "leftist" in our judgments. He never specifically identified what the newspaper had done to irritate him, but we could guess that he probably wasn't happy that we were independent, foreign and reasonably unaccountable. Furthermore, as we had a large foreign circulation, when we ran articles that he didn't like, he knew that information about him was reaching an important audience: the potential investors and policy makers overseas. What's more, we were a group of foreigners making often incorrect judgments about a country a lot of us didn't understand. There were many times when reporting in *The Prague Post* or *Prognosis* was slipshod or mediocre at best. But *The Prague Post* was not the only news organization to draw his wrath. On August 18, Klaus blasted the Czech press, especially the television networks, for propagating what he said was "confusion" about the breakup of the country.

Klaus told Czech radio that the right to democratically voice one's opinion was being confused with the right to present one's opinion on prime-time television. "Obviously no one has that right," he said. "It is quite natural that ... people meet to express their views on this or that. But what seems to me inappropriate is that they are provided excessive space by the major mass media." He went on to criticize recent television coverage of the left wing parties. Klaus said he wondered why, since his party had the largest share of votes in the election, they weren't given the most amount of time on TV![1]

New foreign goods continued to flood into the country on a weekly basis: Uncle Ben's Rice. Palmolive. Pampers. One afternoon while shopping in Kotva, Prague's largest department store, Renáta and I encountered a woman handing out free samples of Tampax tampons. Little white tampons were heaped everywhere.

"Why are you displaying these like this?" Renáta asked.

"Because people have never seen these before, and they're afraid of them," the yellow-smocked salesgirl explained, while handing out free samples to passing customers. "Some people think they are giant firecrackers or some kind of snack for dogs!"

At some point around the second anniversary of my arrival in Prague, I finally dreamed in Czech. My sketchy notes indicate that it wasn't much: a few broken sentences of Czech sandwiched into the rest of the dream. I greeted the event with a certain amount of relief and interest, in that it seemed to have taken a long time for my subconscious to catch up with the maddening pace the conscious other had been working. Any private time I had with Renáta seemed all too rare, as I was generally at work.

For me, Prague had changed dramatically, as I was living a totally different life than the first two years. The city seemed less mysterious and I found myself instead being more drawn to the news and constant changes being thrust upon the country by the various important issues: *lustrace,* the Czech and Slovak confrontation and privatization.

Our temporary lease expired and we were forced to go out hunting for another apartment. Unless one is lucky enough to know someone with an empty apartment who will let you live there on the normal rent, generally one must pay grossly inflated rents, which owners rarely pay taxes on. The legality of subletting an apartment is murky, but it is a generally accepted practice. We spent several months going from various apartment to apartment trying to find a reasonable deal, but there were few to be found. After awhile, Renáta went alone because bringing me along only seemed to increase the rent.

The same month, Renáta's grandmother died in a small *panelák* in a town outside of Nymburk. Under the terms of the apartment, Renáta technically "lived" there with her grandmother, even though she was only there several times a month. Some people didn't even live at their future apartments at all.

After the various probate papers had cleared, Renáta took possession of the apartment. Since she couldn't live there—she worked in Prague—she set about trying to sell the apartment. Due to the large number of people who wanted flats, it only took one weekend. First, she exchanged her flat for another one in a cooperative nearby. Under the rules of the cooperative, she was then allowed to sell the flat to another family. She received 150,000 crowns for the flat, which she then used to "buy" her new flat in Prague.

We spent the better part of a weekend emptying the grandmother's apartment and doing the things one does after a family member dies: taking away clothes, cleaning the furniture, sifting through books and things acquired over a lifetime. The grandmother had lived to a ripe old age and had been witness to a truly amazing period of history. Born at the beginning of the century in the times of the Austro-Hungarian Empire, she had married a wealthy businessman in Nymburk who had started a distribution network for oil, gas and food when the automobile became a viable mode of transportation in the 1920s. The company had prospered over the years and had grown to service a lot of the territory immediately east of Prague. Someone had taken the time to carefully document the company's growth over the years in a scrapbook that was bulging with photographs and news cuttings. There were faded, black and white photographs from the opening of new warehouses, company picnics and employee weddings. It was fascinating to watch the development of the company as it added more and more workers and trucks. In 1946, the year of major national elections, there was a leaflet from the Communist Party: "Aren't you tired of people like Mr. Novák controlling so much wealth in Nymburk? Shouldn't there be a more equitable distribution of profits? Vote for the KSČ (the Communist Party), and we'll all share together."

The leaflet, which had yellowed with age, was the last entry. The rest of the scrapbook was blank. The company was nationalized in 1948 and Novák was sent to Slovakia to work as a civil engineer. He and his wife were given a small apartment overlooking a cement parking lot and some garbage cans.

After we had cleaned out her grandmother's flat, Renáta set about trying to find an apartment in Prague that she could purchase, which is a little like trying to find a needle in a haystack. Even though 150,000 crowns was a great amount by Czech standards, it isn't much on the Prague housing market. Amazingly, she found two men who needed a lot of cash very quickly to pay off debts from a failed magazine stand. She looked at the apartment, which was located in a generally run-down, working class part of Prague called Žižkov. Even though it was dingy and fairly small—a kitchen and two rooms—it was available for 150,000 crowns. To have an apartment of her own in Prague was a very valuable commodity and Žižkov was slowly being renovated. It would take more than a decade to effect real change in the streets, but people were slowly fixing some of the apartments and businesses.

On a warm summer afternoon in early August, we met the owners at a bar in the main train station and exchanged the money and keys. The owners of the apartment building, who lived in Ostrava, had already given their blessing to the exchange and had signed all the necessary papers. Earlier that morning, I had gone to the bank and withdrawn the 150,000 crowns. There is no checking system, so we were doing the deal in cash. I have rarely been so paranoid as I walked around that day with the money. The next day, we moved into the apartment, which was now Renáta's as long as she wanted.

31

Speeding towards the Velvet Divorce

Considering that the country was headed for its third major shakeup in less than three years, including the revolution and economic restructuring, the country seemed amazingly calm and tranquil. There were no marches in protest, no strikes and few heated debates. On August 26, Klaus and Mečiar announced after a series of long meetings that the country would be formally divided on January 1. National property would be divided on a 2:1 ration according to the population differences.

Although the third anniversary of the revolution was rapidly approaching, few of the student leaders from the protests had time or interest for marking the day in any unusual way. Václav Bartuška had been a student at Charles University when the demonstrations began and had later written a book about the period. With the money he made from the book, which was called *Polojasno* (Partly Sunny), he traveled around the world.

When he returned, I interviewed him in Prague. Wiry and intense, Bartuška had an extremely cynical sense of humor that filtered naturally through his speech.

On the issue of the split, Bartuška said he had already accepted it.

"I'm not thinking about Czechoslovakia," he said. "I'm thinking about the Czech Republic. Because for me, Slovakia is dead. And I'm optimistic about this part of the country, although I know that right now is a hard time and probably the next years will be harder."[1]

As for the change in leadership, Bartuška was quite sanguine. He didn't miss the past, or the dissidents.

"I don't really care about them. I think they found something for themselves," he said. Why should I care? It's (one) thing to stand up and openly say what you are thinking about. But it's quite a different job to lead a country. It's quite a different job to be a hero and it's quite a different job to make millions—to make five bucks. So that's probably the difference."

Perhaps most interesting was Bartuška's impressions of Americans, whom he said never "had much fun." A self-confessed "lazy person," Bartuška said he couldn't easily relate to the American work ethic.

"I don't see many common things between Czechs and Americans. There are many more similarities between, let's say, Czechs and Australians or Czechs and New Zealanders. Their lifestyles and attitudes towards work. Americans are struggling much more than we are, struggling all the time to pay the rent or to pay the mortgage or to pay a loan or to pay for something. Running all the time and not really having much fun."

Viktor and Jarka returned from America in October. They both said they were relieved and happy to be home. But they both realized it had changed.

"I thought I would never be so happy to come back to Prague after that year," Viktor said in his careful, slow way. "In America, everyone was always talking about money or the things they had to do or the work. And then I came back here and found that everyone else I had known was becoming the same. Now I don't know where to go or what to think."

The Federal Assembly passed the constitutional law ending the 75-year-old Czechoslovak Republic on November 25. The measure carried by just three votes. Largely symbolic, since most of the major issues had been hammered out previously, the large opposition to the vote was due in large part because many of the deputies still believed there should have been some sort of a referendum to decide the actual future of the nation. Klaus and Mečiar and the sympathetic coalitions wanted to get on with the process of the split as quickly as possible, while the left, Socialist and Communist parties, all vigorously protested the lack of a citizens' vote.

As Czechoslovakia was rushing towards the split, Jiří Svoboda, the president of the Communist Party of Bohemia and Moravia, was stabbed on December 5 in front of his home by a masked assailant. As it was Mikuláš—St. Nicholas' day—the day in which children are deemed to be angels of devils in preparation of Christmas, the attacker was wearing a carnival mask. Svoboda's wife hit the attacker over the head with a vodka bottle and a pot and the man ran off into the night. Svoboda did recover, and although a man was eventually arrested and charged, he was never prosecuted for lack of evidence. The case remains unsolved to this day.

Very few people I talked to were unhappy at the loss of the federation, and the Slovak nationalism had seemed to create a new chasm between Czechs and Slovaks.

"I think this whole split is sick," one of my Czech translators told me at *The Prague Post.* "My parents never cared one way or the other about the Slovaks. Now they throw things at the television when Mečiar comes on. This is bad. They have taken the first step. They have learned how to hate people they couldn't have cared less about."

Renáta's grandfather, a normally placid gentleman who had usually nice things to say about people, was more specific in his thoughts: "Mečiar can go into the stinking toilet," he said violently, waving his hand through the air.

On Dec. 18, the Federal Parliament officially dissolved itself, leaving only the Chamber of the Nations of the Federal Assembly in operation until Dec. 31. Meanwhile, in Slovakia and in Prague, the search was on to name officials to posts previously held by Slovaks or Czechs. New ambassadors had to be named, judges had to be recalled from Prague and officials from the various federal offices had to begin shutting down their operations. It had all gone smoothly—so smoothly in fact—that people were calling it the "Velvet Divorce."

On New Year's Eve, Prague slowly built into a deafening roar as everyone emptied into the streets to let off firecrackers, bottle rockets and huge, thunderous M-80s. We had dinner at home and then walked downtown to Wenceslas Square where the main celebration was. It was like a war zone, with Roman candles exploding and fizzling out at my feet and other assorted forms of pyrotechnics whizzing past my head. I stuffed cotton in my ears to keep me from being deafened by the cacophony around me.

The square was packed with people, mostly Germans and Italians, and nearly everyone was drunk or on their way to becoming drunk. Czechs standing in the crowd told us that the atmosphere was merely drunken and foreign and that the celebration lacked the happiness of 1990 when the revolution was still underway.

"You know, then, we were free, but now we are splitting the country and so I don't think we are quite so happy tonight," a woman said as she swigged from a beer bottle.

Down in Slovakia, 25,000 people jammed the center of the town for a celebration that was more heartfelt and intense than in Prague.

Midnight came and there was a mighty, almost salacious, roar from the crowd, and the air exploded with even more fireworks.

We opened several bottles of champagne and kissed each other and greeted the first day of the Czech Republic.

On New Year's Day, Klaus addressed the nation about the future of the country.

"We are at a crossroads again, a crossroads which is no less important than November 1989," he said, speaking before an audience at Prague Castle. "We've prepared the celebration of this day as a sober celebration, one without bombast, without hysteria. Restraint is in the Czech character."[2]

While some Czech and Slovak journalists mourned the loss of the federation, others looked to the future.

"The disconnection of the two republics also has the effect of a rope pulled in two opposite directions which has suddenly been cut," wrote Jiří Hanák in *Lidové Noviny*. "The Czech Republic, telescoped by its German neighbor anyway, will jump even further westwards."[3]

Mečiar gave no clear picture of the future in his New Year's Day address to the Slovak people, except to say that he wanted to "build up a society based on a balance of social and market forces.

"We refused socialism; we also refuse the ideas of capitalism of the last century," he said, speaking from their castle high over the city in Bratislava.[4]

The same day, new Value Added Taxes were going into effect all over Prague, immediately causing prices to jump again. The VAT, which would have been implemented with or without the split of the country, was yet another major step towards a full market economy. Stores and businesses remained closed for the first several days while managers tried to figure out how to implement and account for the new taxes. As the closed stores became more and more inconvenient, the Czech finance minister, Ivan Kočárník, finally exploded in frustration and said the "laziness" of the Czechs had prevented most from bothering to learn about the tax when it had been announced earlier in the year.

The newcomer to Prague walking the streets that first week would not have known the country had been cut in two. After all, the money and the postage stamps were all the same. Only at the borders had new crossings been set up, along with rudimentary customs offices. On February 7, the currency was divided.

In early February, Havel was elected President of the Czech Republic after a bruising battle in which members of the extreme left and right both presented alternative candidates and also criticized Havel on the Parliament floor to the point of slander. He was called many things—a traitor for allowing the division of the country, a drunkard and a liar. Finally, in the early evening, he was confirmed.

While Havel's election was never in doubt, the ugly mudslinging in Parliament showed just how far Havel, and the country, had come from November, 1989. Some had said they believed Havel should not run for the presidency as he had exhausted much of his political credibility over the split of the nation. Others argued that it was demeaning for Havel to carry on, as the powers of the presidency were so weak that Havel would be little more than a figurehead.

"He reentered politics too soon," said Father Václav Malý, priest and former dissident. "If he had waited patiently, the politicians would have come to him themselves. This was a political mistake."[5]

But regardless of whether Klaus and the other members of his party considered Havel too liberal, there was still no other person in the Czech Republic who could provide the same kind of leadership and prestige at home and abroad.

"I don't feel that I am a person enchanted by power, someone who longs for power, who wants to hold any office," Havel told *Newsweek*'s Andrew Nagorski at the time of his election. "The point is that I want to work for something, that I cherish some values, that I want to continue this struggle or work."[6]

Former dissident Jiří Ruml wrote several days before the end of the federation that the time had come for Czechs and Slovaks to find their own way.

"How many times we reproached them for how much it cost us before backward Slovakia became an industrial country," he wrote. "But why emphasize that, if we sincerely intended the unity of the common state? We should say goodbye to all this, that our farewell should be kind and sincere. Perhaps by the end of the century, we will meet again. God willing, in Europe. So goodbye."[7]

32

Endings and New Beginnings (Fall 1994)

Five years after the change in governments, one doesn't see so many grand gestures like the Pink Tank. Instead the golden arches of McDonald's loom in downtown squares, the Marlboro Man rides tall in his cigarette saddle on billboards and Pizza Hut and big department stores like K-Mart—yes, K-Mart!—are drafted onto the urban landscape like out of place *objets trouves* amidst the centuries old assembly of cobblestones, castles and Renaissance architecture.

In January, 1994, Bill Clinton came to Prague for several days to help sell his "Partnership For Peace" program. As opposed to Bush's visit, there was no grand speech in the middle of the town. Instead, it was a much quieter, more substantive affair that lasted three days. While Prague was predictably turned upside down by Clinton's presence, it seemed the country was slowly learning to stage major events with class. The government led by Klaus is reasonably assured in its leadership. During the three days that Clinton was here, there was a sort of calm order. Perhaps the most sensational thing Clinton did was play the saxophone at a local jazz club with several Czech musicians. Earlier in the evening, he had been taken to a traditional Czech pub and ate potato pancakes and cabbage. He drank two beers and was introduced to the Czech writer Bohumil Hrabal. On the final day of his visit, Clinton visited K-Mart and spoke with American business owners and investors in Prague.

So what of the Czechs and their nation? As I have outlined earlier, the nation appears to be well positioned for a strong economic
revival. In addition, the ruling politicians are keen to see the Czech
Republic accepted into the Economic Community (EC) and NATO
by the end of the decade. For now, the country is taking the first steps
by acting as an Associate Member in the EC and as part of President
Clinton's "Partnership For Peace" initiative.

There are some who still continue to denounce what they say was
the illegal split of the nation by two political parties that both had
tremendous amount of political capital at stake in their own territories.

"It is executive power that is dividing the federation, not people
power," said Pavol Kanis, a Slovak left-wing politician, shortly before
the split was finalized in December, 1992.[1] As much as I loathe the
left-wing, Kanis and others have a point, as the people were never
given the chance to openly cast ballots deciding what should be done
with the federation. Shortly before his death of a heart attack in 1994,
Karel Kryl, a popular folksinger and former dissident-in-exile, invoked
the "they decided about us, without us" statement in angrily ascrib-
ing the breakup of the country to people who had no legal authority
to negotiate such a division.

Whether or not the split was legal seems to have become a moot
issue, as the Czech Republic continues to move swiftly towards developing a stronger economic base. The Paris-based Organization for
Economic Cooperation and Development predicted the country's GNP
would grow by 5 percent in 1995 and that inflation will be at about
10 percent.[2] The popularity of the government and a reasonably optimistic future has obscured the question of division. Polls show a majority of Czechs now support division, while more than a handful of
Slovaks say they believe the split was rushed and not a good idea.

Klaus raised some eyebrows in 1993 when he announced that privatization was essentially over and all that was needed was some "fine
tuning." A number of politicians and commentators called Klaus'
statement premature.

"From his words one can infer even that it is the definitive end of
the post revolution era," a commentator wrote in *Mladá Fronta Dnes,*
the largest independent newspaper in the Czech Republic. "A new era

316

is impatiently knocking on the door, the era of everyday politics."[3] The writer went on to list a staggering number of problems which still have yet to be addressed by the government—child care, bankruptcies, doubtful leadership and corruption in city halls, and reform of various ministries.

The average Czech with a family still cannot afford to purchase many high quality Western products on a regular basis, even though polls indicate so many of them dearly would love to be able to buy brand-name goods. Pavel, who continues to work as a photographer and an editor for the Czech News Agency, told me not long ago he is unsure how long the average Czech is willing to be patient. Those who know the country's potential and who believe in the economic restructuring certainly have been quiet so far.

But for how many years will they be silent before expecting a return on these difficult times? Will people be willing to accept the various complications that come from a market economy, including unemployment, homelessness, the domination of corporate life, inflation, competition and uncertain job markets? Certainly, there will be bad years. There will be recessions, boom and busts in various industries.

The older generation has been weaned on a comfortable, cradle-to-grave socialist economy; will a younger generation still in school rise to the challenges posed by the free market, competitive economy? Certainly few expect any return to the past, but will the country continue to embrace a right-wing, free market economic platform or will the center-left, which is currently moribund, make significant inroads to the parliament?

The economic transformation since the revolution has wrought immense changes in the cultural and social fabric, so much so that a cynical minority believes that once again, outside forces are dictating to the Czechs how they will dress, act, shop and eat.

Once again, it is argued, Czechs will be submerged, only this time in a sea of fast-food restaurants, Disney, MTV, Kodak Cameras and banal television commercials. But the difficulties resulting from the shift from a closed, socialist society and economy to a democratic, capitalist state are so enormous that to focus on the issue of available consumable goods is to miss the major issue: People are again allowed to make real choices about what they want in their lives and where they want to travel.

With so many Americans in town, bringing in McDonald's and Disney and American-styled restaurants, Czechs speak of losing control of their culture, their children and their lives as they are forced to spend more and more time working just to pay the bills. A speaker on a panel discussion show is quoted in 1990 as saying: "There are two things Czechs are afraid of. One, they will lose their jobs. Two, they will have to work."[4]

Czechs sometimes seem overwhelmed, not only by the forces of capitalism, but by some unknown force that is dragging people apart and making them less friendly, less sociable.

"There was a time when we all went to the pub together without thinking about it," a friend tells me one night. I hadn't seen him in months, and although our visit was a happy one, there was a distinct feeling that things had changed. "It seemed like we all had more time a few years ago."

He is right. There was more time for people to be together, to socialize after work and celebrate. But now, many people are driven by the need to make money, to get on with a new way of life and move away from the past.

Some Czechs are scared for the future and are thrashing about in vain for new scapegoats. Gypsies and Jews are good in a pinch. After a routine soccer match between Sparta Prague and Slavia Prague, the emotional equivalent of the Brooklyn Dodgers and the New York Giants, an obscenely drunk Sparta fan lurches unsteadily around a parking lot declaring, "All Slavia fans are Jews who should be sent to the gas chambers." Some people laugh. And yet this is a country that was torn literally in half by the Nazis.

One major hurdle for the current government will be crossed if the Czech crown increases in value against Western currencies. But as the international currency market is a volatile beast, inspiring trust in the Czech crown once it becomes fully convertible in the next several years will depend on a whole range of unpredictable factors, including the health of domestic and international economies, the amount of foreign reserves amassed by the Czech Republic, and imports and exports.

If anything, Czechs have been extremely lucky over the last several years. They have managed to dodge several of most virulent problems to hit these reforming nations, including extremist nationalism. Those who have been unlucky enough to witness the living hell known as Yugoslavia would happily embrace the worst elements of Prague: the dirty streets, broken phones and inefficient service. These things don't kill you, and Czech children can walk in the streets without having to fear taking a sniper's bullet. Although inflation in the Czech Republic has been running at more than 15 percent a year, the money is still valid and not imitating the Weimar Republic. The stores are full of all sorts of products that simply didn't exist before the revolution.

In Slovakia, Mečiar was forced to resign as Prime Minister after spending most of 1993 rowing in circles, avoiding privatization, firing ministers left and right and watching a number of key deputies from his party grow unhappy with his increasingly autocratic leadership. New elections were held in the fall of 1994, more than two years ahead of schedule. After the poll, none of the various political parties emerged with enough votes to form a stable or even slightly credible government. Like the fighter he has always been, Mečiar's party did gain the largest percentage of votes and there was a good chance he would be the Prime Minister of Slovakia once again.

In perhaps the strangest irony, some former dissidents, the people who fought the government clandestinely and always in great danger, speak wistfully of the past, feeling as though a great serial has finished, a chapter closed, and they are no longer necessary.

Like prisoners released on the street, their feelings are understandable. The future is uncertain. The past was secure—horrible to be sure—but secure and known. Some who fought the regime remark that life for them today is less unified, less dramatic. Before they were united in what they disliked. Opposition to the government brought together members of the left and right, scientists, educators, waiters and workers. All for a cause. Now the arguments are less clear, the solidarity diffuse and thinning.

Sadly, the band Půlnoc never recorded another album. The group struggled with personnel changes and a demo tapes they had submitted to their American record label were rejected as being "too depressing."[5]

Their leader, Milan Hlavsa sensed that the end had come for Půlnoc.

"During the last five years, Půlnoc has always had the same sound," Hlavsa said in 1993. "In the two years since we toured the United States, the band has stagnated." The record label's rejection of the new music was the last straw for the bassist. "I don't play music that the market wants," he said, "but music that my heart wants. Each concert was a big event for musicians and fans alike. Now it's changed and players have more concerts. The fun and the joy has disappeared. It all had a social connection. Now, bands just get together to record an album and sell it."[6]

Rock & Pop magazine has also had more than its share of problems. The newspaper that supported magazine ran into financial problems of its own and was forced to divest itself of most of its spinoff projects. *Rock & Pop* has continued as a private enterprise, but has battled numerous problems, including a declining and fickle readership, internal battles and the soaring cost of printing.

As for my fellow Westerners in Prague, the myth of the Left Bank shows no signs of abating, especially following the visit of President Clinton to Prague. Every so often a news crew wanders through, seeking a story about the crazy young Americans, Canadians, Brits or Australians. A number of the initial businesses, like *New York Pizza,* have failed, sometimes from inexperience or an overdependence on the tourist market. Others, like *The Globe* bookstore and cafe have brought a much needed touch of class to the Western businesses in Prague. When *The Globe* opened in the summer of 1993, the often critical Czech press was kind to the bookstore, saying that for once, Westerners were bringing a higher level of culture to Prague than Mickey Mouse and McDonald's. *Prognosis* is still chugging away. It has become a weekly newspaper and renamed itself *Prognosis Weekly.* With a third English-language newspaper, the business-oriented *Central European Business Weekly,* having joined the fray two years ago, the competition for advertising and readers gets tighter all the time.

If one wants to draw a unique parallel between Czechs and Americans, it is that for the first time since before World War II, people are *coming* to Prague and the country, rather than trying to find ways to leave it. Some of them, like the large number of westerners, are actually staying. Moreover, people from even poorer countries look to the Czech Republic as a place to immigrate to and Czechs don't have to leave their country with the idea that it will be forever.

What concerns me most is the large number of reporters, especially from the television networks, who want to cover the superficial story and generally don't dig into the unpredictable issues affecting an entire group of countries and societies that stretch from Berlin to Korea. Foreign journalists have a responsibility to properly cover these people and the chilly issues at hand: extremist nationalism, nuclear proliferation, anti-Semitism, resurgent totalitarianism and poverty. Without a better understanding of just who the people of Central and Eastern Europe really are, I fear Americans will not have the tools at hand to help them make decisions in dealing with conflicts in nationalistic countries among ethnic groups.

The many friends I made when I arrived, including Jarka and Viktor, are now scattered. When I do see them, it is usually on rare occasions and even then not everyone is able to make it. Recent marriages, divorces, new children and the inevitable pressure of work has meant the once intimate circle around Jarka and Viktor has fractured. Nikola and Dora are still living in Prague and Dan is in Belgrade, working as a reporter for a major news service and covering the seemingly endless war in Yugoslavia. The school where I taught has been partially reconstructed, and by most accounts, is flourishing under the guidance of the principal, who has been able to attract grants and donations of computers from foreign corporations and foundations.

I myself have become gradually more and more confused by the various inequities of rampant socialism and capitalism. Socialism can never work properly, simply because it implies people will willingly and happily allow their personal lives and careers to be reduced to that of mere machines. It assumes that all work is equal and that people will generally accept this inequality. This is folly, of course, because people are not machines. Pure socialism creates a wealth of misery, laziness and inefficiency. And hopelessness.

Capitalism, on the other hand, is sometimes just as problematic. Certainly the problems facing Western countries today, including sky-rocketing crime, the decay of the inner cities, the collapse of the family unit, rampant drug abuse and the leftover greed from the 1980s must be addressed in the context from which they sprang. The sheer number of cheap gambling halls, ugly bars and make-a-buck-quick companies that have sprung up in Prague is disturbing and unnecessary. Flag-waving conservative friends of mine tell me that the marketplace will take care of these blights, but I doubt it. All one needs to do is go to Los Angeles' Main Street and see an ugly world that has existed for decades. It won't go away.

But if the economy, like politics, must be about making choices between the lesser of two evils, I will gladly stand aside and allow people to make choices for themselves in a capitalist society. I will shut my eyes, hope for the best, and try and dwell on the possibilities of what I call "simple capitalism"—the ability of people to take control of their lives in most proper and libertarian ways.

There is a man, who I'll call George, living in a small village outside of Prague who has been working at the same factory for more than 30 years. Every morning, the factory gates open at 5:30 in the morning and the workers line up like robots in front of breathalyzer machines so the factory can see whether any of them are sober enough to work. The men work until 2 P.M. and then they go home and generally loll about until it is time to pursue some simple projects around the house in the late afternoon or go to the pub. When they return home from the pub after it closes at 10 P.M., most are so drunk they fall directly into bed.

Recently, George decided he had had enough of this sodden routine and saved some money so he could buy himself a rug shampooer and other tools for cleaning houses. In the afternoons, after he returns from the factory, he has a full slate of appointments in homes where he provides a cleaning service. He also sells the homeowners various cleaning supplies.

"I'll be glad when I can retire so I can stuff the factory and get on with my other projects," George said recently. He still has two more years to go until he will qualify for a pension, so he will be staying at the factory. He says he is happier than he has ever been, simply because he has the chance to get out and do something for himself. All his life he has been stamped, numbered and identified by a government which wouldn't allow him to make simple decisions on his own. George once suggested to the factory manager that perhaps they should open the factory a bit later—6:30 say—and that way the workers might come to the job sober. George said the manager looked at him like he was crazy. The workers would get confused. They've been coming at 5:30 A.M. for forty years.

"As I said," George continued, "I'll be happy when I can stuff the factory."

To me, George is the best example of "simple Capitalism," a man who wants to get on with it and not wallow about in pity or wait for other people to make decisions for him. He said he knows that others in the village have complained that he is too smug, too happy and satisfied. But, then again, being openly charitable and privately envious, snide and cruel is something of a Czech trait. In fact, there is a Czech expression, usually said after someone you envy leaves the room: ". . . and may your pig die."

After nearly four years here, my life is ordered in a way I could never have expected when I first arrived. I can properly ask for bread and tins of yogurt from the small food store on my street and say hello to the neighbors, who all know me as *ten americký muž*—that American man. I know where to take the clothes to the laundry and how to explain what I need to the old women there. But as for truly understanding Czech society, I think much of their culture remains a mystery to me, and any Westerner—not because of the obvious linguistic barrier, but because another culture is a enigma that cannot be solved. One can't precisely define the many facets that make up American society, either, or what makes people in this culture act the way they do.

In preparing material for this book, I have asked the question "who are the Czechs?" a hundred times and received at least a hundred different answers. Still, I believe I have been lucky to have seen a good deal of the Czech character. I'm comfortable not being able to receive a series of properly coded answers.

It is a beautiful cool day in early March. I step out onto the sidewalk in Prague and gaze up at a sky cut with swaths of puffy white clouds and traces of blue sky. After so many months of cold, icy wind, it is strange to walk down the street and feel the sun on my face. The wind is blowing slightly, ruffling my hair. I walk down the street and can see the huge Hradčany castle out in the distance. After living so long in its shadow, I can not imagine being anywhere else.

Just as in the old days, I walk for more than an hour, with no particular urge to go left or right. I have no destination; I am happy enough just to be twisted subtly by the streets and through the narrow walkways and arching buildings that surround me.

After awhile, I bumble into a new cafe that seems vaguely inviting. Looking around the restaurant with its gleaming brass and renovated, varnished windows and tile floors, it seems a million miles from the generic "snack bar" I first went to across from the school.

Hunting through my bag, I pull out the battered, faded notebook into which I had originally recorded my first observations of Prague. Tracing my finger through the pages, I recall the early days four years ago and the images come in a rush: the Dům, the little blue Škodas belching blue smoke, the children, running, always running. And this: "Ukončete výstup a nástup, dveře se zavírají." It is the tongue twisting recording from the metro that confounded me so long ago.

As I stir my tea, I mouth the sentence and discover that it rolls easily off my tongue. It has ceased to be a demon. I try it again. I sit back and feel extraordinarily happy. So much of my journey here has been an endless set of beginnings, of limitless encounters with new people and places. I have been blessed to have been witness to an astonishing period: a time of Pink Tanks and Velvet Hangovers. Like the good people of Pilzen, who never forgot the American soldiers who liberated their town, I shall never forget this wondrous country.

Bibliography and Additional Source Notes

The following texts and articles have proved invaluable to me in the preparation of this book. They contain excellent accounts relating to specific periods of Czechoslovakia's development. I have expanded on some of the texts to give the reader additional starting points for research about the Czech Republic and Slovakia. Some of the texts listed below have gone out of print (op), but may be found at used bookstores or in academic or well-stocked libraries.

1. A Train into Bohemia

1. Academic American Encyclopedia, Grolier Electronic Publishing, Inc., 1990.
2. "Czechoslovakia: Where The Suppression Of Human Rights Led To The 1989 Democratic Revolution," edited by the Czechoslovak News Agency, September 1991. p. 3; and Sharon L. Wolchik, *Czechoslovakia in Transition: Politics, Economics & Society,* Pinter Publishers, London and New York, 1991. p. 212–214. A concise and important collection of material relating to the economic and social life of the country immediately before and after the revolution.
3. George J. Kovtun, *Masaryk & America: Testimony of a Relationship.* (Washington D.C.; Library of Congress, 1988), 65.
4. When President George Bush visited Prague in November, 1990, there was an elaborate ceremony held at Hlavní nádraží to restore Woodrow Wilson's name once again. Nearly four years later, the name change has not taken place on maps and at the station itself. The directors of the station say they don't have the money to pay for the high cost of changing signs, maps, train schedules and other documents. Nonsense, say a lot of other people, who suggest that several die-hard Communist officials at the station are behind a plot to keep Wilson's name off the station.

4. The Czechs

1. Karel Čapek, *Toward the Radical Center: A Karel Čapek Reader* (New York, Catbird Press, 1990), 399. The selection listed is drawn from Čapek's essay, "At the Crossroads of Europe" Those interested in Czech literature and the creation of the Czech state in 1918 would do no better than begin with Čapek's works, including his essay, "Why I Am Not A Communist" (also found in the Čapek reader). Čapek was responsible for popularizing the word *robot* and also produced a three-volume series of interviews with T. G. Masaryk called *Conversations With Masaryk*. Čapek died of pneumonia only months after the Munich decision of 1938. Some say he really died of a broken heart. Čapek's brother, Josef, who was an artist and illustrated some of Karel's works, later died in a Nazi concentration camp during World War II.

2. Tad Szulc, *Czechoslovakia Since World War II* (op) (New York: The Universal Library, Grosset & Dunlap, 1971), 25. The only complete history of Czechoslovakia available in English covering the period from 1945 to 1971.

3. Kovtun, *Masaryk & America: Testimony of a Relationship,* 24.

4. Ivan Sviták, *The Czechoslovak Experiment: 1968–1969* (op) (New York: Columbia University Press, 1971), 173. Sviták is a controversial and provocative historian whose sometimes dogmatic views are not shared by everyone. His work is very well researched.

5. Václav Havel, *Summer Meditations* (Letní přemítání) (New York: Alfred A. Knopf, 1992), 126. Anyone doing research on the Slovak separatist issue should delve into this book, especially the essay, "In a Time of Transition."

6. R. H. Osborne, *East-Central Europe: An Introductory Geography,* (op) (New York, Frederick A. Praeger, 1967) 129–138. Material in this text is useful for those interested in the physical characteristics of the Czech Republic and Slovakia.

6. Havel: A President for the People

1. Jiří Otter, *The Evangelical Church of Czech Brethren,* (Prague: Church of Prague, 1992), 10.
2. Václav Havel, *Disturbing The Peace* (Dálkový výslech), (New York: Vintage Books, 1990), 187–188. This book-length interview is one of the best places to begin a study of Havel; also see Mark Hertgaard, "Havel's Progress," *The Los Angeles Times Sunday Magazine,* 20 October, 1991, p. 20.
3. Stephen Schiff, "Havel's Choice," *Vanity Fair,* August, 1991, p. 124. Both this article and the Hertgaard story about Havel (See "Havel's Progress") are reasonably well-balanced, if sometimes naive, profiles of the man and the changing face of Czechoslovakia. For a profile of Havel during the time he was out of office in late 1992 and early 1993, see Guy Martin's "The Short, Happy Exile of Václav Havel,"*Esquire,* February, 1993, p. 85.
4. Andrea Chambers and Toby Kahn, "Life Turns Upside Down For Václav Havel," *People Magazine,* 22 January, 1990, p. 44.
5. Nell Scovell, "Miloš Forman," *Vanity Fair,* February, 1994, p. 140.
6. Václav Havel, *Letters To Olga* (Dopisy Olze) (New York: Henry Holt & Company, 1989), 141.
7. Ellen Pall, "Czech Writer Under Arrest," *Christian Science Monitor,* 19 July, 1989, p. 19.
8. Andrew Borowiec, "Czech Authorities Brace For Anniversary of '68 Invasion," *The Washington Times,* 21 August, 1989, p. A8.
9. *The Collapse of Communism,* by the correspondents of *The New York Times* (edited by Bernard Gwertzman and Michael T. Kaufman, (New York: Times Books, Random House, 1990). p. 226. Summaries from major articles published about the fall of various governments in the Warsaw Pact and the student uprisings in China in 1989.
10. Ibid, 26; also see Jonathan Kaufman, "Opposition Snubbed in Czech Cabinet," *The Boston Globe,* 4 December, 1989, p. 1.; and Kaufman, "Power Struggle Seen Within Czech party," *The Boston Globe,* 23 November, 1989, p. 2.

11. John Tagliabue, "Upheaval in the East," *The New York Times,* 10 December, 1989. p. 1.

12. R. C. Longworth, "Czechs Embark on New Economic Road," *The Chicago Tribune,* December 3, 1989. Section C, p. 3.

13. Frederic L. Pryor, *East European Economic Reforms: The Rebirth of the Market,* Hoover Institution, Stanford University, 1990. p. 44

14. Longworth, "Czechs Embark on New Economic Road." Section C, p. 4.

15. Havel, *Open Letters,* p. 395–396. A collection of material from 1965–1990. Far more difficult is *Living In Truth* (Faber and Faber, London, 1989), which contains some of Havel's most detailed writing from the 1970s, including "Letter To Dr. Gusáv Husák," which opened the most vivid phase of Havel's clashes with the police in 1975. Havel's comment about power being returned to the people is drawn from Jan Amos Komenský, the "teacher of nations" who founded the basics of modern education in Europe during the first half of the 17th century. Komenský was appointed by various governments around Europe to reform their systems of education and create proper education for all generations.

16. Interestingly, farm cooperatives had been used illegally to shield a number of quasi-private ventures during the late 1980s. A noted co-op called Slušovice produced computers and textiles and even shared control of a race track. For more on this subject, see Pryor.

17. At one time, Klaus floated plans for a more radical voucher system in which coupons could be exchanged for a certain amount of national wealth. People could use these vouchers to purchase their apartments or shares in ownership of stores and companies where they worked. See Pryor.

18. Wolchik, *Czechoslovakia in Transition,* 250.

19. Craig R. Whitney, "Evolution In Europe," *The New York Times,* 3 June, 1990. p. 14.

20. Edward Lucas, "East Europe Elections," *The Independent,* 7 March, 1990. p. 11.

8. Into the Golden City

1. John Perrotta, "The Hungry Tourists of Prague," *The San Francisco Chronicle,* 21 January, 1991, p. C2.
2. Sam Bingham, "Czechoslovakian Landscapes," *Audubon Magazine,* November, 1990. p. 92–93.

9. Covering Up the Past

1. Herbert Mitgang, "In Czechoslovakia, A Literary Revolution Follows The Political One," *The New York Times,* 20 December, 1990, p. B1.
2. "Prague's Velvet Hangover," *The Los Angeles Times Sunday Magazine,* 12 May, 1991. p. 35.

10. Had Enough Beer?

1. Sarah Shaw, *The Prague Pub Guide,* (op) Pragolem and Art Agency Scena, Prague, 1992. Also see Joshua Benjamin Meisler, "Beer Drinking Is A Respected Tradition In Prague," *The Los Angeles Times,* 22 November, 1992. p. L16.
2. Jeff Kaye, "Transatlantic Fight Brewing Over Right to Budweiser Name," *The Los Angeles Times,* 1991; also see Ferdinand Protzman, "A Czech Cousin Haunts Budweiser," *The New York Times,* 5 April, 1990. Section D, p. 1; "Budweiser vs. Budweiser in Europe," *The San Francisco Chronicle,* 29 January, 1991. p. C1.
3. Staff report, *The Prague Post,* 26 May, 1992. p. 2

11. Our Wild Life

1. Bingham, "Czechoslovakian Landscapes," *Audubon Magazine,* November, 1990. p. 92–93.
2. IPI Survey: *The Press in Authoritarian Countries.* 1959
3. Ibid
4. *1990 Gannett Foundation Report on Freedom of the Press in Central and Eastern Europe.* pps. 45–53.

12. Americans in Retreat

1. Peter Hames, *The Czechoslovak New Wave,* University of California Press, Berkeley, 1985. p. 36. For those interested in exploring the long history of Czech and Slovak film, Hames' book is one of the few documents available. Fanatics may wish to search out Josef Škvorecký's *All the Bright Young Men and Women,* (Toronto, Peter Martin Associates, 1971). Though it is out of print, the original Czech version, *Všichni ti bystří mladí muži a ženy,* is available in Prague.
2. Ibid

13. Growing Pains

1. Havel, *Open Letters,* p. 392.
2. Wolchik, *Czechoslovakia in Transition: Politics, Economics & Society,* 89.
3. Ibid, 90; also see "Czechoslovakia: Where The Suppression ..."

14. Meeting the Parents

1. Steve Hochman, "Czech Rockers Půlnoc Put Music Over Politics," *The Los Angeles Times,* 8 May, 1989. Calendar, Part 6, p. 1.
2. Garry Mason, "Půlnoc: The Other Side of Midnight," *The Prague Post,* 7 July, 1993. p. 11.

15. Mr. Bush Comes to Town

1. Havel, *Summer Meditations,* xviii.
2. Staff report, "Staff Plays Numbers Game on Bush's Crowd In Prague," *The Los Angeles Times,* 18 November, 1990. p. A14.
3. M. B. Christie, "Capitalism a grind for busy Czech Women," *The San Francisco Examiner,* 1 November, 1991. p. 1.
4. According to a survey by the Dema Research Co., 44 percent of Czech men and 26 percent of women consider extramarital sex "natural and normal," while close to 50 percent of women and more than two-thirds of men have been unfaithful to their partners (*The Prague Post,* 16 March, 1994. p. 2).

5. Alexandra Burešova, "Czechoslovakia 1991: Abortion & Contraception," *Planned Parenthood in Europe,* Vol. 20, no. 2. Other articles about feminism and women's issues in Central and Eastern Europe can be found in Slavenka Drakulić's *How We Survived Communism and Even Laughed* (New York: W. W. Norton, 1991).

16. Winter Blues

1. Ann Marsh, "Ball Season Has Egalitarian Roots," *The Prague Post,* 26 January, 1994. p. 9a.

17. Klaus: Privatization Architect

1. Boris Gómez, "Klaus: Pragmatism Over Intellectualism," *The Prague Post,* 30 December, 1992. p. 5.
2. Jonathan Kaufman, "Velvet Revolution Not Going So Smoothly In Czechoslovakia," The Boston Globe, 15 November, 1990. p. A4.
3. Burton Bollag, "Czech Communists Gain Seats in Local Elections," *The New York Times,* 27 November, 1990. p. A11.
4. Staff report, "Czechs In Favor of Legal Discrimination," *The Prague Post,* 30 March, 1994. p. 2. Wolchik, *Czechoslovakia in Transition.* p. 183–185.
5. Jefferson Morley, "Midnight Journey: the timely death of the Plastic People," *The Village Voice Rock & Roll Quarterly,* Fall 1988. Also of interest is an account of Paul Wilson's time as a singer with the Plastic People in ("What It's Like Making Rock n' Roll in a Police State," *Musician,* February, 1983). Wilson, who today serves as Havel's official translator, lived in Czechoslovakia for much of the 1970s before being deported by the state for his association with the Plastics. Those interested in the history of rock n' roll behind the Iron Curtain might want to read *Rock Around The Bloc* by Timothy W. Rayback (Oxford University Press, New York, 1990), which is fairly interesting, although it is fast going out of date and appeared to have been researched mainly from newspaper and magazine accounts. However, it's one of the few works available about the influence of

rock music in Central and Eastern Europe.

6. Staff report, "Underground Poet Fined," *The Prague Post,* 26 May, 1992. p. 2; see also *The Student Paper: Independent Magazine of Czechoslovak Students,* Summer, 1990.

7. Havel, *Disturbing The Peace.* p. 126–127.

8. Josef Škvorecký, *Talkin' Moscow Blues,* Faber and Faber, London, 1989. p. 89. An absorbing collection of essays about various issues in Czechoslovakia from World War II to 1988. Of particular interest is a well-researched history of Czech involvement in the American Civil War.

18. Christmas and Fried Carp

1. "Carp For Christmas," *The Prague Post,* 23 December, 1991. p. 10.

2. As opposed to Poland, where the Catholic church played a large role in people's lives, the church in Czechoslovakia was more suppressed. The late Cardinal František Tomášek, was originally secretly consecrated in 1949 and later was arrested and convicted of anti-state activities. Later, after he was released, he served in several small parishes until he was named as a Cardinal in 1977. During the 1980s, Tomášek was heavily involved in the Charter 77 movement and later gathered more than 600,000 signatures in 1988 asking the government to allow more religious freedom. After the revolution, a number of priests who had been secretly ordained under communism were fully integrated into the church. "We feel gratitude towards these people, who during the time to totalitarian rule labored at risk and put themselves in danger, and we will first of all deal with them," said Miroslav Vlk, an Archbishop in Prague (*Czechoslovak News Service Daily Summary,* 3 March, 1992, p. 6). Vlk had worked as a window cleaner after having had his priestly license revoked in 1978.

19. The Winter Grows Colder

1. M. B. Christie, "Czechs scurry to beat increase in price of coal," *The San Francisco Examiner,* 24 December, 1990. p. A7.

20. The Pink Tank

1. Staff report, "The Pink Tank," *Studentské Listy International Edition,* July, 1991, p. 11.
2. Matt Welch, "The Politics of Pink," *Prognosis,* June, 1991, p. 3. See also staff report, "Havel," *Mladá Fronta Dnes,* 20 May, 1991, p. 3
3. "Head for the hills girls—Easter's here," *The Prague Post,* 30 March, 1994. p. 1.
4. Carol J. Williams, "Czech Businesses On The Auction Block," *The Los Angeles Times,* January 28, 1991. See also David Rocks, "Bizarre Buys on Czech Auction Block," *The San Francisco Chronicle,* 30 September, 1991. p. 1.
5. M. B. Christie, "Czech Reforms Called Tainted," *The San Francisco Examiner,* 30 December, 1990, p. A11.
6. Jan Macháček, "Privatization: More Than An Economic Goal," *East European Reporter,* January–February, 1992. p. 55–56.

21. Remembering a Liberation

1. "Czechs say cheers to the unmentionable liberators," *The Daily Telegraph,* 7 May, 1990, p. 10.
2. Szulc, *Czechoslovakia Since World War II.* p. 107.
3. IPI Survey: *The Press in Authoritarian Countries.* 1959
4. Ibid. See also *Prague Farewell.*
5. Erin Kelly, "Štěpán: Next Time We'll Be More Clever," *The Prague Post,* 18 November, 1992. p. 4.
6. Dan DeLuce, unpublished interview, 1991.

23. Anniversary One

1. Originally known as *Rowboat To Prague,* it was re-published as *So Many Heroes,* (Second Chance Press, Sagaponack, New York, 1980) This is an excellent account, and still perhaps the only one in English, of the events leading up to and after the Warsaw Pact invasion.
2. Hames, *The Czechoslovak New Wave,* p. 92–115. Hames discusses the "vibrant realism" of Czech film, especially during the

1960s New Wave.

3. Alan Levy, "Dubček: End of an Era," *The Prague Post,* 10 November, 1992. p. 1.

4. Author interview, *The Prague Post..*

5. Alan Levy, "Dictator Husák's Death Fans Political Flames," *The Prague Post,* 26 November, p. 3.

6. Charles T. Powers, "Land of Opportunity," *The Los Angeles Times,* 13 January, 1992. p. E1. There have been many, many articles about the Americans in Prague, but sadly most of them are shoddily reported. Seek out Henry Copeland's "Wild, Wild, West" (*Details Magazine,* June, 1992. p. 22); also see Jason Goodwin, "Prague," *Departures Magazine,* Spring 1992. p. 84. Those who can read Czech should consult Zdeněk Procházka's "Hej Hou, Hej Hou, Yankeeové Jdou" (Hey Ho, Hey Ho, Yankees Are Going), *Mladý svět,* 19 June, 1992. p. 35.

25. Lustrace: Cleaning Out Communists

1. Dan DeLuce, "Alleged StB Collaborators Barred From Public Office, *The Prague Post,* 8 October, 1991. p. 1.

2. Ibid.

3. Dora Gallagher, "Witch Hunt In Prague," *The Los Angeles Times Sunday Magazine,* 29 September, 1991. p. 23. For an even more thorough analysis of the Kavan situation, refer to Lawrence Weschler's long profile of Kavan in *The New Yorker* (25 October, 1992). To date, this article may be the single best piece of reporting on life after the revolution in 1989.

4. Ibid.

5. Ibid.

6. Dan DeLuce, "Flips and Flops As Kavan Is Cleared and Uncleared," *The Prague Post,* 3 March, 1992. p. 1.

7. Dan DeLuce, "Panel Finds Kavan Guilty," *The Prague Post,* 20 October, 1992. p. 1.

8. Staff report, "President Havel's Message: To Find Ourselves Anew," *The Prague Post,* 7 January, 1992. p. 3.

26. A Country Breaking Apart

1. Dan DeLuce, "Mečiar," *The Prague Post,* 30 December, 1992. p. 5.
2. Dan DeLuce, "MPs Skeptical of Havel's Bid," *The Prague Post,* 26 November, 1991. p. 1.
3. Charles T. Powers, "Slovak Issue May Imperil Prague's Economic Reforms, Havel's Future," *The Los Angeles Times,* 23 February, 1992. p. A5.
4. David Rocks, "Sentiment Appears Strong For a Separate Slovak State," *The San Francisco Chronicl*e, 28 November, 1991. p. A11.
5. Dan DeLuce, "MPs Give Havel Cold Shoulder," *The Prague Post,* 10 December, 1991. p. 1.
6. Ellen Hale, "Communism's Dirty Secret," *Gannett News Service,* 5 August, 1990.
7. Ibid.
8. Ibid and also see Dan Stets, "Czechs now ready to face disastrous pollution poisoning population," *Knight Ridder Newspapers,* 25 January, 1991.

27. Olga

1. A note about style here: in Czech, as with other Slavic languages, the wife or daughter adds "ová" to the family name to distinguish between male and female.

28. Cranking Up Capitalism

1. Daniel Arbess, "Legal Aspects of Privatization and Foreign Investors," speech at the *Third CERGE Lecture on Practical Aspects of Privatization,* December 4, 1991.
2. Boris Gomez, "Voucher Schemes," *The Prague Post,* 14 January, 1992. p. 7.

29. Fateful Election

1. "Havel, Hoping to Save Federation, Will Run Again," *The International Herald Tribune.* Thursday, 21 April, 1992. p. 2.

2. Throughout 1991 and 1992, there was pressure from some groups —most notably the anti-communist party Klub Angažovaných Nestroníků (KAN)—to publish the entire list of agents and collaborators with the StB. Despite the government's refusal to release the material, a "list" of questionable repute was eventually leaked out and printed in a quasi-satirical, political magazine called *Rudá Krávo (Red Cow)*. Essentially just a long list of names, the document did little to clear the air. The government's investigation of journalists was much more severe and controversial. Several well-known journalists were accused of being collaborators, including a photographer who worked for *The Prague Post*. This photographer steadfastly maintained his innocence and disputed the information in his file; he said that he had been contacted by agents but he had not done any work with them. The charges against the photographer were, like so many others, open to question.

3. Susanna Cooper, "Republics Choose Different Courses," *The Prague Post,* 9 June, 1992. p. 1.

4. Dan DeLuce, "Deadlock Puts Federation in Danger," *The Prague Post,* 16 June,1992. p. 1.

5. James O. Jackson, "Can This Marriage Be Saved?" *Time,* 6 July, 1992. p. 24.

6. Ibid

7. Ross Larsen, "Czechs Don't Want Detour to Division," *The Prague Post,* 14 July, 1992. p. 1.

8. Mitch Mitchell, "Slovak Leaders Rejoice As Nation Forges Future," *The Prague Post,* 21 July, 1992. p. 1.

9. Staff report, "Broken Pledges Drive Havel Out," *The Prague Post,* 20 July, 1992, p. 4.

10. Markéta Špinková, "Slovaks Raise Warning To Flag Debate," *The Prague Post,* 25 November, 1992, p. 1.

30. Czechs vs. Americans

1. "Czech premier blames mass media for public confusion," *ČTK daily news and press survey,* 19 August, 1992, p. 3.

31. Speeding towards the Velvet Divorce

1. Author interview, "For Rich People, Americans Don't Have Fun, *The Prague Post,* 2 December, 1992, p. 11.
2. Boris Gómez, "Somber Czech State Looks To Job Ahead," The Prague Post, 6 January, 1993, p. 1.
3. Press Survey, *The Prague Post,* 6 January, 1993, p. 2.
4. Mitch Mitchell, "A New Nation," *The Prague Post,* 6 January, 1993, p. 5.
5. Andrew Nagorski, "Homecoming at Hradčany," *Newsweek,* 1 February, 1993, p. 24.
6. Ibid.
7. Ross Larsen and Leslie Chang, "New Nations Start Living Apart," *The Prague Post,* 6 January, 1993, p. 3.

32. Endpoints and New Beginnings

1. Carol J. Williams, "Few Slovaks Enthused over Break With Czechs," *The Los Angeles Times,* 26 December, 1992, p. A4.
2. Money & Markets, *The Prague Post,* 6 April, 1994, p. 15.
3. Jiří Leština, "Reforma skončila, co s porevoluční kocovinou?" *Mladá Fronta Dnes,* 19 October, 1993, p. 6.
4. Lewis Dolinsky, "Glimpses of Fledgling Democracy," *The San Francisco Chronicle,* 18 November, 1990, p. 13.
5. Garry Mason, "Půlnoc: The Other Side of Midnight," *The Prague Post,* July 7, 1993. p. 11.
6. Ibid. p. 11.

For complete discussions of the revolution itself, readers are directed to several texts, including:

Timothy Garton Ash, *We The People: The Revolutions of '89* (London: Granta Books, Penguin, 1990). This contains a good insider account of the formation of Civic Forum after Nov. 17.
Misha Glenny, *The Rebirth of History* (London: Penguin Books, 1990). Like Ash's book, this is an overview of the changing Warsaw Pact

countries. People interested in gaining a better understanding of the Yugoslav crisis are also directed to Glenny's excellent account of the war, *The Fall of Yugoslavia: The Third Balkan War,* (London: Penguin Books, 1994).

Deset pražských dnů (Ten days in Prague) (Prague: Academia, Prague, 1990) Although unavailable in English, this text contains one of the most complete set of documents dating from November 17–27, 1989.

Jeffrey Goldfarb, *After The Fall* (New York: BasicBooks, 1992) While more analysis and perspective than actual historical recounting, Goldfarb's text considers the changing democracies and resurgent nationalism in Central Europe.

Several worthwhile books about Prague and the region for travelers:

J. V. Polišenský, *History of Czechoslovakia in Outline* (op) (Prague: Bohemia International, 1947). This short book was reprinted after the 1989 revolution and contains a quick and excellent history of the Czechs and Slovaks up to World War II.

Rob Humphreys, *Czechoslovakia: The Rough Guide* (London: Harrap Columbus, 1991).

Stephen Brook, *The Double Eagle: Vienna, Budapest and Prague* (op) (London: Hamish Hamilton Ltd., 1988. An interesting travel book about life in the three cities in the mid-1980s. An account of a May Day celebration in Prague is of particular interest to anyone seeking a detailed description of what life under "normalization" was like.

For perspectives on feminism and women's issues in the Warsaw Pact:

Slavenka Drakulić, *How We Survived Communism and Even Laughed* (New York: W. W. Norton, 1991). Drakulić is an excellent Croatian writer and journalist who has also produced several fine novels and *The Balkan Express* (London: Penguin Books, 1993), an interesting collection of essays about the Yugoslav conflict.

Finally, anyone interested in gaining an understanding of life from before World War II to after the 1968 invasion should read:

Heda Margolius Kovaly, *Prague Farewell* (London: Gollancz, 1988). Sent to various concentration camps as a Jew, she survived and married after the war, only to see her husband, Rudolf Margolius, tried and executed as part of the Rudolf Slánský show trials. A different translation and shorter version of the book has also been published as *Under A Cruel Star* (Plunkett Lake Press, 1986).